Power
and the Powerless

Power
and the Powerless

MICHAEL PARENTI

St. Martin's Press   **New York**

To my Father with my love

Acknowledgments

"Look, this System is not Working" by Jonathan Kozol, from *The New York Times,* April 1, 1971. © 1971 by the New York Times Company. Reprinted by permission.

Excerpt from *Labor and Monopoly Capital* by Harry Braverman. © 1974 by Harry Braverman. Reprinted by permission of Monthly Review Press.

Preface

"Power politics" has become a pejorative term in the popular ocabulary. But it is also something of a redundancy, for what other kind of politics is there? The condemnation of "power politics" implies that there can be a "nonpower politics" untouched by questions of control, coercion, manipulation, and competition. I would not rule out the possibility, indeed, the eventual necessity, of developing a social order whose institutions and decision-making forms are essentially cooperative and nonhierarchical. But the anticipations of tomorrow are no substitute for the study of today.

Many of us prefer to believe as we have been taught—that the important decisions of society are arrived at by a natural process of give and take, with different groups having their say along the way. "From time to time," comments Grant McConnell, "we have cherished the illusion that power need not exist, sometimes even that it is a myth. Parts of our political tradition seem to encourage these beliefs."[1] Yet the use of great concentrations of power in the pursuit of interests other than our own by persons beyond our reach is one of those inescapable realities affecting us no matter how inattentive we choose to be.

The subject of this book is power in American society or, specifically, the relationship of power to social structure, political consciousness, and powerlessness: how and for whom power is organized and what its institutionalized roots are; how power serves interest and how it defines interest; why certain social alternatives are chosen and others ignored; how change and protest are contained; how in the face of all inequities and abuses the prevailing social order maintains itself. Also treated is the question of how our social system evokes the loyalty, consciousness, and empowering responses of masses of people, many of whom—as they will tell you—are living lives of little security or gratification. Attention is given to such important determinants of socialization as social structure, class dominance, institution, role, and ideology. The momentous scope of these questions is reason enough for a sensible scholar to shy away from them. Yet without hoping that definitive answers can be formulated, I believe such topics are worthy, indeed, demanding, of investigation.

This book can be viewed as a sequel to my *Democracy for the Few*,[2] although it is written in a somewhat different style, takes a different approach, and is intended to be read independently. *Democracy for the Few* deals with the American political process in a detailed, descriptive, substantive, and essentially basic manner. This book treats some of the same subjects but gives primary attention not to a description of political practices and outputs, but to those social arrangements, usually seen as antecedent to the political process, which play a salient role in political socialization, class dominance, and social control.

Power operates throughout the entire social context from which political actors and issues emerge—or fail to emerge. Hence, the maneuvers of particular actors engaged in the decision process should not be treated as the sum of political life. Of what significance is a tighter defense budget when its continuing purpose is to maintain a global police force to protect American interests abroad, interests that are defined by a select number of people whose perspectives do not change much with the changing administrations in Washington? How important are competing fiscal policies when together their first intention is the support of corporate enterprise? Of what democratic import are the squabbles among giant producers over public appropriations if the interests of the great bulk of the population are left out of such considerations? How vital are human services programs when their funds are channeled through a politico-economic structure that consistently deprives those most in need? If most decisions only alter the margins of policy, then it is time we begin to examine the social and ideational context that gives policy its fundamental direction.[3]

With this book the reader is invited to think of power not only as a relationship arising among persons with each new political contest but as a pattern of relations inhering in the social system itself, persisting over long periods of time. To anticipate a specific point discussed later on: established institutions are not "just there" but are largely the causes and effects of highly inequitable organizations of power and interest. It follows that the values and social roles propagated by these institutions are not neutral, innocent entities but get their meaning from the predominant interests within institutional hierarchies. In later pages I shall explore how an institution's control of role behavior and socialization, and the links between different institutions, are themselves momentous resources of socio-political power. And I shall discuss some of the ways that ideologies and institutions support each other with circular effect, thereby serving the class interests of those who occupy the institutional command positions.

Some people fault an author for writing his own book rather than the one *they* wanted to see written. In the hope that I might save myself from some irrelevant criticisms, I would like to say what this book does *not* do. First, it does not explore every aspect of *intra*group dynamics, nor the psychology of leadership, nor techniques of leadership, as such. Nor is it an inquiry into the moral questions relating to power. A study of the ethical ramifications of power in modern capitalist (or socialist) societies would be a worthwhile undertaking but is not attempted in the pages ahead. Likewise, the political activist should understand that this volume is not designed as a handbook for either transforming or defending the status quo, but one hopes it might help us advance our understanding of the power realities within the existing social system—and no activist, or scholar, should be indifferent to that undertaking.

I would add that rigorous, precise theory building—assuming there is such a thing—is not my central concern. The style herein is that of a somewhat discursive scholarly essay and not of a formalized "hypothesis hunt." This book is not strictly behavioralist in that there is no attempt to build elaborate models or collect highly abstracted propositions. Thus, there are very few sentences like this: "Persons with low resources but high output expectations are more likely to resort to deviant modes of political expression than either persons with high resources and low output expectations or persons with low resources and low output expectations." One could spin a good number of such hypotheses from the materials presented here, and some of these might even lead to fruitful kinds of research. But that is not the task I have chosen.

This book is concerned neither with delineating the intricacies of the political decision-making process, nor with giving a complete description of the substantive outputs of the political system. As previously noted, I have treated such questions more fully in *Democracy for the Few*. However, here I do try to keep in mind that the struggle for outputs is, after all, what politics is all about. One should not talk about power divorced from interest nor political process divorced from costs and benefits.[4]

To say that this work is primarily analytic rather than descriptive is to claim, among other things, that the propositions offered are generalizable rather than fixed to particular moments in history. Yet I would not pretend that this analysis transcends all boundaries of time and place. Anyone who writes about generalizable phenomena has a set of particular data in mind and the generalizations made from these are usually less than universal in their application.[5] The primary focus here is on United States society and to a lesser extent on Western capitalist nations.

Some of my observations touch on things common to many kinds of social systems. Elite dominance, unequal distribution of power resources, and the propagation of orthodoxy exist in societies other than the United States. But it is our own society I have chosen to study, critically comparing the officially propagated image to what I consider to be the reality. The fact that other social orders produce their own abuses is no excuse for not trying to develop as realistic and accurate a view of our own as we can.

This is no place to argue comparative systems, but I would suggest that what are called "socialist" societies today are in many ways more productive, more secure, and happier places, and therefore less oppressive for the common people than is the United States. In other ways, life in such societies may be less satisfying and more constricting than life in the United States for many American citizens. This question is in real need of investigation, but it is not one I will be dealing with here. My concern is with power in American society, and what my analysis reveals about this system is not to be dismissed as of no significance because other societies are presumed to be "just as bad' or "worse." The social reality of this country should be compared to the image paraded before us by its apologists. Furthermore, even if only implicitly, this system should be compared to what it *could* develop into were it not for the constraining, distorting effects of a capitalist, elite-dominated mode of power and interest. The sense of what *has been* in other societies is no excuse for ignoring the vision of what *could be* in our own and no excuse for assuming that the status quo is the immutable sum total of the human condition.

There is no attempt to offer conclusive proofs for all the ideas developed herein, many of which have been exhaustively treated by others. While a good deal of evidence is introduced, these pages are leaner than they might have been. Data that might have lent further documentation to my observations can be found in the supporting citations. Much of the evidence to support what I say about the inequities, exploitations, and repressions of the United States ruling class can be found in *Democracy for the Few*. Here I try to advance the analysis to include the entire social structure, offering a way of looking at power that has been neglected by those academic and journalistic investigators who, fixing their gaze on the trees, have managed to overlook the unhappy things happening in the forest.

Michael Parenti

NOTES

1. Grant McConnell, *Private Power and American Democracy* (New York: Knopf, 1966), p. 29. As we shall see, it is more than "our political tradition" that encourages this.

2. Michael Parenti, *Democracy for the Few*, 2nd ed. (New York: St. Martin's, 1977).

3. See Douglas Rosenberg, "Dimensions of Military Growth," in Bruce Russett and Alfred Stephan (eds.), *Military Force and American Society* (New York: Harper & Row, 1972), p. 141 ff, for a discussion of this point in regard to the ideological context of American foreign policy.

4. See chapter 3 for further comments on this point.

5. The converse is also true, of course: anyone writing about particular phenomena is implicitly guided by general assumptions, even when claiming to be influenced only by "the facts."

Acknowledgments

The late Richard Warner provided much valuable criticism and encouragement during an early stage of the writing. Stating my gratitude for his efforts does little to ease the loss I still feel over his untimely death. A word of appreciation is also due sociologist Benjamin Nelson, a former colleague of mine who years ago taught me to think systemically, and sometimes even systematically, about the social structure. Although he had nothing directly to do with the preparation of this manuscript, he might well recognize his influence on these pages.

Special gratitude must be expressed to Theodore Lowi, who provided a detailed, lengthy critique. His effort, partly impelled but never diluted by a personal friendship that has transcended our political differences, was of major benefit to this book. So unselfishly did Lowi insinuate his talents into these pages that I feel compelled to credit him not only with a share of whatever merits the book might possess but also with a portion of its shortcomings. I'm sure he will not shrink from the responsibility.

My thanks to Dorothy Ives, who did most of the typing and whose corrections and clarifications brought a kind of literacy to the manuscript I could not have achieved on my own. Robert Allen Ackerman deserves thanks for his careful copy editing and valuable substantive criticisms of the text. Once more I feel indebted to the staff at St. Martin's Press, especially Thomas Broadbent, Glenn Cowley, Bert Lummus, and Carolyn Eggleston.

An earlier version of the first five chapters, which I had sent to several professional colleagues for their critical comments some years ago, was published without my knowledge or consent by one of them in a book of his own. That book has since been removed from circulation by its publisher. I mention this only to protect my own professional reputation and that of my publisher. I would not want the reader to arrive at the mistaken notion that materials here were taken from someone else. Rather, it is the other way around.

Contents

Power
and the Powerless

Part One

On Power

1

What We Mean by "Power"

The concept of "power" has an elusive, almost intangible, quality. As Kaufman and Jones wrote: "We 'know' what it is, yet we encounter endless difficulties in trying to define it."[1] Yet for all its elusiveness, the concept of "power" remains irresistible. Just as soon as some social scientists decide to discard it, out of a suspicion that it raises too many semantic problems, "power" creeps back into their pages wearing such disguises as "influence," "control," "dominance," and so forth. When a concept continues to prove so troublesome yet so compelling, it is usually because it refers to phenomena that crave explanation. And whereas we may dismiss the term as bothersome, this does not satisfy the craving.

GETTING WHAT ONE WANTS

Power as a concept is fundamental to the analysis of political affairs, "in the same sense," Bertrand Russell suggests, "in which Energy is the fundamental concept in physics."[2] Neither power nor energy is an object of the sensate world; both are hypothetical constructs. One does not see or touch energy as such, but one may observe its manifestations in heat, light, motion, growth, and decay. Thus we say that energy has been expended when in fact what we see is a bird taking flight or a rock falling. So with power: it is a construction of the mind introduced because it is useful in describing and explaining important empirical phenomena. One cannot actually reach out and touch power but one observes its manifestations in every human relationship and social arrangement—or one does not, depending on how broadly the term is defined. The boundaries of a concept are human-made and are drawn for the purpose of lending clarity to whatever the researcher is attempting to explore. "Every way of classifying a thing," William James reminds us, "is but a way of handling it for some particular purpose."[3]

Out of an understandable desire for precision and comprehension, the investigator may contrive a model of power that is so elaborate as to be unfathomable to the reader and sometimes unmanageable for the researcher, thereby defeating the purpose of models, which is to make the subject more tractable and comprehensible.[4] A model can reveal links between phenomena not usually drawn together by casual observation. As Baran and Sweezy point out, the test for any thesis, perspective, or model is: "Does it help to make sense of the real world? . . . Does it help us see connections to which we were previously blind, to relate effects to causes, to replace the arbitrary and the accidental by the regular and the necessary?"[5] I shall be sparing in my model building in regard to the concept of power. Ultimately my concern is not to develop a monumental model of power but a better understanding of socio-political life.

Let me begin by defining power as a *relationship* between a person and his environment; specifically let us say that power is the ability to get what one wants. Or as Thomas Hobbes stated it several centuries ago: "The POWER *of a Man* (to take it Universally,) is his present means, to obtain some future apparent Good."[6] In keeping with the sense Hobbes gives to the term, "good" is used here to signify any object or objective which one desires. Whether it be morally good is not considered; suffice it to say that goods are the *desiderata* pursued by social actors, the things actors define as being in their interest to attain.[7]

The ability to get what one wants frequently implies the ability to outdo those whose interests might conflict with one's own. Since the demand for many desiderata exceeds the available supply, we might expect some degree of competition, and one person's (or group's) gain frequently involves another's loss, especially if the society is organized along privatized, competitive modes of production, distribution, and acquisition. Thus a corollary measure of one's self-serving power is the ability to deal helpful or hurtful effects on others, effects which may be produced *intentionally* or *unintentionally*. For instance, the corporation that moves its factory to a new locale, causing unemployment in the community from which it departs, is motivated by an intention to maximize profits and not by the desire to leave people destitute. Yet an impressive influence intentionally or unintentionally has been exercised by corporate leaders over the material welfare of the abandoned community even if they do not wish to claim responsibility for such an influence.

Thus far, my emphasis has been on the *effects* of actions rather than on the alleged *intentions* or *motives* of the actors. For the purpose of understanding how social desiderata are allocated in society, evaluations of the sincerity or insincerity of motives (assuming we, or the actors themselves, can accurately determine their motives) seem of less importance than the actual effects. Indeed it is a rare political actor who does not profess the highest motives even as his actions bring misery to others. Having taken notice that noble intentions and ignoble effects exist in equal abundance, I will concentrate on the latter, that is, on the question of who enjoys and who suffers what effects, rather than on who claims what intentions.

GETTING OTHERS TO SERVE ONE'S INTERESTS

Lest it be thought that one should consider only effects and outputs, I would add that besides looking at who gets what, we might also consider who and what *determines* who gets what. Since the successful pursuit of scarce desiderata by any one person, group, or class often involves engaging the efforts of others, we might think of power as A's ability to get others to act or think in ways they would not otherwise act or think, specifically *in ways which maximize A's interests.*

The italicized specification is important. If we conceive of power as being only the ability to influence the behavior of another in any way whatever, then we find ourselves sharing the position held by Richard Merelman, who seems to argue that *all* participants in a transaction exercise power, including those who are defeated in any conflict because they have been able to induce the victorious group to expend the effort needed to vanquish them! "Even if those planning to initiate policies hostile to an 'elite' become subject to its power and are constrained to desist," he argues, "they still have exerted power of their own. The elite has been forced to anticipate them and exert power of their own."[8] By that view, a conquered people exercises power by inducing the invading army to take forceful measures; a murder victim exercises power by resisting and causing his assailant to expend energy in the act of cutting his throat, and so forth.

One may define power as Merelman does but then it becomes difficult to imagine any situation, even the most brutally suppressive one, as anything other than a sharing of power. All interactions, after all, involve expenditures by participants and therefore some modification of their actions, including the actions of those who emerge totally triumphant. But to give power "any differentiating meaning," David Easton observes, "we must view it as a relationship in which one person or group is able to determine the actions of another *in the direction of the former's own ends*."[9] It is the implied conditions of dominance, gain, and loss which make the concept of power of compelling interest to students of politics.

Although the definitions offered here have referred mostly to individual actors, one may conceive of interrelations involving large groups, classes, and whole nations of people, where many of the individuals involved will have no direct contact with, or knowledge of, each other. All sorts of interpersonal relationships can be seen as involving power, including those between lovers or between parent and child. But I shall focus primarily on the kind of interest relationships involving issues of aggregate social significance.

No concept dealing with complex social forces can be defined with absolute precision and no definition will satisfy every desired use of the concept. So with power. One can readily think of some marginal conditions that are not well covered by the definitions offered here. And one can detect new boundaries to the use of the word as the analysis moves forward.

THE DEFINITION OF INTERESTS

Power, as I have defined it, is not a substance emanating from a person, although in popular parlance we evoke that kind of imagery by saying "He is a powerful figure" or "One can feel her power." The personal qualities of a leader, while counting among the things determining his or her ability to influence others, should not be mistaken for the interpersonal relationship itself. For if power emanated from the self, how could we explain the immense disparities in power among people? Hobbes once noted:

> Nature hath made men so equall, in the faculties of body, and mind; as that though there bee found one man sometimes manifestly stronger in body, or of quicker mind than another; yet when all is reckoned together, the difference between man, and man, is not so considerable, as that one man can thereupon claim to himselfe any benefit, to which another may not pretend, as well as he. For as to the strength of body, the weakest has strength enough to kill the strongest, either by secret machination, or by confederacy with others . . .[10]

Nor can greatness of mind, which exists in very few, be taken as the cause of great power. For even if one were to argue that every person of great intellect could become a wielder of power, one would still be hard put to convince us of the more relevant proposition that every wielder of power is a person of great intellect.

Whatever the case, we should still need to distinguish the personal attributes which are part of the resources of power from the interpersonal responses that create power relationships. What makes one person so much more powerful than others are those very others who give him or her their empowering responses. Socio-political power is not self-generated but acquired through the attachments of many individual energies, strengths, and talents (what Hobbes called the "natural powers") to one or a few wills. We recognize this condition when we speak of a person as having power "given" to or "taken" from him/her.

Why do people devote some portion of their time, energy and fortune to the will of others, thereby empowering others? They do so because they anticipate some kind of psychic or material reward for compliance or some deprivation for noncompliance, or because they have been socialized into "the habit of obedience," into an acceptance of orderly compliance as "right and proper" behavior, carrying its own justification. This is clearly seen, for instance, in those values associated with patriotism. Loyalty to the nation-state becomes an end value, and the question "Why should I be loyal to my country?" is treated as inherently suspect. Patriotism, to use Weber's description of a category of belief, is either "a purely affectual" response of "an emotionally determined loyalty," or "a rational belief in the absolute validity of the order as an expression of ultimate values."[11] In either case, patriotism, like virtue, is taken as its own reward.

As the reference to patriotism might indicate, not all interests are self-interests in the immediate, individuated sense.[12] Individuals have been known to pursue political goals for other than egoistic gain, that is, for ethical ideological reasons, with no direct substantive benefit and sometimes with much risk to themselves. Consider the many who have agitated against slavery, capital punishment, child labor, and overseas military interventions or on behalf of labor reforms, prison reforms, and certain economic changes. People may be moved by self-sacrificing long-range collective values as well as individuated hedonistic ones. This sometimes seems true both of those who would die defending their government and those who would die overthrowing it.

Rewards for obedience may include anything from casual approval to physical survival, while deprivations may range from mild expressions of disapproval to loss of life. To put the matter differently, we might say that A can exercise influence or control over B *when A has something which B wants*, something which B cannot acquire at will but only by entering into some kind of exchange relationship with A. Should one person have nothing desired by others, then others are unlikely to enter a relationship with that person since they have no *interest* in so doing. Thus the occasions of power are determined in part by the *definition of interests* people bring to a situation.

Unless A can engage B's interest, A cannot wield power over B. If B no longer wants what A has, at least not to the extent of having to behave as A dictates, then A cannot control B. The threat to withdraw affection or fire one from a job or fling one into prison or take one's life are effective constraints only if one is interested in maintaining oneself as an object of affection, holding one's job, or preserving one's freedom, health, or life. And since most people are indeed interested in such things, then controls over conditions of esteem, work, health, and safety become important means of determining the behavior of others; they are resources of power.

The worker who obeys the directives of her boss may want the psychic reward of a superior's approval or at least the peace of mind that comes from avoiding disapproval. She also may want more substantive returns, such as security in her job, a promotion, a day off, and the like. Her behavior being dictated by these considerations, we can say that she is "in the power" of her superior for certain hours of the day in regard to certain functions. She complies because it is in her *interest* to do so, at least as she defines her interest. The employer controls those things which the employee wants and therefore controls the latter.

Should the worker no longer desire what the boss possesses, then the boss's power to regulate the employee's work behavior is no longer operative. By reordering her own priorities, by redefining her interests, the employee can change the power relationship. However, her readiness to do this is seldom exclusively a matter of personal volition, but will depend on such conditions as her ability to find other employment opportunities, sustain a temporary loss in income, etc. *Her very capacity to give a certain definition to her interests is related to the wider objective conditions of her social environment as well as to what are considered her "personal" attitudes and needs vis-à-vis her job.* A power relationship gets its definition from the interests of the participants but these interests, in turn, are defined in part by wider economic and cultural forces—a point that will be developed further.

Many power relations are to be likened to exchange relations, with each participant having something for the other. The boss has control of the livelihood which the worker wants, and the worker has the labor and skills which the boss wants. That there is an exchange of interests, however, does not mean the relationship is an equitable one. The slave master and the slave are engaged in an exchange of interests: the command of the latter's body and soul in return for a miserable survival and momentary relief from the former's whip. The gunman offers an exchange to his victim—"Your wallet or your life"—and the victim trades his wallet for that which the gunman temporarily but decisively controls—his physical safety.

In some extremely asymmetrical power relationships the weaker party may lose everything and gain nothing. One, then, cannot speak of an "exchange" in any sense of the word. The thief who does not give his victim a choice but rather shoots him dead to get his wallet is exercising power by the first definition offered earlier: he is getting what he wants, and is intentionally or unintentionally hurting the interests of another. But he is pilfering a corpse rather than, as with most power relationships, commanding the behavior of another living being (the second definition). In any case, there is no interest exchange.

Usually the least powerful party in an exchange relation is the one who stands in greatest need. The worker who is desperate to maintain his job, and who can easily be replaced by someone else, has a greater interest in the relationship than the employer who can readily replace him. The boss, having a lesser need for the worker than the latter has for his job, enjoys an advantage in the relationship. That is what has been described as "the principle of least interest,"[13] or, if taken from the perspective of the underdog, what I would describe as "the principle of the greater need."

The choice for people in subordinate positions is more apt to be one of *relative deprivations*, that is, the lesser of two undesirable choices, than one of relative advantages. Indeed, one way we determine that a person *is* in a subordinate or weaker position is by observing that her choices vis-à-vis another are predominantly ones of relative deprivation, for instance, compliance in an underpaid, exhausting job as opposed to unemployment. Implicit in such exchanges is the element of *coercion*, for if the subordinate party had her way, presumably she would choose neither of the deprivations. She submits to conditions not to her liking out of fear of having to face worse ones. Habit and custom are such, however, that we frequently do not recognize the element of coercion involved in most social relations. But once divested of the affirmative aura of legitimacy, these exchanges reveal their asymmetrical and coercive quality.

Consider one of the more blatant examples of social coercion, a relationship traditionally represented as one of glory and duty by those who do the coercing: specifically, that situation in which a ruling sovereign (whether king, dictator, or elected assembly) demands two or more years of a young man's life in military service under penalty of law. Whether he chooses the army, jail, or exile, he is confronted with an exchange relationship not of his making; he is the weaker party faced with a coercive choice of relative deprivations. In such situations, assuming the absence of irrational ties to ultimate and purely affectual values of the kind Weber mentioned, the individual will comply only as long as he remains convinced that obedience has its returns, specifically the "reward" of being able to escape a still greater deprivation.

The deprivations suffered by less fortunate persons in an asymmetrical exchange relationship are not immutable, that is, the exchange could get better or worse. If the fortunes of the superior take an ill turn, the fortunes of the subordinate may suffer also. Hence, one can speak of a "forced collusive interest" between both parties, as between the slave and master, serf and lord, worker and owner. I say "forced" because the subordinate party accepts the relationship at great cost to himself only because the alternative threatens an even greater cost: painful obedience instead of death, poor wages instead of starvation, and the like.

To pursue the earlier example: suppose a young man decides to go into the army rather than suffer imprisonment or exile, or suppose he selects jail or exile as the preferred course, in what sense can it be said that he has chosen what is "best for his own interests"? In fact, his *own* interests, as he might want to define them, would rule out all three choices and would demand a situation free of compulsory military service. His "real interest," that is, his real or *first* preference, *were he free to set his own agenda*, might be to have nothing to do with conscription. But that alternative is, in the immediate situation, an "unrealistic" one, and he does not get the opportunity to consider his real preference. In facing the draft, he finds his interest range has been defined by others. The point is that power is used not only to *pursue* interest but *is a crucial factor in defining interest or predefining the field of choice within which one must then define one's interests.* You are free to "worship at the church of your choice," or "vote for the party of your choice (Republican or Democratic)." The exercise of choice may be so narrow, so much a matter of relative deprivations, so tightly circumscribed by power conditions serving interests other than one's own that the "choice" may be more a manifestation of powerlessness than of power.

A distinction should be made between one's immediate interests within a narrow range of alternatives fixed by politico-economic and institutional forces (e.g., procuring a job with a firm that manufactures a highly profitable and ecologically damaging product) and one's long-term interests (e.g., protecting the environment from damage by the manufactured product, working in a kind of productive system that rules out profits as the primary goal, etc.). A characteristic of our social system is its ability to oblige people to make choices that violate their broader long-term interests in order to satisfy their more immediate ones.

To give no attention to how interests are prefigured by power, how social choice is predetermined by the politico-economic forces controlling society's resources and institutions, is to begin in the middle of the story—or toward the end. When we treat interests as *given* and then focus only on the decision process in which these interests are played out, we fail to see how the decision process is limited to issue choices that themselves are products of the broader conditions of power. A study of these broader conditions is ruled out at the start if we treat each "interest" as self-generated rather than shaped in a context of social relationships, and if we treat each policy conflict as a "new issue" stirring in the body politic.

POWER AS A SYSTEMIC FORCE

Thus far I have defined power as (1) the ability to get what one wants (frequently exercised with an intentional or unintentional effect upon others) and (2) the ability to influence others in ways that further one's own interest. But the foregoing discussion of interest should tell us that there is yet a broader dimension to power. The preceding definitions treat power as an interpersonal phenomenon involving the overt behavior of persons engaged in the pursuit of specific decisions. Yet decisions themselves take place in a social and systemic context that prefigures what will and will not be considered a policy choice or a social alternative. The crucial question, Theodore Lowi recently suggested, is not "Who governs?" but "*What* governs?" The social system itself, its organizational structures and institutions, its long-standing beliefs and shibboleths, and the imperatives of its economy can shape developments in ways not readily understood even by many decision makers. These broader forces often bring results that differ from the intentions of individual actors.

To move from the question "Who prevails in decision X?" to the question "Why was decision X on the agenda rather than decision Y or Z?" is to begin to go beyond interpersonal definitions of power. To ask further: "What are the objective forces that impel social actors to act in ways that are not of their own choosing?" is to introduce a wider contextual dimension to power, one which says that regardless of individual personalities and predilections, people will be limited in their policy choices by various systemic imperatives. An enlightened businessman might wish to initiate progressive changes in his firm, including improved safety standards, work conditions, and wages, but he finds himself caught by the pressures of competition, the need to invest surplus capital in new markets so as not to diminish the profit margins of old ones, the need to hold down wages and cut production costs, and other such factors. These force him to move in a more conservative direction or face economic collapse. When liberal principles come into conflict with basic class interests, the principles are the more likely to give way. The power of the system operates even over those who are among its more powerful participants.

This is not to say that the impersonal dynamics of the system are innocently or neutrally evolved, devoid of political bias or class interest. If the market limits the possibilities of reform for an individual capitalist, it is still a creation of capitalism and still serves capitalist interests. Systemic constraints have evolved in particular ways, operating more in the service of the propertied and wealthy than the propertyless, and this development has been too one-sided and too consistent to be due merely to historical chance—so it will be argued in the chapters ahead. No matter how impersonally the system operates, its business and political elites consciously strive to maintain the conditions allowing for its continued operation. The structural constraints of the capitalist political system are not so absolutely compelling, do not work so automatically, as to turn its elites into mere caretakers and functionaries who carry out policies imposed upon them by the system.[14]

NOTES

1. Herbert Kaufman and Victor Jones, "The Mystery of Power," *Public Administrative Review*, 14 (1954), 205.

2. Bertrand Russell, *Power, A New Social Analysis* (New York: Norton, 1962), p. 9.

3. William James, "The Sentiment of Rationality," in *Essays in Pragmatism* (New York: Hafner, 1948), pp. 7–8.

4. For instance, see Harold Lasswell and Abraham Kaplan's *Power and Society* (New Haven: Yale University Press, 1950), an entire book dedicated to the construction of a model, along with derivative definitions and propositions, which despite its great elaboration, or because of it, has been little used in empirical research.

5. Paul A. Baran and Paul M. Sweezy, *Monopoly Capital* (New York: Monthly Review Press, 1966), p. 15.

6. *Leviathan*, ed. C. B. Macpherson (Baltimore: Penguin, 1968), chap. 10, p. 150.

7. Whether these desired goods and values in turn actually advance one's welfare, or the welfare of others for whom one is an advocate, is a question dealt with in the next. chapter.

8. Richard Merelman, "On the Neo-Elitist Critique of Community Power," *American Political Science Review*, 62 (June 1968), 455.

9. David Easton, *The Political System* (New York: Knopf, 1953), p. 143. (Italics added.)

10. *Leviathan*, chapter 13.

11. Max Weber, *The Theory of Social and Economic Organization* (New York: Oxford University Press, 1947), pp. 126–127.

12. See William E. Connolly, "On 'Interests' in Politics," *Politics and Society*, 2 (Summer 1972), 462–463.

13. Willard Waller and Reuben Hill, *The Family* (New York: Dryden, 1951), pp. 190–192; also the discussion in Peter Blau, *Exchange and Power in Social Life* (New York: Wiley, 1964), p. 78 ff; and E. A. Ross, *Principles of Sociology* (New York: Century, 1921), p. 136.

14. Ralph Miliband, "The Capitalist State: Reply to Nicos Poulantzas," *New Left Review*, 59 (January-February 1970), 57.

2

Interests and Consensus

If we decide that interests are neither randomly distributed nor purely self-generated by individuals in a social system but are shaped to some extent by the objective forces of the society that determine the limits of consciousness, then it would seem that people do not always decide in accordance with their own best interests, that at times they may be suffering from what has been called "false consciousness," that is, adhering to beliefs damaging to their interests.

THE QUESTION OF FALSE CONSCIOUSNESS

Some social scientists hold that whatever people define as being in their interest at any given time must be taken as such. To postulate that individuals pursue goals which do not serve them or their group or class, that they suffer from false consciousness, is to presume to know better than they what is best for them. In order to avoid superimposing one's ideological or otherwise subjective expectations on others, the neutral observer should take people's expressions of interest as the only given components of interest—so the argument goes.

This supposedly "neutral" position rests on an unrealistic view of the way people arrive at their beliefs. It denies the sociological fact that people's awareness of how they are affected by issues and events are, as Gamson points out, "subject to social control."[1] In judging what is in their interest, they are influenced by many factors other than interest,[2] among these being the influence of social forces greater than themselves. To quote C. Wright Mills:

> What [people] are interested in is not always what is to their interest; the troubles they are aware of are not always the ones that beset them. . . . it is not only that [people] can be unconscious of their situations; they are often falsely conscious of them.[3]

To assume that the absence of opposition to the existing social order is evidence of a freely arrived at consensus is to rule out the possibility of a manipulated consensus. It is to assume there has been no indoctrination, no socialization to conservative values, no control of information, no limitation of the agenda, no predetermination of interest choice, that power has not been operative in the shaping of interest definition.

If no overt conflict exists between rulers and ruled this may be because (1) the ruled are satisfied with things because their interests are being served; (2) they are dissatisfied but acquiesce reluctantly because they do not see the possibility of change; or (3) they accept the existing order out of lack of awareness that alternatives exist and out of ignorance as to how the rulers are violating their interests. The more conservative social scientists would have us treat (1) as the only condition of consciousness which can be empirically studied because it is supposedly the only one that exists. In fact, with some extra effort one can empirically study and document instances of (2) and (3). What the proponents of (3) are saying is that people's "wants may themselves be a product of a system which works against their interests," and that their interests are what they would really want, were they aware of the choice and free and able to choose.[4]

The rejection of false consciousness as being an "ideological" (read: "Marxist") superimposition leads the orthodox social scientists to the conclusion that no distinction should be made between perceptions of interests and what might be called objective interests. The notion of interest is taken as synonymous with any subjective value choice, no matter how ill-informed or self-defeating the choice might be for the one who chooses. The reduction of interest to a subjective state of mind leads us not to a more rigorous empiricism but to a tautology. "People act in their own interests" becomes "People act as they are motivated to act."[5] Whatever individuals are motivated to do and believe, or not do and not believe, is taken as being in their interest because, by definition, their interest is their motivational condition. This mistakenly presumes that one's awareness of one's social relations is the sum total of those relations.

Without making judgments about people's beliefs we can still inquire as to how they came to their preferences rather than treat these preferences as irreducible and unexaminable givens. For instance, Americans are not congenitally endowed with loyalty to a particular order of competitiveness, acquisitiveness, consumerism, militarism, and hierarchy. The definition they give to their interests is shaped in part by the objective forces determining their life chances.[6] And their life chances may be limited by all sorts of larger forces acting beyond their awareness. Their objective interests have not been translated into a personal perception.

Even if we accept people's subjective awareness as the sum total of their interests, we can still observe false consciousness in the way they pursue these interests—unless we assume they act with infallibility. (Indeed, infallibility *is* imputed by those theorists who insist that whatever policy preference a group articulates must be taken as its interest.) But once we acknowledge that people sometimes make choices that do not maximize even their articulated interests, as when they are uninformed or misinformed, then we are saying that they are exhibiting false consciousness.

People might value good health as a prime life value, and most do, yet unknowingly continue to eat carcinogenic chemicalized foods, breathe colorless, odorless, but lethal air pollutants, ingest dangerous prescription drugs, and suffer the radiation leaks of neighboring nuclear reactors. Their sense that they are enjoying a safe, sanitary life situation, when they are not, leads them to pursue choices and policies harmful to their interests, while remaining oblivious to ones that might better serve them. As Connolly writes:

> Misinformation, poor calculation, or failure to consider feasible but unarticulated policy alternatives might lead one to prefer a policy which

does not, on a comparative basis, maximize his "opportunities to get what he wants." A low-income citizen, for example, might want to maximize his disposable income but then favors a state sales tax over [a progressive] income tax because of a mistaken view about the relative effects of each type on the amount of his disposable income. His policy preference, in this instance, would be at odds with his interest.[7]

THE INNOCENCE OF CONSENSUS THEORY

Not all exchanges of interest involve a choice of relative deprivations for one of the parties. We know individuals and groups exchange resources to further their mutual interests. A general uses his position to persuade the Congress that a defense contract is necessary for national security, and the firm that gets the contract provides him with a high-paying executive post upon his subsequent retirement to civilian life—a not uncommon occurrence. The extended series of collusive actions and pronouncements between the military and the defense industry is enough to show, as Talcott Parsons noted, that not all power is to be interpreted as the efforts of one group to prevent other groups from getting what they want. Power, according to Parsons, can be "the capacity to mobilize the resources of the society for the attainment of goals for which a general 'public' commitment has been made, or may be made."[8]

Parsons may be overstating his case, however. Much of his writing, as is true of that of other social scientists, is dedicated to showing how power is not an instrument of conflicting interests but rather a facility which functions on behalf of "society as a system." This view of human society is comparable to Hobbes's view of ants and bees: private pursuits naturally coalesce into an all-abiding collective interest, a description which Hobbes felt was distinctly not applicable to human society, certainly, one might add, not to any society with deep interest-group divisions. It may be that "every functioning social structure is based on a consensus of values among its members," as Parsons and other exponents of "consensus theory" have argued,[9] but the question remains, whose interests are served by that consensus? A stabilized consensus, an "integration" of values, can well serve as an instrument of authority, conformity, and oppression.

We should also question what is meant by Parsons' contention that the characteristic exercise of power in society serves the "general public" or advances "the society as a system." For even when *certain* groups are exchanging resources to achieve mutually beneficial goals, their actions frequently generate effects which conflict with the interests of others. The interests supported by military-industrial collusion work against the interests of those who might benefit from military budget cuts. Few, if any, exchanges serve every interest in the general public, although partisans are wont to make universal claims for their particular interests.

Any one group will have interests of varying scope. A corporation has (1) interests that are immediately important to it (e.g., winning a certain government contract); (2) interests that are shared by its class (e.g., maintaining high investment profitability); and (3) interests that might be shared by everyone (e.g., avoiding the total destruction of the natural environment). Usually, the more diffuse interests, applicable to the largest number of people, are least likely to receive consideration. For even though all of us may have a common interest in a collective benefit like preservation of the environment, we have no individual interest in paying the costs.[10] The corporation's profit interest is to minimize costs including those relating to pollution control and environmental cleanup, and to continue a high-profit production that happens also to be polluting the environment. To pursue a general good having *diffuse* benefits for everyone but *particular* costs for oneself would be to violate one's immediate and essential financial interests in a serious way. This may explain why corporate heads say that the costs of environmental cleanup should be borne by the public because "industry is not big enough to do the job." With each firm acting individually, industry is, of course, big enough to pollute the environment but when it comes to ecological repair, the particularistic competitive interests of each firm, and the profit-maximizing class interests of industry in general, conflict with society's broader ecological needs. Thus in 1975, the Environmental Protection Agency abolished the award it gives to "the business enterprise that does the most for the environment" because in five years, no business enterprise had done anything to win it.

In sum, consensus theorists notwithstanding, even the most universally embraced interests are not given the same priority by everyone. "It is essential to recognize," Lenski observes, "that all [people] do not share the same goals and even those who do, do not always rank them the same."[11] All of us have an interest in breathing clean air but industrial firms place a higher priority on profit goals. A community which allocates funds for a public library is serving a "public interest" but those of its citizens who have no interest in reading—and there are many—must contribute to the necessary taxes and reap no direct benefit, while still others who look favorably upon a library nevertheless might feel the money would be better spent improving the local hospital.

There is some point, then, at which the cooperative efforts of some groups will conflict with the priorities advocated by others. Indeed, it is the anticipation of such opposition which frequently draws various groups into cooperative effort. Thus we might distinguish between *collusive* power relations involving a mutually advantageous exchange of interest, and *competitive* power relations involving conflicts among interests in which the exchange is asymmetrical and the relationship is antagonistic rather than symbiotic, "situations in which a better bargain for one means less for the other,"[12] otherwise described by game theorists as "zero-sum" decisions.

In his critique of C. Wright Mills, Parsons explicitly rejects the "zero-sum" or "constant-sum" notion of power. As just noted, he sees power as the ever-expanding "capacity of a social system to get things done in its collective interest."[13] Parsons's presumption that there is an articulated collective interest in present-day American society that is expressed through the integration of common values allows him to emphasize the *collusive* aspects of power while neglecting the *competitive* dimensions. By that view, the power of some people seems not to involve the powerlessness of others, and the society has moved beyond class conflict. What is also overlooked is that collusive power relations are frequently a response to, or an anticipation of, competitive ones and the ability to construct collusive relations greatly determines the ability to prevail in competitive ones. *The ideal purpose of collusion is to build such a preponderance of support for a particular interest as to forestall the emergence of competing interests, thereby sustaining the appearance of an unopposed "collective interest."* Indeed, since subordinate groups are frequently coerced into choosing between relative deprivations, much of what passes itself off as cooperative endeavor is on closer examination a coercion of subordinate groups by stronger groups.

Even when benefits are diffusely distributed among large sectors of the public there are often striking inequalities in distribution. A multibillion-dollar highway program brings less driving time to many motorists and jobs to Detroit workers, but more particular and highly profitable benefits go to the oil, automotive, trucking, tire, and motel industries. Furthermore, the existence of a diffuse benefit does not mean that the policy is equitable, democratic, or optimal for the public. A comprehensive mass-transportation program might bring greater diffuse benefits at fewer costs in taxes, lives, and pollution than highway programs.

Theorists like Parsons, who define power as the engagement of a collective grand-positive-sum game in which benefits are wisely distributed within the society and no one ever really loses much, also are inclined to view social problems as resulting from impersonal and innocent causes rather than from the politico-economic inequities that are both the cause and effect of maldistributions of power. Since power, in the Parsonian world, is defined as the collusive efforts of persons directed toward the accepted goals of the entire society, then social problems are treated as little more than the symptoms of insufficient efforts or the results of unavoidable natural developments.

THE SCIENTISTIC PRETENSE

It is often assumed that the important problems of society can be resolved by applying the techniques of science to them. Science will supposedly give us a better understanding of things and more effective strategies for solution. What is missing from this technocratic, scientistic view is the essence of politics itself, an appreciation of the inescapability of interest and power in determining what solutions will be deemed suitable and what goals and methods supportable. Instead it is mistakenly assumed that decision makers and, for that matter, scientists, operate outside the matrix of vested interests.

The presumption that there is a scientifically discoverable "correct" solution to problems overlooks the fact that social problems involve conflicting ends and often irreconcilable interests; thus one person's solution can be another's disaster. A "correct" proposal for some political actors is one which resolves the threat of an opposing interest without causing any loss of privilege, profit, or status to oneself. For other advocates, a "correct" program is one calling for nothing less than momentous reallocations in the substance and process of the entire politico-economic system.

Unlike mathematical problems, which might be resolved by procedures unrelated to the subjectivities of mathematicians, the actual solutions to social problems cannot be treated except in the context of vested and conflicting interests which give vested and conflicting definitions to the problem. This is true whether the question is rebuilding ghettos or withdrawing troops from Vietnam: the solutions are potentially "at hand" or "nowhere in sight," depending on the priorities and interests of various proponents.

The scientistic approach presumes that problems exist because of the ignorance of the would-be problem solvers rather than because of the conditions of power among social groups. But, again, unlike mathematical problems which begin and end on paper, social problems are never resolved by study alone; they need action also. Many of the social ills we live with have been studied repeatedly, but since they have not been resolved it is assumed by the proponents of scientism that they need further study. Here we have an uncharacteristic instance of social scientists pretending to an *ignorance* they do not possess, for the last thing some of our problems need is further study.

Witness the hundreds of studies, reports, surveys, and exposés done on Appalachia by a variety of commissions, committees, economists, and journalists, extending back more than half a century. Neither history nor the historians have "bypassed" or "neglected" the people of Appalachia. Some of the forces of history, in this case the timber and mining companies that swindled and coerced the Appalachians out of their land, exploited their labor, and wreaked havoc with their lives, were all too attentive to the destinies of that region even though never held accountable for the social costs of their actions. The plunder and profit which is the history of the region have been duly documented,[14] yet Appalachia is still treated as a kind of historical mishap, a presumably innocent development of the "changing times," a "complex situation" needing our "concerted attention."

The President's Task Force on Prisoner Rehabilitation said in its 1970 report: "We concluded early that there was no need to search for new ideas about rehabilitating prisoners. The voluminous literature on the subject overflows with excellent ideas that never have been implemented nor, in many cases, even tested."[15] Similarly the plight of the urban poor in various Western industrial societies has been studied and documented by official and unofficial sources for more than a century, and in recent decades we have traced the web of interests, the private and public forces at the national and local levels which have contributed to and perpetuated Black ghettos. The story is well known to us, but our discoveries have brought forth no solutions.

The poor themselves have become increasingly aware of the difference between scientific study and social action. Low-income Blacks in various cities have voiced their opposition to the intrusions of well-financed social scientists. In Champaign, Illinois, to cite one example, a Black community leader protested: "The poor people of Champaign County and our state have found themselves the target of research. Large sums of monies are obtained for research on the conditions of poverty, with those conditions not being changed one bit after the completion of this research."[16] At least one noted political scientist echoes this view: "Although the nation may seem preoccupied with racial vicissitudes, its principal outlet has been little more than a series of paper programs and endless conferences, commissions, and committees."[17]

To be sure, an essential step toward remedy is to investigate the problem. But if no other measure is taken, no move toward action, then the call for "a study of the problem" is justifiably treated as nothing more than a symbolic response, an "appropriate reciprocal noise," designed to convey the impression that decision makers are fulfilling their responsibilities[18] The commissioned "study" becomes an act which violates its own professional purpose: rather than inducing change it is designed to mitigate the demands for change. Appearing before the Kerner Commission on racial disturbances, the psychologist Kenneth B. Clark noted:

> I read that report . . . of the 1919 riot in Chicago, and it is as if I were reading the report of the investigating committee on the Harlem riot of '43, the report of the McCone Commission on the Watts riot.

I must again in candor say to you members of this Commission—it is a kind of Alice in Wonderland—with the same moving picture re-shown over and over again, the same analysis, the same recommendations, and the same inaction.[19]

By incorporating Clark's admonition into its pages, the Kerner Report may have achieved the ultimate in cooptation, for it, itself, was a prime example of that kind of official evasion and obfuscation designed to justify the very status quo about which Clark was complaining. The Kerner Report demanded no changes in the way power and wealth are distributed among the classes; it never got beyond its indictment of "White racism" to specify the forces in the political economy which brought Black people to riot; it treated the obviously abominable ghetto living conditions as "causes" of disturbances but never really inquired into the causes of the "causes," namely the ruthless enclosure of southern sharecroppers by big corporate farming interests, the subsequent mistreatment of the Black migrant by northern rent-gouging landlords, price-gouging merchants, urban "redevelopers," discriminating employers, low wages, underemployment, insufficient schools, hospitals, and welfare, brutal police, hostile political machines and hostile legislators, and finally the whole system of interests and public power distributions on the state and federal levels which gives greater priority to haves than to have-nots.[20]

To treat the *symptoms* of social dislocation (e.g., slum conditions) as the *causes* of social ills is an inversion commonly practiced by government commissions and other social investigators. Unable or unwilling to pursue the implications of their own data, they tend to see the *effects* of a problem as the problem itself. The victims, rather than the victimizers, are defined as "the poverty problem." A haphazard variety of federal, state, and local programs are initiated, focusing on the poor and ignoring the system of power, privilege, and profit which makes them poor. It is a little like blaming the corpse for the murder.

To conclude: many theorists emphasize the symbiotic and functional features of American society. In such an approach, power is treated as a mutually beneficial force advancing the collective performance of the social system. While not denying that power can be, and has been, mobilized for widely popular purposes, it is suggested here that we also begin to appreciate the highly asymmetrical and coercive qualities of many social relationships. Rather than thinking of the social system as a grand-positive-sum game in which everyone gains, we should recognize that interest conflict and constant-sum allocations are more often the rule than the exception, and we should alert ourselves to the causes of deprivation and inequality immanent in the system.

Similarly, we might observe that by underplaying the coercive and exploitative features of social action, and by neutralizing the causes of social problems, we have presumed the existence of neutralized solutions. The traditional conservative view that social problems, by their nature, have no solutions ("The poor shall always be with us") allows little room for rational change. The modern scientistic view that almost all problems are subject to solution by rational investigation and manipulation seemingly allows all the room in the world. Yet both views have certain things in common: both avoid the *political* reality; both fail to draw any link between the social problems of the have-nots and their powerlessness, or more generally, between social problems and power distributions; both accept the existing politico-economic social order as an immutable given, operating with neutral effect. By evading questions of power and interest, investigators who "search for solutions" stay within the safe limits allowed by the powers that be. One reason they fail to find solutions, then, is that they are part of the problem.

NOTES

1. William Gamson, *Power and Discontent* (Homewood, Ill.: Dorsey, 1968).

2. Reinhard Bendix, *Work and Authority in Industry* (New York: Harper & Row, 1963), p. 7.

3. C. Wright Mills, *White Collar* (New York: Galaxy, 1956), p. *xix*.

4. Steven Lukes, *Power: A Radical View* (Atlantic Highlands, N.J.: Humanities Press, 1974), p. 34; an impressive empirical work along these lines is Matthew A. Crenson, *The Un-Politics of Air Pollution: A Study of Non-Decisionmaking in the Cities* (Baltimore: Johns Hopkins University Press, 1971); also John Gaventa and Richard A. Couto, "Appalachia and the Third Face of Power," paper presented at the 1976 annual meeting of the American Political Science Association; for a discussion of objective interests, see William E. Connolly, "On 'Interests' in Politics," *Politics and Society*, 2 (Summer 1972), 462–463.

5. Francis X. Sutton et al., *The American Business Creed* (New York: Schocken Books, 1962), p. 13. Isaac Balbus discusses the tautological nature of defining interest as only that which a person says is in her or his interest. See his "The Concept of Interest in Pluralist and Marxian Analysis," *Politics and Society*, 1 (February 1971), 151–177.

6. Balbus, "The Concept of Interest," p. 153.

7. Connolly, "On 'Interests' in Politics," p. 446. This may be true not only of the common populace but of people of great power and wealth, except that those who control the large economic and political institutions are in a far better position to perceive their interests and control how interests are defined and pursued. Those pluralists who reject the concept of false consciousness as an ideological invention frequently fall back on it. Thus when trying to refute the notion that citizens can designate who are the power elites in their community, Raymond Wolfinger was moved to observe that people "cannot perceive accurately the distribution of political power in their communities." See his "Reputation and Reality in the Study of Community Power," *American Sociological Review*, 25 (1960), 638. But if they have no accurate sense of the distribution of power, then how can we presume that they can make an accurate assessment of what their community interests might be?

8. Talcott Parsons, *Structure and Process in Modern Societies* (Glencoe, Ill.: Free Press, 1960), p. 221.

9. See Ralf Dahrendorf, *Class and Class Conflict in Industrial Society* (Stanford, Calif.: Stanford University Press, 1959), p. 161.

10. See Mancur Olson, Jr., *The Logic of Collective Action* (New York: Schocken Books, 1965).

11. Gerhard Lenski, *Power and Privilege, A Theory of Social Stratification* (New York: McGraw-Hill, 1966), p. 36

12. Thomas C. Schelling, *The Strategy of Conflict* (Cambridge, Mass.: Harvard University Press, 1960), p. 21.

13. Parsons, *Structure and Process*; for a critique of the "consensus theorists," see Lewis Coser, *The Functions of Social Conflict* (New York: Free Press, 1956).

14. See Harry M. Caudill, *Night Comes to the Cumberlands* (Boston: Little, Brown, 1962) for one of the best of many studies of Appalachia.

15. Quoted in *Crime and the Law* (Washington, D.C.: Congressional Quarterly, 1971), p. 13.

16. Remarks by John Lee Johnson reported in *The News Gazette* (Champaign-Urbana, Ill.), December 17, 1969.

17. Andrew Hacker, *The End of the American Era* (New York: Atheneum, 1970), p. 108.

18. See Murray Edelman, *The Symbolic Uses of Politics* (Urbana: University of Illinois Press, 1964) for an explanation of the ritualistic and control functions of political acts.

19. Clark's testimony is quoted in the *Report of the National Advisory Commission on Civil Disorders* (New York: Bantam, 1968), p. 29 ("Kerner Report").

20. See Andrew Kopkind's excellent critique of the Kerner Commission, "White on Black: The Riot Commission and the Rhetoric of Reform," *Hard Times* (no. 44, September 15–22, 1969), 1–4. Often the victims are accused of being the cause of their own conditions. See William Ryan, *Blaming the Victim* (New York: Vintage, 1972).

3

A Farewell to Pluralism

A vast amount of political science research has concentrated on political parties, Congress, the presidency, pressure groups, public administration, and certain of the conventional aspects of public opinion and voter participation. The image that emerges from this literature is of an array of groups competing on an array of issues. Conflict is seen as multilateral and ever-changing, and the bulk of the population is said to consist of diverse interests endowed with "a multitude of techniques for exercising influence on decisions salient to them."[1] Some groups are recognized as being more powerful than others, but political decision makers supposedly operate "on the principle that everyone should get something and no one should be hurt very much."[2] And "all active and legitimate groups in the population can make themselves heard at some crucial stage in the process of decision."[3] If there are elites in our society, they are numerous and specialized and they are checked in their demands by the established "rules of the game" and by the competing demands of other elites, all of whom represent varying, if sometimes overlapping, constituencies.

THE REFRACTED VISION OF
PLURALISM

The emphasis in the academic literature is on the bargaining strategies of contestants, the ways that conflicts are mediated. The government is envisioned as arbiter, stabilizer, and readjuster, trying as best it can through institutional arrangements and the consensus building efforts of political leaders to maintain stability while allowing for gradual change. The United States, in the eyes of political scientists who subscribe to this view, is a "pluralistic" society.[4]

In recent years the pluralist vision of society has been called increasingly into question. If by "pluralism" we are referring to the many regional, class, and ethnic associations which busily make claims upon state, local, and national governing bodies and which compose a multiplicity of public and private interests and identities, then the United States, like any modern society of size and complexity, is pluralistic. (In the Soviet Union, for instance, there are diverse groups within the bureaucracy, the Party, the military, the intelligentsia, etc., all competing for scarce resources, forming alliances according to shifts in priorities and ideology, jockeying for position, and trying to protect their domains against encroachments. But to my knowledge, no American pluralist has declared the "totalitarian" Soviet Union a pluralist society.)

Used in an all-encompassing sense, the term "pluralism" is not a particularly arresting one for those interested in determining whether *power* is democratically operative. However, if by pluralism we mean that the opportunities and resources necessary for the exercise of power are *inclusively* rather than exclusively distributed, that benefits are widely allocated, that institutional and economic elites are subjected to effective controls by the constituencies whose welfare they affect, that neither the enjoyment of dominance nor the suffering of deprivation is the constant condition of any group, and that political and administrative officers operate as guardians of popular needs rather than as servants of wealthy interests, then the assertion that ours is a pluralistic society is not so easily accepted.

What is missing from the pluralist view, among other things, is any sense of how diverse interest groups are related to the social system in which they function. Issues and cleavages are taken as givens rather than as symptoms of broader systemic conditions which themselves might be of concern to students of power. The politico-economic structure is seen as a neutral backdrop against which issues are contested and seldom as a crucial factor of power.

The many community power studies written by pluralists clearly exemplify this deficiency. While mayors and city managers complained that the problems confronting the cities were decisively influenced by corporate and governmental powers whose resources extended far beyond the boundaries of the municipalities, pluralists continued to study cities and towns as if they were autonomous entities in which "key issues" were presumed to be readily detectable and, once studied, productive of theoretical insights about power in America. But the picture that emerged left much to be desired. For instance, in his study of political influence in Chicago during 1956 and 1957, Edward Banfield was able to discover only six controversies of city-wide importance (mostly disputes about the location of various facilities),[5] thereby causing Allen Schick to comment: "The community power studies often were exhaustive in their coverage but they covered little."[6] Despite detailed case studies, most of the questions about how and why resources were, and were not, allocated were never answered because they were never asked.

By insisting that power can be seen only in situational terms, each situation being treated as something new and particular, as a separate case study, the pluralists are able to avoid the whole reality of institutional structure, both public and private. How can one see structured patterns of influence if one refuses to look for them and rules out their existence at the onset? Many pluralists also assume that the most significant political decisions are made publicly and that diverse interests, including those of unorganized voters, influence these decisions either through the pressure of public opinion or through their elected representatives. It may sometimes be so, but it remains to be demonstrated as the case, not assumed as the rule.

In addition, the pluralists overlook the tremendous importance of privately made decisions which might have profound consequences in determining the life chances of millions of people. By so narrowing the scope of inquiry, they conclude that the totality of power is reflected in the visible political arena, in the pursuance only of those decisions which run into enough open conflict as to be defined as "issues." Yet in recent years, with revelations like the Pentagon Papers, Watergate, the secret air war in Cambodia, the outrages of the CIA and the FBI, the manipulations of grain markets, the rigging of oil prices, and the many other unlawful doings of giant corporations, we repeatedly, if belatedly, are discovering that all sorts of covert operations have been going on for years, involving the use of illicit, unaccountable power by the few at the expense of the many, an entire nether world of secret money, plunder, deception, swindle, collusion, intimidation, break-in, political repression, and assassination, a world whose existence the pluralists not only failed to anticipate but blithely dismissed as the "conspiracy fantasies" of the power-elite theorists.

Not a word in the pluralist literature can be found in regard to that kind of power which predetermines the *direction* of policy, not the particulars of policies themselves but the very definition of the policy situation, the definition of what is "possible" and what is "impossible." The pluralist approach, for instance, denies the possibility that some of the most effective uses of power involve the prevention of decisions, the muting of issues, the avoidance of conflict by pre-emptive advantage, by limiting the agenda to suit prevailing interests. Nondecisions are a form of decision, it has been pointed out often enough. The difficulties of empirically observing the "nondecisional" exercise of power should not lead us to the conclusion that it does not exist and that no strategies can be devised for studying it.'

There are many social phenomena, like acts of God or nature, which are beyond human capacity to shape. But should scientific knowledge, historical development, and social organization advance to the point where a particular problem once considered to be independent of human will, for example, poverty, is now within the possibility of solution by a reordering of social goals and reapplication of resources (as demonstrated in certain socialist countries), then "the failure to act with regard to it becomes a deliberate decision."' In other words, implicit in any analysis of why government does certain things is the question of why it does *not* do certain other things—a question ruled out by the pluralists on the grounds that they study only "what is." But the avoidance of certain policy directions, the denial of certain social interests, are as much of "what is" as anything else.

The presumption that all political power is encompassed in the bargaining and decision-making processes also caused pluralists to neglect the muted and less favored groups whose power resources were so limited that they rarely achieved entry into the decision process. The *politically* visible—as defined by a narrow concept of the "political"—was taken as encompassing all that was *empirically* visible. And grievances which lacked political visibility were considered to lack empirical existence. Thus, Nelson Polsby, in his compendium of pluralist presumptions, assures us: "Most of the American communities studied in any detail seem to be relatively healthy political organisms . . ."[9] That the pluralists have been able to investigate so many urban communities and find so little wrong tells us more about their modes of analysis than about urban communities. By defining the conventional arena of politics as the only proper study for students of power, the pluralists avoid the whole question of powerlessness. Thus the pluralism of the late 1950s had no way of anticipating the rage and riot of the 1960s.

The pluralists' stress on close-up empirical investigation of specific decisions arose partly in reaction to the political science of an earlier generation, one that was considered either too "journalistic" or too legalistic or too filled with prescriptions and preachments. But in moving toward what they considered to be a more scientific treatment of political life, the pluralists committed some grievous sins of their own. As early as 1957, Robert Lynd, criticizing the newly arrived "behavioral" group theorists, wrote:

> The present operational approach tends toward analysis of the tactics of power without a theory of power other than the traditional liberal doctrine of the flux of competing forces. Here we see the haven that refined empiricism can provide for the modern social scientist confronted with the problem of power in society: bits of power may be analyzed in detail as tactical moves in an endless game of competing parties and pressure groups, of trends in opinion polls, of the impact of state and regional issues on voting in national elections, and so on, without ever confronting directly the massive, over-all structure of power as a weighting built into the social structure and the institutional system of the society.[10]

Consider Earl Latham's description of America as the "one pluralist world." "Because the relations of people are myriad and shifting," Latham writes, "subject to cycles of deterioration and decay, because the environment itself changes with each passing hour, there is a ceaseless struggle on the part of groups to dominate, neutralize or conciliate that part of their environment that presses in upon them most closely . . ."[11] It is enough to point out that far from being "myriad and shifting," social relations, be they classified as economic, cultural, or political, are limited by time, space, class, occupation, age, and income and are fixed by law, custom, power, and interest, enduring over long periods of time. Latham's world is a free-for-all in which, like so many marbles rolling about on a plate or like bacteria oozing about in a culture whose temperature changes with every minute, we fluidly interact. It is hard to imagine how such a society could survive, let alone function.

For Latham, American society is "an aggregation, a collection, an assemblage, a throng, a moving multitude of human clusters, a consociation of groups, a plurality of collectives, an intersecting series of social organisms, adhering, interpenetrating, overlapping—a simple universe of groups which combine, break, federate and form coalitions and constellations of power in a flux of restless alterations."[12] This undulating, almost orgiastic image of society begs the whole question of structured, institutionalized power, as Lynd notes. It suggests that the loci of power are everywhere and nowhere, and it conjures an invisible hand acting, as in the free market, as a natural regulator of group demands, keeping things flowing and "interpenetrating" more or less for the best interests of all.

PROCESS WITHOUT INTERESTS

The inclination among those who concentrate on the intricacies of the decision process is to treat process as an end in itself (who governs?) while ignoring the substantive effects (who gets what?) and the systemic dimension (*what* governs?). But the substantive effects are what make the decision process a meaningful topic of study, and they are an important force in shaping the efforts of political actors. To study only the antecedent stratagems of a given decision is to impose a rather imperfect understanding of "process," one which does not recognize that outputs are as essential to an understanding of political process as inputs.

The study of policy outputs also is important when treating those groups which seldom achieve visibility in the formal decision process, those people who fare least well in the allocation of social desiderata and whose low index of power ("powerlessness") can be measured by the deprivations suffered, that is, by effects. To be concerned, as are Dahl and Polsby, only with the decision maneuvers that led to the urban-redevelopment program in New Haven without giving any attention to what interests were benefited and what interests were hurt is to give us a most incomplete picture of the purposes of interest-group politics.[13]

The pluralists' emphasis on process and their neglect of class interests are partly motivated by a professed desire to keep empirical descriptions free of normative considerations. Austin Ranney explains that some social scientists "think that focusing on [policy] content is likely to lead to evaluations of present policies and exhortations for new ones."[14] But this fear of the normative produces a rather curious conceptual framework, *one which sometimes overlooks the difference between trying to neutralize oneself as a scientific observer and trying to neutralize one's subject matter.* This confusion is widespread in the social sciences and can have quaint effects. Thus some clinical psychologists, when referring to patients who have sexual desires, speak of "clients" who "cathect their affects onto libidinous objects." It is not clear how the cause of science is advanced by such nomenclature. What *is* clear is the scientistic affectation: having "neutralized" his subject matter with the introduction of an inflated but no more precise vocabulary, and sometimes at a cost to the intrinsic meaning of the subject, the observer mistakenly thinks he has neutralized himself.

In political science, the same confusion persists. The desire to appear dispassionate when dealing with an inherently passionate phenomenon like politics has led to a concentration on topics which are often marginal to political life. *It is one thing to attempt a nonnormative investigation of political processes and another to treat politics itself as a nonnormative process.* Politics, as Marx said, is frequently concerned with "the most violent, mean and mailignant passions of the human breast, the Furies of private interest."[15] Politics is the engagement of purposive persons and institutions capable of the most ruthless measures on behalf of the most noble or ignoble ends, but one does not get that impression from much of the academic literature.

Some pluralists argue that the study of outcomes is a futile task because social outputs cannot be accurately measured and do not readily reflect decision-making interests.[16] This shyness about a subject because it is not readily measurable curiously does not extend to input factors, which usually are far more elusive and less visible than outputs. Indeed, in this age of records and statistics probably the most readily observable dimension of public policy is who gets what. And even if there is no perfect relationship between input influences and output distribution, given the diffuse quality of certain social goods and services, there is certainly *some* kind of important relationship— unless we assume that people always pursue frivolous goals and have no interest in substantive payoffs.

The pluralists' unwillingness to study substantive effects can be ascribed not only to their desire to avoid normative questions but to their assumption that the right normative conditions already obtain. As Schick observes, the pluralists assume that "if the process is working properly, the outcome will be favorable. Hence, there is no need for an explicit examination of outcomes; one can evaluate the process itself to determine its performance and desirability."[17] That groups engage in, and consent to, ongoing allocations is taken as sufficient evidence of the value of the decision process.

Since the distributions effected within the political system are assumed to represent the best of all imperfect worlds, there is no felt need to pursue the question of "who gets what?" The pluralist stance, then, is far from normatively neutral; there is an implicit and often explicit acceptance of the presumed optimal qualities of our sociopolitical system, *an acceptance which forecloses the possibility of important kinds of empirical investigations.* While professing a "behavioralist" dedication to studying only "what is," pluralists treat the system as a structural-functional necessity, or even a desirability, rather than as an object inviting analysis. This approach imparts a conservative vision of political life.

My main complaint is not that pluralists have inserted values of their own while insisting that their investigations are value-free, although this is often the case, nor that they have ignored important normative questions which need serious discussion, although this too is often the case. The present argument with pluralism is conceptual and not one of fact versus value. In this book there is no quarrel with the pluralist dictum that we observe only the observable, but I suggest that what the pluralists have defined as observable is not all that meets the eyes of other researchers. Despite their concentration only on "what is," the pluralists in fact fail to take in all of "what is." What is questioned here are not the precepts of the pluralists' *normative* theory (which, by their own insistence, are afforded no systematic presentation in their work), but the analytic range, operational schema, and conclusions of their "empirical theory."

I will forego the temptation of offering a more detailed critique of the pluralist literature in the pages to follow, partly because so many excellent and devastating evaluations have already been written,[4] and also because my intention is to develop a statement of my own on power in American society.

NOTES

1. Nelson Polsby, *Community Power and Political Theory* (New Haven: Yale University Press, 1963), p. 118.

2. Edward Banfield, *Political Influence* (New York: Free Press, 1961), p. 272.

3. Robert Dahl, *A Preface to Democratic Theory* (Chicago: University of Chicago Press, 1956), p. 137.

4. To cite examples of the "pluralist" view of American politics is to offer a bibliography of the great bulk of traditionalist and behavioralist literature in political science over the last twenty years. A few specific titles might be referred to: Robert Dahl's *Who Governs?* (New Haven: Yale University Press, 1961), offers an interesting and intelligently developed statement on behalf of pluralism. Other pluralist views may be found in Earl Latham, *The Group Basis of Politics: A Study in Basing-Point Legislation* (Ithaca: Cornell University Press, 1952); David Riesman et al., *The Lonely Crowd* (Garden City, N.Y.: Doubleday, 1955); David Truman, *The Governmental Process* (New York: Knopf, 1951); Arnold M. Rose, *The Power Structure* (New York: Oxford University Press, 1967); Polsby, *Community Power*; Banfield, *Political Influence*.

5. Banfield, *Political Influence*, passim.

6. Allen Schick, "Systems Politics and Systems Budgeting," *Public Administration Review*, 29 (March/April 1969), 138.

7. For a study which measures nondecision influence, see Matthew A. Crenson, "Non-issues in City Politics: The Case of Air Pollution," in Marvin Surkin and Alan Wolfe (eds.), *An End to Political Science: The Caucus Papers* (New York: Basic Books, 1970). A longer work by Crenson is his *The Un-Politics of Air Pollution* (Baltimore: Johns Hopkins University Press, 1971).

8. Robert Paul Wolff, *The Poverty of Liberalism* (Boston: Beacon Press, 1968), p. 90.

9. Polsby, *Community Power*, p. 134.

10. Robert S. Lynd, "Power in American Society as Resource and Problem," in Arthur Kornhauser (ed.), *Problems of Power in American Democracy* (Detroit: Wayne State University Press, 1957), p. 3.

11. Latham, *The Group Basis of Politics*, p. 31.

12. Ibid., p. 49; also quoted in Lynd, "Power in American Society," p. 28.

13. Neither Dahl nor Polsby has much to say about the reactions of people displaced by the New Haven urban renewal program. Polsby speculates (*Community Power*, p. 71): "Who wanted urban redevelopment? By 1957, practically everyone who had anything to say in public strongly favored this program." Dahl (*Who Governs?*, p. 244) makes a passing reference to those who did not have "anything to say in public": "several hundred slum dwellers without much political influence" and a handful of small businessmen.

14. Austin Ranney, "The Study of Policy Content: A Framework for Choice," in *Items* (publication of the Science Research Council), September 1968.

15. Marx's comment is found in the preface to the first German edition of *Das Kapital*, vol. 1.

16. See for instance Polsby's unconvincing arguments in *Community Power*, p. 132; also Yehezkel Dror, *Public Policy Making Reexamined* (San Francisco: Chandler, 1968), p. 36 ff.

17. Schick, "Systems Politics," p. 138.

18. Among the many fine antipluralist works, one might cite Grant McConnell, *Private Power and American Democracy* (New York: Knopf, 1966); Ralph Miliband, *The State in Capitalist Society* (New York: Basic Books, 1969); Paul Baran and Paul Sweezy, *Monopoly Capital: An Essay on the American Economic and Social Order* (New York: Monthly Review Press, 1966); Peter Bachrach, *The Theory of Democratic Elitism* (Boston: Little, Brown, 1967); Theodore Lowi, *The End of Liberalism* (New York: Norton, 1969). For detailed critiques of the pluralist literature see the articles by Bay, Kim, Schwartz, Petras, Ono, Gitlin, Bachrach and Baratz, Duncan and Lukes, Davis, Walker, Goldschmidt, and Greaves reprinted in Charles A. McCoy and John Playford (eds.), *Apolitical Politics, a Critique of Behavioralism* (New York: Thomas Y. Crowell, 1967); also Thomas J. Anton, "Power, Pluralism and Local Politics," *Administrative Science Quarterly*, 7 (March 1963), 425–457; Philip Green, "Science, Government and the Case of RAND," *World Politics*, 20 (January 1968), 301–326; G. William Domhoff, *Who Rules America?* (Englewood Cliffs, N.J.: Prentice-Hall, 1967). The essays in Philip Green and Sanford Levinson (eds.), *Power and Community: Dissenting Essays in Political Science* (New York: Pantheon, 1970), especially those by J. Peter Euben, Sanford Levinson, Kenneth Dolbeare, and Michael Rogin, offer further criticisms of pluralism. See also Michael Parenti, "Power and Pluralism: A View from the Bottom," *The Journal of Politics*, 32 (August 1970), 501–530, an expanded version of which is found in Marvin Surkin and Alan Wolfe (eds.), *An End to Political Science: The Caucus Papers* (New York: Basic Books, 1970), 144–166. Also Crenson, *The Un-Politics of Air Pollution*, and Steven Lukes, *Power: A Radical View* (Atlantic

Highlands, N.J.: Humanities Press, 1974). A fine critique already referred to of pluralist assumptions in budget analysis is Schick's "Systems Politics." Also Harold V. Savitch, "Powerlessness in an Urban Ghetto," *Polity*, 5, no. 1, pp. 19-56, offers a good critique in regard to urban policies, as does Jewel Bellush and Stephen M. David (eds.) *Race and Politics in New York City* (New York: Praeger, 1971). Also the writings of Robert Alford, Isaac Balbus, William E. Connolly, Marilyn Gittell, and many others contain important critiques of pluralism. The evidence and arguments raised by the antipluralists over the last dozen years have gone largely unanswered, and in many cases unread, by the pluralists. Raymond Wolfinger made a dismal attempt at defending pluralism by ignoring the more salient criticisms, analyses, and data presented in the above literature. See his "Nondecisions and the Study of Local Politics," *American Political Science Review*, 65 (December 1971), 1063-1080.

Part Two

On Belief and Social Structure

4

The Nature of
Orthodoxy

As noted in chapter 1, power is exercised not only when A is able to get B to *do* something but also when A is able to get B to *think, feel,* or *believe* something, to place a positive value on certain things and a negative value on other things so that B defines his interests and priorities in a way most suitable to A's own interests and priorities. The ability to control the definition of interests is the ability to define the agenda of issues, a capacity tantamount to winning battles without having to fight them.

ORTHODOXY IN THE "OPEN SOCIETY"

When Georg Simmel wrote, "Superordination may be exerted by an individual, by a group, or by an objective force—social or ideal,"[1] he was introducing the notion that the sources of power are found not only in the interactions of individuals but in the context in which they act. The society's belief system, whatever its ambiguities, should not be treated as a mere backdrop of shared attitudes before which actors play out their competitive roles. By defining the limits of legitimacy, by providing the normative guidelines which treat some demands as "essential" and some as "outrageous," the belief system itself becomes one of the resources of power, and itself one of the objects of competition. Indeed, much of political conflict might be described as a struggle among competing perceptions for the privilege of defining the acceptable beliefs about reality.[2]

By virtue of being a *system* (i.e., sets of selective valuations and dedications which bear some relationship to each other, as opposed to a random encyclopedic listing of values), no belief system can give equal accommodation to all human proclivities. The conventional beliefs of a society (the "credenda") compose a value-priority system and as such cannot claim to operate with perfectly inclusive effects but must perforce skew value priorities in one or another direction. The very definition of a society presupposes an ordering of values which favor certain beliefs at the expense of other beliefs. Even in a nation such as the United States which makes great claim to being "open," "pluralistic," and peculiarly "free of ideology," one discovers many and sometimes quite severe limitations placed on heterodoxy, and one soon realizes that certain beliefs are to be pursued only at one's own risk.

Among the factors determining the predominance of particular beliefs, we might take into account the peculiarities of climate, geography, collective temperament, and such factors as seem to have their origin in the age-old accumulations of history and culture. The relationship between culture and historic material conditions is not perfectly isometric. Ideas from one civilization can, with some minimal mutation, be transported over great distances in time and space to another. Today there are people residing in New York City who practice traditional Buddhism, or as close an approximation as might be allowed under the survival imperatives of midtown Manhattan. Also some ethical beliefs, laws, art forms, literature, and cuisines of other societies find their way into our own, lending new and old flavor to our life-styles.

Nevertheless, having observed that cultural transplants and syntheses are possible, we must consider a culture's overall thrust: what are its central themes, its overriding operational codes? For all its residual and deviant side features and plagiarized exotica, our cultural system offers a configuration of traits and values that is anything but haphazard.

Our awareness that extraordinarily complex and sometimes unfathomable antecedents help shape the ideational content of any society should not mislead us into thinking of a belief system as being solely an impersonal, innocent product of time and custom. Cultural beliefs do not just "happen"; they are mediated through a social structure and are, to a large degree, the products of those groups which control the material resources of a society, those who control the institutional and communication systems and who enjoy special access to the symbolic environment and to mass constituencies. In Marx's memorable words:

> The ideas of the ruling class are in every epoch the ruling ideas; i.e., the class, which is the ruling material force of society, is at the same time its ruling intellectual force. The class which has the means of material production at its disposal, has control at the same time over the means of mental production . . .[3]

Weber said it somewhat differently when he noted: "There is a close connection between the prestige of culture and the prestige of power."[4]

The predominant belief system in the United States and much of the Western capitalist world remains the "Lockean ideology," which teaches that individuals are free to make their own way; that freedom is to be defined in competitive, individualistic terms; that "equality of opportunity" means the right to move ahead of others and become unequal to them in life chances; that our goal is self-advancement rather than collective betterment; that private property and the profit system are the mainstays of society, essential to democratic freedoms; that business enterprise and giant corporatism are not a danger to democracy but among its pluralistic components; that democracy is defined as a process encompassed in party elections and parliamentarianism, functioning with presumably meaningful substantive effect regardless of the immense inequalities in wealth and power; that the people are self-governing and free to change social arrangements through properly regulated procedures. "The bounds of the Lockean ideology define for the American mass the limits of legitimate debate, of conceivable alternative."[5]

One axiom of the Lockean theory itself is proscribed, however, namely that people are free to make war against their government should it become oppressive, unaccountable, and indifferent to their woes. Little has been said about this principle since Jefferson's day. In fact, to advocate the forceful overthrow of the government nowadays is a felony. Thus an originally revolutionary ideology hardens into a status quo orthodoxy.

THE APPEARANCES OF HETERODOXY

To say our society offers a "market of ideas" is to apply a misleading metaphor, for ideational wares are seldom afforded the kind of equal currency given goods at an old-time bazaar. The ideational "market" of this society is more like a modern capitalist consumer market. Ideas are distributed the way products are, to mass audiences by those few who have the financial resources to create and control a mass market. The "free competition of ideas," like its counterpart notion of free economic competition, exists more as a legitimating myth than as a material practice. A few ideas and images that are critical and others that are even pornographic, flagrant, violent, and shocking can win access to the business-controlled mass media so long as they do not challenge the legitimacy of the capitalist system. Anticapitalist ideas find what exposure they can in a handful of "little magazines" which function under the constant threat of financial extinction.

"Many values of importance to a democratic society," Robert Lynd writes, "are relatively fragile things. Such values must be granted some measure of genuine freedom as to the areas of experience to which they apply; and they need encouragement and support for what they are and can mean in the society."⁶ Rather than receiving "encouragement and support," politically heterodox ideas and their proponents repeatedly are the objects of concerted attack.⁷

The claims of patriotic oratory notwithstanding, what we have in the United States in regard to the politico-economic system is not the cacophony of many varied and challenging voices but the monotony of the chorus, the straining toward conformity. Yet the illusion of heterodoxy is maintained amidst the practice of orthodoxy by various means. Much of what is considered to be an untrammeled interplay of ideas really involves differences of opinion which seldom stray beyond the acceptable framework of belief. Such differences are treated as evidence of the free flow of opinion when in fact ideas operating outside the pale of ideological respectability are seldom allowed a hearing. Genuine tolerance, Barrington Moore, Jr., reminds us, does not "exist where various nuances of orthodoxy pass for academic freedom."[8]

The gingerly circumscribed treatment sometimes accorded competing ideologies ("Let us consider for a moment what the extremists preach") leaves the impression that alternatives are being open-mindedly entertained, and are being dismissed only after rational investigation. In this way, the ongoing belief system, supposedly having withstood the test of its critics, emerges all the more legitimated in the eyes of its proponents. Heterodoxy is patronized (in both senses of the word) for the implicit purpose of affirming orthodoxy. "For indoctrination to occur it is not necessary that there should be monopolistic control and the prohibition of opposition: it is only necessary that ideological competition should be so unequal as to give a crushing advantage to one side against the other."[9]

Most people have neither the awareness nor the opportunity to construct values and models which transcend the familiar arrangements of the dominant political culture. Even when "all sides" are given a hearing in an occasional discussion group, college lecture, television panel, or news column,

> the people exposed to this impartiality are no *tabulae rasae*, they are indoctrinated by the conditions under which they live and think and which they do not transcend. To enable them to become autonomous, to find by themselves what is true and what is false . . . in the existing society, they would have to be freed from the prevailing indoctrination (*which is no longer recognized as indoctrination*).[10]

This last point should not be passed over. Socially acceptable vocabularies and symbols are so enshrouded with positive affects as to preclude responsiveness to competing symbols. Without the individual's awareness, foreclosure occurs both in the symbolic environment that mediates the stimuli and in the internalized self-censoring mentality which the recipient superimposes upon his or her own perceptions.

The "truth" and "objectivity" of one's view of social reality find reinforcement in the perceptions of other individuals similarly indoctrinated and in the familiarity which custom lends to experience. As William James wrote:

> Philosophers long ago observed the remarkable fact that mere familiarity with things is able to produce a feeling of their rationality . . . To explain a thing is to pass easily back to its antecedents; to know it is easily to foresee its consequents. Custom, which lets us do both, is thus the source of whatever rationality the thing may gain in our thought . . . Novelty *per se* becomes a mental irritant, while custom *per se* is a mental sedative . . .[11]

The most effective ideologies are not those that prevail against all challenges but those that are never challenged because in their ubiquity, in their cultural entrenchment, they appear more like "the nature of things."[12]

"When orthodoxy examines something new from its entrenched position, from its own assumptions and beliefs—whether in politics, religion, or science—it inevitably finds only heresy."[13] Accusations of "partisanship" and "lack of objectivity" are leveled against those who challenge—but rarely against those who reinforce—ongoing social, economic, and political orientations. Thus we are warned against the dogmas of the left and of the right, but not a word is uttered about the dogmas of the center, since these are perceived not as dogmas but, again, as the nature of things.

The ruling ideas gain such a legitimacy and long-standing support as to become a force of their own, internalized in the minds of millions, supposedly defining the difference between ideas that are "realistic," "moderate," and "unbiased" and ideas that are not. In time, the ruling ideas serve not only as an *effect* of class power, they become a *cause*, acting as a support for the very class interests sustaining them.

Legitimated ideas and institutions allow for a double standard of political perception. Repressive and "extremist" actions which are treated as evidence of tyranny in other societies are accepted as necessary steps to ensure the security of one's own. Thus the widespread violations of law committed by intelligence agencies and security forces and the organized police violence perpetrated against dissenters are treated as isolated and aberrant happenings—on the occasions they are publicized—rather than as inherent manifestations of our social order. But the same practices in certain other lands are seen as predictable and necessary components of "totalitarian" systems. The German invasion of Poland in 1939 is fascism in action; the American invasion of Vietnam is a "blunder," an "overextension," or at worst an "immoral application" of power. The indoctrination of children in Nazi Germany or the Soviet Union into the myths and rituals of the nation-state is taken as a typical trait of totalitarianism, but our own grade school indoctrination, replete with flag salutes, national anthems, and history books espousing the myths of American virtue and American superiority, is "education for citizenship." Many repressive social arrangements which would evoke strongly negative sentiments if defined as products of some foreign undemocratic state become by their proximity and familiarity no cause for alarm when practiced at home.

The orthodox center is frequently characterized, by those who occupy it, as a democratic force fighting a war on two fronts against the extremes of right and left. Certainly the center has had its differences with the right as when the conflicting interests of the ruling classes of centrist and rightist capitalist nations devolved into armed conflict in World War II. (Although even in this instance, the main fear of the United States Congress up until the eve of the war was not Nazi Germany but Communism. Throughout the 1930s, attempts by the Soviet Union to form a left-center coalition against Germany and Japan were repeatedly rebuffed by the Western capitalist nations.) In most domestic conflicts and overseas interventions, the center has been more inclined to make common cause with the right against the left than oppose both with equal fervor. This has been so even when the right has been fascist and the left has been democratic as was the case with United States intervention in places like Guatemala, Iran, Indonesia, the Dominican Republic, and Chile. Far from being a blameless victim when fascism emerges, the center is something of an active accomplice. Be it Weimar Germany or the present-day United States, the repressive forces of the state have been used vigorously against the left and rarely against the right.[14]

The collusion between center and right is understandable. Despite their differences in emphasis and method (differences that are not always to be dismissed as insignificant), the center and right share a common commitment to the capitalist system and the ongoing class structure and institutional hierarchy, along with a common hostility toward socialism of whatever variety.

While capable of extensive repressive actions at home and abroad, including the waging of genocidal wars against Third World peoples, those of the orthodox center consider themselves incapable of the extremism ascribed to the right and left "dogmatists." Indeed, the very linear model they apply to politics (extreme left/left/center/right/extreme right), like any line or spectrum, can extend itself at both ends to allow for limitless extremes but makes no spatial provisions for an extreme center. The extreme, according to Webster's dictionary, is "the utmost part, the utmost limit, an extremity." Therefore, the very notion of an extreme center is a contradiction in terms. The extremes of the center on a linear political spectrum, to the extent they can be imagined, are nothing more than the beginnings of a "moderate" left and "moderate" right.

But "extreme" has another meaning, to quote Webster's again, "an excessive or immoderate degree, condition or measure." Implicit in the second definition is the image of the intransigent, dogmatic, and violent extremist, and in common parlance, this second meaning is often blended into the first so that the spatial relationship of extreme-moderate-extreme as placements on a schematized linear model takes on a moral quality. By way of a spatial metaphor, the center retains its virtue, becoming incapable of political extremism. The center is a place inhabited by "moderates" who by definition cannot be immoderate.

Yet, in truth, it does not follow deductively that those who occupy the extremes of a linear model, a placement made in accordance with beliefs about changing the established politico-economic order, must perforce be extremists in the pejorative sense, nor does it follow that those who occupy the mainstream center of any political spectrum are thereby incapable of the kind of immoderate, brutal, repressive, destructive, intransigent actions usually associated with "extremists." It was not right-wing fascists who tried to bomb Indochina into the Stone Age, who developed the policy of free-fire zones, used thousands of tons of antipersonnel and napalm bombs against civilian populations and resorted to the widespread systematic assassination of Vietnamese dissenters; it was "the best and the brightest" of the mainstream center.

In sum, the dominant myths, symbols, vocabulary, and belief orientations which envelop the minds of people and set limits to their political struggles and perceptions become important resources of power worthy of systematic study. The function of the dominant ideology is to legitimate the ongoing social order. One method of legitimacy is to deny the very existence of a dominant ideology and profess a commitment to the market of ideas. Yet in practice, heterodoxies are accorded only the most limited kinds of exposure. The socializing institutions of the society, the public school, the pulpit, the professions, the press, the political parties, the police, the courts, and other agencies of the capitalist system lean hard in the direction of the established ideology, propagating acceptable values, muting and discrediting unacceptable ones. In the chapters ahead more will be said about these socializing institutions.

NOTES

1. Georg Simmel, *The Sociology of Georg Simmel*, ed. Kurt H. Wolff (New York: Free Press, 1964), p. 190.

2. Stanley Hoffman, "Perceptions, Reality and the Franco-American Conflict," *Journal of International Affairs*, 21, no. 1 (1967), 57.

3. Karl Marx, *The German Ideology* (New York: International Publishers, 1947), p. 39.

4. Max Weber, "Structures of Power," *From Max Weber*, edited by Hans Gerth and C. Wright Mills (New York: Oxford University Press, 1958), p. 448n.

5. Susan S. Fainstein and Norman I. Fainstein, "American Social Policy: Beyond Progressive Analysis," in Dorothy B. James (ed.) *Outside, Looking In: Critiques of American Policies and Institutions Left and Right* (New York: Harper & Row, 1972), p. 226.

6. Robert S. Lynd, "Power in American Society as Resource and Problem," in Arthur Kornhauser (ed.), *Problems of Power in American Democracy* (Detroit: Wayne State University Press, 1957), p. 31.

7. For extensive documentation of this point, see Michael Parenti, *Democracy for the Few*, 2nd ed. (New York: St. Martin's, 1977), pp. 149–175, and the sources cited therein.

8. Barrington Moore, Jr., "Tolerance and the Scientific Outlook," in Herbert Marcuse, Barrington Moore, Jr., and Robert Paul Wolff, *A Critique of Pure Tolerance* (Boston: Beacon Press, 1965), p. 63.

9. Ralph Miliband, *The State in Capitalist Society* (New York: Basic Books, 1969), p. 182.

10. Herbert Marcuse, "Repressive Tolerance," in Herbert Marcuse, Barrington Moore, Jr., and Robert Paul Wolff, *A Critique of Pure Tolerance* (Boston: Beacon Press, 1965), pp. 98–99.

11. William James, "The Sentiment of Rationality," in his *Essays in Pragmatism* (New York: Hafner, 1948), p. 13.

12. See Michael Parenti, *The Anti-Communist Impulse* (New York: Random House, 1969), p. 4.

13. Alain Naudé, in his introduction to George Vithoulkas, *Homeopathy, Medicine of the New Man* (New York: Avon, 1971), pp. 9–10.

14. See Franz Neumann, *Behemoth* (New York: Octagon, 1963), on the Weimar Republic's suppression of the left and coddling of the right; and Michael Parenti, *Democracy for the Few*, 2nd ed. (New York: St. Martin's Press, 1977), for evidence of the same official behavior in the present-day United States.

5

The Organization of Wealth

It is doubtful that an investigation of economic forces will tell us all we need to know about power in society, but our understanding of power and politics would be hopelessly incomplete without some analysis of the organization of wealth.

SCARCITY AMIDST PLENTY

Let us begin with some fundamentals. All people, having an interest in survival, need access to the minimal necessities of life. Even the holy ascetic must maintain his physical existence in order to continue his spiritual pursuits. Satisfaction of basic material needs is the first condition of life. Living in something less than a state of automatic nurturance in their natural environment, human beings find it necessary to involve themselves in productive labor in order to create the material conditions which sustain life. To do so is also to involve themselves with each other. The need for survival, security, food, shelter, sex, companionship, communal living, and caring for offspring require that people enter into various kinds of ordered social relations. Ways must be found to sustain production (that is, sustain the material base that allows life to continue) and regulate the distribution of material and nonmaterial desiderata.

Individual capacities for labor are not perfectly congruous with individual needs. Persons with special disabilities, who often have special needs, are least able to provide for themselves, for example, the very young, the very old, and the infirm. A reliance on personal ability with no provision made for redistribution of resources according to need imposes hardship on those handicapped by endowment or disability. When the rule is dog eat dog, and personal prowess, cunning, brute force, and cupidity become the untrammeled determinants of who gets what and who controls what resources, we can expect sharp inequalities to arise and deprivations to be suffered by many.

This is especially true as wealth accumulates. Gerhard Lenski marshals a good deal of anthropological evidence to support the view that there is a correlation between the amount of material wealth in a society and the degree of inequality.[1] In the subsistence economies of hunting, food gathering, and early horticultural societies, the disparities are not great and the degree of sharing is impressive. *Need* rather than power seems to be the primary consideration in the distribution of resources. The tribe as a collective may know extreme hardship but as long as there is food, there is a place at the fireside for everyone. Observing the Iroquois in 1656, a Jesuit priest wrote: "Hospitals for the poor would be useless among them, because there are no beggars. Those who have are so liberal to those who are in want, that everything is enjoyed in common. The whole village must be in distress before any individual is left in necessity."[2] His observation could apply to many "primitive" peoples. In the subsistence economy some persons may excel in hunting and food gathering, thereby enjoying slight advantages in possession, consumption, and prestige, but usually no one has built up the kind of surplus that enables him to organize large numbers of others in undertakings dedicated to his personal gain.

The accumulation of material surplus,[3] however, as found in the more advanced horticultural and later agrarian and industrial societies, leads to the development of large-scale organizations dedicated to the production and protection of wealth. *Instead of private efforts being mobilized for collective interests, collective efforts are increas-*

ingly mobilized for private interests. Minor inequalities are compounded and the gulf between haves and have-nots becomes more marked as wealth accumulates.

In the subsistence primitive societies only a very limited degree of tyranny is possible. Chiefs may be selfish and abusive but, Lenski notes, "the means are not yet available for the tyrant to protect himself against the reaction which develops if he presses his interests too far." The chief among a tribe of hunters lacks "a staff of dependent specialists whose interests are linked with his. Furthermore, the general democracy in weapons and the universal experience in their use combine to put him at a disadvantage against an aroused opposition."[4] But in the more abundant economy, a portion of the surplus can be used to support retainers and armed guardians whose job is to protect the prosperous and allow them to expand their holdings still further. *Power* rather than *need* becomes the chief determinant of who gets what. Social inequalities deepen as the economic surplus expands and as armed men are organized under the command of propertied interests. Propertyless people are trained and paid to keep other propertyless people in line. The taboos and restrictions of property are codified and sanctified as part of the "public order." In effect, a state is born. The security forces advance in technology to the point where average citizens cannot compete on equal terms in any contest of arms.

The anthropologist Meyer Fortes finds that tribes which have no sharp divisions in status and wealth lack centralized authority and administrative machinery, whereas all those that do have accumulations in wealth and privileges have developed a state apparatus.[5] Writing almost two centuries before Fortes, Adam Smith noted the relative absence of such things as rank, command, and privileged birth in subsistence hunting societies and their emergence with the development of accumulated wealth.[6] As class differences become more pronounced so does the need for a public authority. Smith writes:

> The acquisition of valuable and extensive property . . . necessarily requires the establishment of civil government. Where there is no property, or at least none that exceeds the value of two or three days labour, civil government is not so necessary.

Civil government supposes a certain subordination. But as the necessity of civil government gradually grows up with the acquisition of valuable property, so the principal causes which naturally introduce subordination gradually grow up with the growth of that valuable property.[7]

Through inheritance, the differences in wealth soon became distinctions of birth. The difference between aristocrat and commoner, and most other differences in clan and social rank, originate in the acquisition of wealth. To quote Smith again:

Superiority of birth supposes an ancient superiority of fortune in the family of the person who claims it. All families are equally ancient; and the ancestors of the prince, though they may be better known, cannot well be more numerous than those of the beggar. Antiquity of family means everywhere the antiquity either of wealth or of that greatness which is commonly either founded upon wealth or accompanied with it. . . . There never was, I believe, a great family in the world whose illustration was entirely derived from the inheritance of wisdom and virtue.[8]

PROFIT AS PURPOSE

In modern capitalist societies, millions live in poverty amidst an affluence never before seen in history. This condition cannot be blamed on the innate capacity of productive units but on the way productive resources are used and distributed. While busily trying to create new and somewhat artificial *wants* through advertising, in order to sell the great piles of goods and services that glut the market, private industry inadvertently creates new and quite real *needs*, as when it destroys the natural environment which sustain us. Thus do we begin to surmise that industrialization, at least in its present devotion to private interests, sometimes creates more difficulties than it solves, and we grow increasingly skeptical that technological advances bring us ever closer to the good life so confidently envisioned by earlier generations.

When trying to understand the persistence of poverty in modern capitalist nations, we should keep in mind that under capitalism private profit rather than collective need is the principal determinant of who gets what. As Lichtheim reminds us, capitalism "operates for the benefit of paying customers only and does not recognize the existence of other people."[9] The distribution of rewards is a manifestation of the distribution of wealth and power rather than of needs.[10] Those who have the power, or the buying power, command most of the productive outputs and other desiderata. Hence, in every capitalist society, an endless array of new frivolous indulgences is created while old and essential needs go unanswered.[11]

The overriding, inescapable concern of the businessman is not the general welfare, but, as Veblen puts it, the maximization of pecuniary interests.[12] Technological innovation, improved goods and services, considerations of public safety and social need, these engage capitalist effort only to the extent they serve profits. New modes of production and new areas of investment are often delayed even after having "become patently advisable on industrial grounds" because profit opportunities are not seen as sufficiently promising.

The driving motive behind the emergence of the giant business trusts during the early part of this century, Gabriel Kolko demonstrates, was not to increase technical efficiency—which often did *not* occur with consolidation—but to restrict competition, extend financial controls, fix prices, and thus increase profits.[13] Because of financial considerations, consolidations may not take place even when beneficial for production. It was Veblen's opinion that the consolidation of the American transportation system was retarded by forty years. Josephson comes to a similar conclusion in his study of the "robber barons," pointing out that monopolistic profiteering practices, rather than "rationalizing" the economy, often had a retarding effect on production and technology.[14]

The pursuit of profit may or may not be without beneficial social consequences, but the important point is that social consequences are of secondary consideration when measured against the financial interests of the business enterprise. To quote Werner Sombart:

> Production for exchange (as opposed to production for use) is the motto of economic activities. As much profit as possible is their ideal; consequently what matters is not the goodness or the kind of commodities produced but their salability. How they are sold is secondary, so long as they are sold. Consequently the undertaker [i.e., entrepreneur] is wholly

indifferent to the quality of his wares; he will make shoddy goods or cheap substitutes, if only it pays . . . [There] are cases where there is more profit from high-class goods than from inferior articles. The greatest gain is the only criterion in these matters, and an undertaker will make now cheap goods, now dearer, according as the one or the other yields more profit. From the capitalist's standpoint that is only natural.[15]

Certainly, businessmen are not totally immune to what Veblen called "the sentimental factors": a sense of equity, fair dealing, and a desire to bring some creditable improvement in the industrial process; but these laudable impulses are severely circumscribed by the necessities of competition and profit seeking.[16] On rare occasions, managerial elites might even go out of their way to heighten the serviceability of their product in ways contradictory to their pecuniary interest. "Such aberrations," Veblen writes, "are, of course, not large, and if they are persisted in to any very appreciable extent the result is, of course, disastrous to the enterprise. The enterprise in such a case falls out of the category of business management and falls under the imputation of philanthropy"[17]—not the preferred destiny of most firms. "The vital point of production" for management "is the vendibility of the output, its convertibility into money values, not its serviceability for the needs of mankind,"[18] a fact we may bemoan or applaud but should not ignore.

The managerial-capitalist elites who control the livelihoods and well-being of large numbers of people are in an advantageous position to maximize their own influence over both economic and non-economic life; that is to say, material resources can be parlayed into (1) control of still more material resources, and (2) control of non-material resources.

To consider the first: those who have capital goods not needed for personal exchange or consumption (i.e., capital surplus) have the best, indeed, usually the exclusive, ability to compete for other highly valued capital goods. Theorists as disparate as Marx and Weber have noted how the opportunities for capital accumulation are monopolized by the owning class.[19] Those who own wealth are able to enter into advantageous relations with large numbers of people, making claim to their physical and mental labor. "Whereas the employer buys labor power," Peter Blau notes, "just as he buys raw materials, by investing money to make a money profit, the employee's income represents his whole livelihood, not simply one of many profitable transactions, and what he invests is not money at all but a good part of his life."[20]

The means of production (the farm, mine, shop, store, factory, and office) are, for the propertyless, the means of labor. Being without capital resources of their own on which to work, employees must pay for access to the capital of others.[21] Thus a major portion of the wealth they produce is left to the owners of the capital. Under such a system the worker can be assured that those who give him this limited access to their capital (discounting instances when family favor is the prime consideration) do so with the intention of making money from his labor. The tenant farmer who surrenders half his crop to an absentee landlord, the factory laborer who works on the assembly line for a set wage, even the high-salaried scientist in a company laboratory all have this in common: some substantial portion of the product of their physical or mental labor remains with those who control the means of their labor, those who control the capital.

In return for their efforts, workers receive wages that may or may not provide a comfortable livelihood but which rarely allow for the creation of large-scale productive units or for competing modes of capital accumulation. The relationship between employer and employee, as measured in material terms, is to the former's advantage. It is an asymmetrical exchange of interests insofar as the net wealth created by labor is not returned to the laborer but is distributed so as to augment the surplus wealth of the owner, thereby further increasing the latter's opportunities for investment and profit. Quite simply, as the history of capitalism demonstrates, possession of wealth increases the opportunities for acquiring still more wealth. In a free-market system knowing few of the communal restraints of primitive traditional societies, "small inequalities tend to generate greater inequalities and great inequalities still greater ones."[22] Or, as the saying goes, nothing makes money like money.

In modern times, corporate leaders and their spokesmen have fostered the notion that business firms are run by "public-minded managers" and "neutral technocrats" whose first concern is "public well-being rather than private avarice."[23] Thus one noted sociologist proclaims, "Never has the imputation of a profit motive been further from the real motive of men than it is for modern [corporation] managers."[24] The separation of ownership from management supposedly has created a benign service-minded corporation. In reality, corporate managers are themselves usually wealthy men and big investors with direct interests in big profits. Their careers depend upon their ability to advance the fortune of their firms. The economist James S. Earley observes:

> The major goals of modern large-scale business are high managerial incomes, good profits, a strong competitive position, and growth. Modern management does not view these goals as seriously inconsistent but rather, indeed as necessary, one to the other. Competitive strength and even survival, management believes, require large innovative and substantial growth expenditures in the rapidly changing technical and market conditions of the present day. Since growth by merger is hazardous and frequently impossible, large and more or less continuous capital expenditures are necessary. For well-recognized reasons, management wishes to minimize outside financing, so the funds for most of these expenditures must be internally generated. This requires high and growing profits above dividend levels. So, too, do high managerial rewards. High and rising profits are hence an instrument as well as the direct goal of great importance.[25]

Profit rather than philanthropy remains the ultimate measure of corporate success and the raison d'etre of business.

During the late nineteenth century some tycoons anticipated a time when the expansion of business would no longer be necessary. But men like Andrew Carnegie and John D. Rockefeller invariably discovered that to delay expansion was to invite regression. "It frequently happens," Sombart wrote, "that [the entrepreneur] really does not want to expand further, but he must."[26] The imperatives of a modern market economy—the accumulation of profit and the need to invest surplus capital, the need for strategic overseas materials and new markets, the emergence of new wants and the instabilities of old markets, the development of important new productive methods, the threat of recession and depression, the pressures of domestic and foreign competition—all these force capitalism into its restless, endless expansion.

Growth itself creates the demand for new capital. "The more the business grew," the first Rockefeller once remarked, "the more capital we put into it." Growth may often follow investment but, just as readily, investment follows growth. A kind of monomaniacal imperative sets in, as Sombart observes: "Capital is piled on capital *because* the business grows."²⁷ And so people are caught in a system of action because others are similarly caught.

> In the olden days, when industry was preached as a prime virtue in the tradesman, it was necessary to implant a solid foundation of duties in the inner consciousness of men . . . Today all this is changed. The businessman works at high pressure because the stress of economic activities carries him along in spite of himself. He is no longer exercising a virtue; necessity drives him to this particular course. The general business pace determines what his own business pace shall be. He can no more be idle than a man at a machine. . .²⁸

FROM WEALTH TO
NATIONAL POWER

The ceaseless investment of profit for the making of profit, the endless search for new markets and resources all lead to overseas expansion and to the expropriation of one nation's labor, land, and natural resources by another nation's ruling class, a process known as "economic imperialism" although its apologists have variously described it as "the white man's burden," "exporting the American Way," "bringing prosperity to the less fortunate," and "closing the gap between rich and poor nations." In fact, the gap continues to widen because the net effect of capital expansion is to increase the wealth of the investors at the expense of the "recipient" nations. The result is usually a maldeveloped, one-product economy in the exploited nation which serves the productive interests of the exploiter and leaves in its wake high unemployment, illiteracy, poverty, disease, massive neglect of essential human services, and a worsening of the life chances and material conditions of Third World peoples.

The capitalist plunder of the Third World's land and labor is a process that has gone on for five centuries, so that today "underdeveloped" nations would be better described as "overexploited."²⁹ Rebellions against foreign intruders are as old as the first European incursions into Africa, Asia, and South America. But in the twentieth century these rebellions have taken on newly rationalized forms of national liberation and have won some resounding successes against Western capitalist power, causing a country like the United States vastly to increase its repressive state apparatus around the world.

If, as noted earlier, there is a net transfer of wealth from those who must pay for access to the means of labor to those who own the means, there is also a transfer of social power and prestige. Those who own the means of labor (or means of production), and who thereby control the means of sustenance and survival, begin to accumulate prerogatives extending well beyond their original domain. Since they are presumedly burdened with the awesome responsibility of sustaining the entire community ("Where would we be without the company?"), they—and the incorporated entities they have formed—are given special considerations.

Exceptional responsibilities are accorded exceptional privileges. These privileges soon steal into many areas, and it is not long before the use of public resources, the setting of communal priorities, the defining of social statuses, and the shaping of institutional and cultural life including important dimensions of law, politics, religion, and education are affected by the "socially responsible" elements of the corporate class. In actuality the corporation's "social responsibility" is not to maintain the health and welfare of society but of "society's" productive units. Thus, the corporation's social responsibility is nothing more than to itself, to its own system of production and accumulation.

We might conclude by observing that individuals amass great wealth in the same way they amass great power: by enlisting the skills and energies of many others. Power is derived from the loyalty of others and wealth is derived from the labor of others. What is significant is the connection between the two: to command the talents, energies, and options of others in matters of material survival and well-being, to determine who gets what, is to exercise an essential power over their lives and loyalties.

NOTES

1. Gerhard Lenski, *Power and Privilege, A Theory of Social Stratification* (New York: McGraw-Hill, 1966), passim.

2. Quoted in *Akwasane Notes* (a Mohawk Nation publication), May 1971, p. 24.

3. Lenski defines "surplus" as those "goods and services over and above the minimum required to keep producers alive and productive," *Power and Privilege*, p. 44. Baran and Sweezy define economic surplus as "The difference between what a society produces and the costs of producing it. The size of the surplus is an index of productivity and wealth, of how much freedom a society has to accomplish whatever goals it may set for itself. The composition of the surplus shows how it uses that freedom: how much it invests in expanding its productive capacity, how much it consumes in various forms, how much it wastes and in what ways." Paul Baran and Paul Sweezy, *Monopoly Capital* (New York: Monthly Review Press, 1966), pp. 9–10.

4. Lenski, *Power and Privilege*, p. 140.

5. Meyer Fortes and E. E. Evans-Pritchard (eds.), *African Political Systems* (London: Oxford University Press, 1940), p. 5.

6. Adam Smith, *The Wealth of Nations* (Chicago: Encyclopedia Britannica, Inc., 1952), book 5 and passim.

7. Ibid., p. 309.

8. Ibid., p. 310.

9. George Lichtheim, "What Socialism Is and Is Not," *New York Review of Books*, April 9, 1970.

10. Lenski, *Power and Privilege*, p. 63.

11. For a good overview of the deficiencies of modern capitalism, see Paul Baran, *The Political Economy of Growth* (New York: Monthly Review Press, 1957).

12. Thorstein Veblen, *The Theory of Business Enterprise* (New York: New American Library, n.d.; originally published in 1904), chapter 3. For case studies of the ways businessmen habitually violate the public's welfare for the sake of profit, see Robert Heilbroner et al., *In the Name of Profit, Profiles in Corporate Irresponsibility* (Garden City, N.Y.: Doubleday, 1972).

13. Gabriel Kolko, *The Triumph of Conservatism* (Chicago: Quadrangle, 1967).

14. Matthew Josephson, *The Robber Barons* (New York: Harcourt, Brace and World, 1934).

15. Selection from Werner Sombart, *The Quintessence of Capitalism*, in Hendrick M. Ruitenbeck, *Varieties of Classic Social Theory* (New York: Dutton, 1963), p. 189.

16. Veblen, *Theory of Business Enterprise*, p. 26.

17. Ibid., p. 193n. He cites instances of businessmen who refuse to deal in deleterious commodities and who consider safety and health factors even when not pressed to do so; also the occasions when the more prosperous entrepreneurs take pride and pain to give not the best service that profit demands, but the best that profit will allow. In some of these instances, of course, there is a disguised pecuniary interest especially when the "altruistic" act involves a minor substantive allocation while promising a real return in market prestige and good will.

18. Veblen, *Theory of Business Enterprise*, p. 30.

19. Marx's position on this question needs no documentation; for Weber's views see his "Class, Status, Party" in Hans Gerth and C. Wright Mills (eds.), *From Max Weber: Essays in Sociology* (New York: Oxford University Press, 1958), pp. 181–182.

20. Peter M. Blau, *Exchange and Power in Social Life* (New York: Wiley, 1964), p. 164.

21. See the comment in C. B. Macpherson, *The Real World of Democracy* (Oxford: Clarendon Press, 1966), p. 48.

22. Lenski, *Power and Privilege*, p. 341.

23. A. A. Berle, Jr., and Gardiner C. Means, *The Modern Corporation and Private Property* (New York: Harcourt, Brace and World, 1932), p. 356.

24. Rolf Dahrendorf, *Class and Class Conflict in Industrial Society* (Stanford,

Calif: Stanford University Press, 1959), p. 46.

25. James S. Earley, an unpublished paper quoted in Baran and Sweezy, *Monopoly Capital,* p. 25. One study finds that the profit orientation of executives in management-controlled companies was more or less as intense as those in owner-controlled firms. See Robert J. Larner, *Management Control and the Large Corporation* (New York: Dunuellen, 1970).

26. Sombart, *Quintessence,* in Ruitenbeck, *Varieties of Classic Social Theory,* pp. 182–183.

27. Ibid. Italics in the original. The quotation from Rockefeller is also from Sombart, *Quintessence.*

28. Sombart, *Quintessence,* in Ruitenbeck, *Varieties of Classic Social Theory,* p. 192.

29. For an historical view of capitalist exploitation of the Third World, see Eduardo Galeano, *Open Veins of Latin America* (New York: Monthly Review Press, 1973); and Ernest Mandel, *Marxist Economic Theory, Vol. 2* (New York: Monthly Review Press, 1968); Baran, *The Political Economy of Growth.*

6

Powerful Resources and Powerless People

A fundamental theme of this chapter and the ones to follow is that the resources of power are not randomly scattered among the population to be used in autonomous ways but are distributed within a social system, and the way the system is organized has a decisive effect on what resources are available to whom. Any listing of the resources of power would include property, wealth, organization, social prestige, social legitimacy, number of adherents, various kinds of knowledgeability and leadership skills, technological skills, control of jobs, control of information, ability to manipulate the symbolic environment, and ability to apply force and violence. This list is not exhaustive and its categories are crude and overlapping, but there probably would be fairly wide agreement among students of various persuasions that its items represent most of the essential power resources.[1]

THE SOCIAL DESIDERATA

Dahl reminds us that when we say someone is powerful, we should specify powerful in respect to what.[2] Most of us exercise some kind of power in one situation or another and no one can claim to be all-powerful in all things. Similarly when speaking of the powerless, we must ask powerless in respect to what. Few people are powerless in all instances, under all conditions. Powerlessness, as used here, means the inability to get what one needs or wants (the social desiderata) and the inability to influence others effectively in ways furthering one's own interests. "Powerless" is a shorthand expression for "low index of power."

Lacking accessibility to power resources, certain classes of people will chronically gain a deficient share of the social desiderata. In modern Western societies the social desiderata are usually thought to include such things as material comfort; financial security; adequate and safe diet; clean natural environment; good health and good medical care; sanitary living conditions; opportunities for recreation, learning, self-development, and self-esteem; autonomy of choice in personal affairs; opportunities for participation in social affairs; gratifying personal relationships; meaningful and useful work, freedom from exploitative and degrading labor, and other such tangible and intangible life values.[3]

What are and are not to be considered desiderata, however, is far from a settled question. Competition for the privilege of defining and ranking the desiderata is itself a point of political contention. Dif-· ferences as to the significance and desirability of particular social outputs vary with class, subcultural context, and ideological commitment. The position people occupy in the social structure shapes much of their social experience, including how they define what are and are not the "good" and "bad" things in life. Consider, for instance, the distinction usually made between the "material and nonmaterial" desiderata. For well-to-do persons who do not have to face the oppressive realities of substandard living conditions, "bad housing" is likely to be categorized as a "material" condition and one of no great urgency in their lives. But for slum dwellers, bad housing is not only a material factor but a way of life. Conditions of overcrowding, infestation, poor sanitation, and lack of proper heat and ventilation represent social and psychological realtities as well as material ones, affecting one's morale, self-expectations, self-esteem, personal relations, life performances, and life chances in ways that are difficult for more comfortably situated persons to imagine.

SOME POWERLESS GROUPS

Groups having the least power also have fewer of the good things in life. The dilemma of the dispossessed is that their material and non-material deprivations leave them at the low end of any index of power and their relative powerlessness ensures their continued deprivation. Those with the greatest needs are thus least capable of satisfying those needs. The pluralist image of an array of groups competing for outputs across the entire breadth of society overlooks the fact that certain groups are so disadvantaged by class oppression, custom, or natural endowment as to be chronically consigned to a low measure of power and a high measure of need. Let us consider some specific categories of people.

As just noted, those who chronically suffer the lowest degree of power are persons who occupy the lowest rungs of the economic ladder. Throughout history, whether they be called the blessed or the damned, whether slave, serf, sharecropper, indentured servant, or "free laborer," they have endured a scarcity of power and an abundance of need. Possessed of little material wealth when wealth has been the greatest determinant of life chances, the lower classes have experienced the harshest exploitation as both workers and consumers; the most disease and the earliest deaths; the least opportunity for comfort, learning, autonomy, self-governance, and self-respect and the sternest mistreatment at the hands of the law.[4] Ralph Miliband describes their condition:

> Like other classes, the working class of advanced capitalist societies has always been, and remains, highly diversified; and there are also important differences in the internal composition of the working class of one country as compared to another. Yet, and notwithstanding these differences inside countries and between them, the working class remains everywhere a distinct and specified social formation by virtue of a combination of characteristics which affect its members in comparison with the members of other classes. The most obvious of these characteristics is that here are the people who, generally, "get least of what there is to

get," and who have to work the hardest for it. And it is also from their ranks that are, so to speak, recruited the unemployed, the aged poor, the chronically destitute and the sub-proletariat of capitalist society. For all the insistence of growing or achieved 'classlessness' . . . the proletarian condition remains a hard and basic fact in these societies, in the work process, in levels of income, in opportunities or lack of them, in the whole social definition of existence.[5]

Many tens of millions in the United States, numbering neither among the very poor nor the rich, compose an amorphous category dubbed "middle Americans," which includes everyone from well-paid middle-level managers to lowly paid clerical workers. The accepted notion is that these people are increasing in numbers as the "service sector" of the economy grows and that they enjoy affluent, comfortable lives. A closer examination of the evidence indicates that while some are well-off, a goodly number of persons in the white-collar and service sectors, like most blue-collar workers, live under the chronic threat of economic insecurity, forced early retirement, unemployment, inflation, high taxes, and heavy debts, and are employed at some of the most underpaid, menial, and mindless jobs any modern civilization could produce.[6] Occupational disability, job insecurity, job dissatisfaction, constant financial anxieties, mental stress and depression, alcoholism, and conflictful domestic relations are common woes among the mass of middle Americans who compose the aching "backbone" of America. Even if not suffering from acute want, few if any exercise much control over the conditions of their lives. If not as severely buffeted and exploited as the very poor, they still number among the powerless in regard to most of the crucial decisions affecting their livelihoods, their communities, and their nation.

The plight of the middle Americans, however, as measured by the consequences of their powerlessness, is nowhere as severe as that of the very poor, who compose about 20 percent of the United States population. Their vague feelings of alienation and estrangement are more bearable than the continued presence of uncertainty and imminent disruption, "the constant threat of having life completely overturned by forces that can be neither predicted nor controlled," which is the condition of very poor people.[7]

The disadvantages suffered by other categories of people, such as the very young, the very old, women, ethnic minorities, and those who are "institutionalized" for physical and presumably mental disabilities are greatly compounded by class position and are partly a function of class. For instance, children of all classes constitute one of the largest and most vulnerable low-power groups. They do not participate as decision makers in most of the arrangements directly affecting their lives. They have no lobbies, no voice in the political system, no appeal from the tyranny of adults. "At a time when they are particularly weak and easily intimidated and manipulated," Mary Kohler notes, "their rights are particularly vulnerable to infringement," often by those who claim to act on their behalf.[8] In the United States and elsewhere in the world, children are frequently the objects of repeated physical abuse and torture. One study estimated that 7 out of every 100 British children are so victimized by neglect and abuse as to require the intervention of social authorities.[9] One health authority estimated that more children died in the United States from injuries inflicted by parents than from all childhood diseases combined, some 200,000 a year being willfully beaten, burned, smothered, or starved.[10] Kohler observes:

> Much of the law now governing the relationship between parent and child relegates the child to little more than the status of a chattel. Parents are described as having "property" rights in children. Children's economic interests are made subservient to those of the parent in almost every instance. Legal concepts of parental control and legal requirements of parental consent leave the child little opportunity for self-determination.[11]

But if all children risk the injustices of the adult world, the offspring of the lower classes are the most victimized of all, a disproportionately high number of battered and abused youngsters coming from homes plagued by poverty, unemployment, and overcrowding. To be conceived in poverty is to suffer risks while still inside the womb. Insufficient prenatal care, poor diet, and difficult working conditions for lower-class women leave them more likely to produce miscarriages, premature births, mentally and physically damaged infants. Once born, the lower-class child faces conditions of malnutrition, infection, and inadequate health care that may lead to maldevelopment of the central nervous system and mental retardation. Indeed, the poor of *all* age brackets suffer proportionally far more than do those of higher income from tuberculosis, rheumatic fever, food poisoning, epilepsy, polio, diphtheria, brucellosis, silicosis, and venereal disease. The physician Norman Bethune once remarked: "There is a rich man's tuberculosis and a poor man's tuberculosis. The rich man recovers and the poor man dies. This succinctly expresses the close embrace of economics and pathology."[13]

Class position becomes an important factor in shaping the life conditions of the elderly. Like the very young, the very old suffer from natural disabilities when attempting to compete for social outputs. In a society that places a premium on beauty, youth, energy, speed, earning power, aggressive drive, and productivity, the old and infirm are easily deprived of their place in the sun. When one's status and security is determined by one's ability either to control wealth or sell one's labor on the market, the superannuated are a surplus people of little use to the productive system, to their families and, as often happens, to themselves. The deference accorded a person of years in more traditional societies is replaced with impatience, patronization, neglect, and finally incarceration in a nursing home. As the elderly are given more years to live, they are given less reason to live.

But in old age, too, the well-to-do fare better than the needy. Reflecting on the relationship between class and age, Simone de Beauvoir sums it up well:

> It is clear that the age at which decline begins has always depended on the class one belongs to. Today a miner is finished at 50, whereas among the privileged, many carry their 80 years with ease. Drained of his forces sooner, the worker also suffers a much more rapid decline. His exhausted body is prey to injuries and sickness even in his prime, whereas an old person who has been able to take care of his body can keep it more or less intact until the day he dies. . .
>
> Even if a [worker] in retirement preserves his health and his mental faculties he is still prey to the terrible blight of boredom. Deprived of his grip on the world, he is unable to regain it because apart from his work his leisure was alienated. . .
>
> It is the fault of society that the decline of age begins prematurely and is precipitous, physically painful and morally terrifying—because

people come to it with empty hands. When their strength deserts them, the exploited and alienated are fatally transformed into discarded rubbish.[14]

Women are another oppressed group, customarily relegated to the more subsidiary and demeaning roles (the "vulgar employments," as Veblen called them), suffering the concomitant mistreatments and inferior stereotypes that go with lowly position. Long denied their own rights to sexual expression, women have frequently been treated as objects of sexual barter and assault. In most cultures they have been debarred from significant participatory roles in hunting, sports, government, war, religion, and the arts. In modern capitalist systems, many women have been confined exclusively to household chores and child care, thereby engaging in "a huge amount of socially necessary production," as Margaret Benson points out. "Nevertheless, in a society based on commodity production, it is not usually considered 'real work' since it is outside of trade and the market place."[15] Domestic toil (except in the case of employed servants) has no *exchange* value, even if it has an important *use* value. "Women's work," therefore, leaves women with few of the resources needed for bargaining in the market, making them dependent on men who command employable resources. When women do enter into the labor market they are channelized in disproportionate numbers to the least rewarding work and confront the disabilities in performance and morale that come with persistent discrimination in recruitment, advancement, and remuneration.

Yet if all women have been oppressed, oppression has meant different things to different classes of women. Whatever else may be said of their lives, upper- and middle-class females are saved from many of the worst abuses and hardships inflicted upon lower-class ones. The latter are far more heavily burdened by toil, drudgery, want, and illness; they enjoy far fewer opportunities for leisure, travel, education, and career, and have little access to good maternal and medical services and child-care assistance. Far from defining their liberation as an escape from the domestic scene, many low-income women, forced to work long exhausting hours for meager wages, would like nothing better than the opportunity to spend time at home with their children. But home life itself can be hazardous. Low-income women are frequently subjected to the kinds of mistreatment from their male counterparts associated with economic oppression, poverty, unemployment, and alcoholism, including abandonment, nonsupport, and physical brutality. The mistreatment of women by men knows no class boundaries but is found most frequently and perniciously among the more economically oppressed groups.[16]

In addition, lower-class women are often the objects of special sexual exploitation by upper-class men. When the landlords of prerevolutionary China wanted a peasant's wife or daughter, "they would simply order her to submit, or rape her outright. There was little the peasants could do."[17] In feudal Europe, the lord's claim to peasant women was institutionalized as the *droit du seigneur* and the practice of White landowners in the South taking their pleasure with Black women, both in ante-bellum times and after, is a well-recorded fact. In almost all lands throughout the ages, the women and even the female children of the lower classes have served as indentured servants, prostitutes, and sexual prey, and have performed the more demeaning, tedious, and physically taxing domestic tasks for the males and females of the propertied class.

Among the powerless we should include those peoples of various races and nations who, because of their smaller numbers, limited command of arms, and possession of fertile lands and coveted natural resources, have been the victims of foreign domination, economic exploitation, rapine, bondage, and genocidal destruction. The racist designation of moral inferiority placed upon the victimized people by their oppressors has served both to invite and justify the atrocities of the imperialist forces. The centuries are so crowded with tragic examples as to leave the impression that history is little more than a succession of mass atrocities. And while many Americans believe the United States managed to remain an island of virtue in this sea of evil, the fate of American Indians, Blacks, Mexicans, Guatemalans, Haitians, Cubans, Filipinos, Vietnamese, Laotians, Cambodians, and others might lead us to conclude that weaker peoples have little cause for rejoicing in our having taken an interest in their destiny.

The sufferings of most Third World peoples have been at the hands of White colonizers bent on expropriating their land and labor. Racial oppression usually contains within it a strong element of class oppression. The massive extermination and enslavement of African,

Asian, and New World populations by European colonizers was done with the purpose of extracting as much profit as possible from their land and labor. Even when the oppressed group survives and is partially integrated into the colonizer's social order, class disabilities operate with cumulative effect on racial oppression. Racial abuses and discrimination in jobs, housing, and education are the common lot of Blacks in the United States, yet the life chances of lower-class Blacks are worse in every way than those of middle-class Blacks.[18] The Black poor are also worse off than the White poor. Racism intensifies the problems of poverty, and poverty aggravates the problems caused by racism. Thus in comparison to poor Blacks, well-to-do Blacks are better able to protect themselves from certain of the effects of racism, and poor Whites are better able to escape certain of the effects of poverty.

Also to be counted among those who suffer particular disabilities and deprivations are the many hundreds of thousands found today in what has been called the "total institutions,"[19] the inmates of local, state, and federal prisons, military stockades, mental asylums, "homes" for the retarded, reformatories, orphanages, and so forth. According to numerous exposés, life among the "institutionalized" is characterized by oppressive controls, supervisory sadism, physical and sexual assault, murder, suicide, overcrowding, filthy living conditions, poor diet, and poor or nonexistent recreational facilities. As measured by almost every criterion, the inmates at these punitive total institutions must be placed at the lowest end of any index of power.[20]

The "institutionalized" offer further evidence of how disabilities are created by, or at least compounded by, class and race. The poorest Blacks, Puerto Ricans, Native Americans, and Chicanos are heavily overrepresented in the prison population in America. The number of people involuntarily confined in American mental hospitals is twice the number of all municipal, state, and federal prisoners and consists of a population "notably devoid of white, middle-class Americans."[21] Legal protections for mental patients are even weaker than those afforded ordinary criminals. In many instances commitment comes without the benefit of investigation, trial, or other procedural safeguards, and is based on considerations and "scientific" criteria which betray a markedly class and racial bias. In the words of one worker in a New York State mental institution: "The hospitals are used merely as junk heaps for poor people who are often abandoned for years to rot, without adequate psychiatric care . . ."[22] A leading critic of the tyrannies of the psychiatric profession writes:

> There is a cynical saying: a person who steals five dollars is a thief, but one who steals five million is a financier . . . The same is true for the human events we call mental illness. The problem that sends the rich woman to Reno is likely to send the poor woman to the state hospital. When the butcher, baker, or candlestick maker thinks that the Communists are after him, he is dispatched to the mental hospital; when a Secretary of Defense thinks so, who will constrain him? . . . How can the weak constrain the strong?
>
>   . . . We still tolerate appalling inequities between our treatment of the rich and the poor. . . . We regard the rich and influential psychiatric patient as a self-governing, responsible client—free to decide whether or not to be a patient. But we look upon the poor and the aged patient as a ward of the state—too ignorant or too "mentally sick" to know what is best for him. The paternalistic psychiatrist, as an agent of the family or the state, assumes "responsibility" for him, defines him as a "patient" against his will, and subjects him to "treatment" deemed best for him, with or without his consent.[23]

EVADING CLASS REALITY

Those who own the means of production are described here variously as the "upper class," "owning class," "corporate class," or "propertied class." Many academicians and social commentators see conflicts existing in American society but not along class lines. *Class* conflict is rejected as a peculiarly Marxist notion supposedly irrelevant to the American experience.[24] "Class" is treated as a sociological category, not as a *relationship* between those who own and those who labor for those who own. Many writers eschew the concept of "class," preferring "more permeable-sounding terms such as 'social groups,' 'status groups,' or 'social strata' . . ."[25]—all of which caused Andrew Hacker to comment:

> Why can't we deal with class? Terms like "upper middle" and "lower middle" refer to style and sophistication, not the deeper divisions of social life. On the whole we prefer to circumvent the question of class.

We think of cities as being composed of "ghettos" and "white ethnics" and "the aged." Discussing families on welfare or crime in the streets, we speak of Blacks and Puerto Ricans. Sociologists neutralize the subject by referring to "stratification." Or they tell us it is "ambiguous" and "complex" . . .

Yet we know that America has classes, and that they are more than temporary way stations. No matter how we divide up Americans according to culture, careers, even income, power is at the heart of the question. Some people have more freedom, more independence than others. Some are buffeted about from birth to death, never in a position to bend events or answer back to authority. Class may confer power over others; but in personal life it affects how you can make the world work on your behalf.[16]

Hacker is alluding to the dual usage of the concept of "class." If "class" refers to the difference between capital and labor, that is, the difference between buying the labor of others for profit and selling one's own labor for wages, between owning and not owning the wealth of society and all the commensurate disparities in life chances and power inherent in that fact, then there is only an owning class and a working class. But when "class" is also used to describe occupational, educational, and income differences among those who work for a living, then there are numerous "classes," variously described as "upper-middle," "middle," "lower-middle," "lower," and "lower-lower."

The refusal to use "class as a concept relating to political power and economic exploitation has led some observers to the conclusion that there are no conflicting interests between classes and, in fact, no classes in this country. Thus one commentator can refer to "the United States' almost classless society, with its powerful promise of upward mobility . . ."[17] But "class" remains as an oppressive reality even if people choose to ignore it as a topic of study. As C. Wright Mills wrote: "The fact that [people] are not 'class conscious' at times and in all places does not mean that 'there are no classes' or that 'in America everybody is middle class.' The economic and social facts are one thing. Psychological feelings may or may not be associated with them in rationally expected ways."[18]

While some social scientists insist there is no such thing as an exclusive, rich, elite-minded upper class in the United States, upper-class persons with their social secretaries, registers, clubs, leagues, and private schools know better and do everything to maintain class boundaries, coopting new members with great care and forgetting intraclass differences when fundamental economic interests are challenged from without. Of owning-class people it may be said that, in their political, professional, and recreational activities, and in the upbringing, education, and marriage of their offspring, most of their essential life experiences are shaped by a commitment to the maintenance of their class styles, privileges, and wealth.[29] The conservative economist Joseph Schumpeter described class reality this way:

> A class is aware of its identity as a whole, sublimates itself as such, has its own peculiar life and characteristic "spirit." Yet one essential peculiarity—possibly a consequence, possibly an intermediate cause—of the class phenomenon lies in the fact that class members behave toward one another in a fashion characteristically different from their conduct toward members of other classes. They are in closer association with one another; they understand one another better; they work more readily in concert; they close ranks and erect barriers against the outside; they look out into the same segment of the world, with the same eyes, from the same viewpoint, in the same direction.[30]

By failing to look at the class dimension of most oppression, traditional social scientists can more easily treat oppression as a phenomenon apart from the very socio-economic system that breeds it. Oppression becomes a reified event, abstracted from class realities, caused by happenstance or by evildoers or by the wrongful attitudes that seem to spring from the human heart. Thus children are oppressed by adults, women by men, Blacks by Whites, and so on. By keeping our vision confined to these general categories no attention is given to systemic forces or class interests, including those which might be oppressing the adult, White male.

Rather than being treated as a cause of group oppressions, the capitalist system is accepted as the neutral framework within which groups try to rectify the inequities they suffer. This approach to oppression is congruent with the prevailing ideological orthodoxy that defines all social injustices as aberrant offshoots rather than as systemic outgrowths. Like other systemic symptoms, be they military spending, pollution, urban decay, fiscal insolvency, inflation, crime, and the like, which are treated as "issues" separate from each other and from the politico-economic system that produces them, each group oppression can be considered a distinct "issue," to be discussed endlessly without ever mentioning class oppression. Jonathan Kozol makes the point as follows:

> The discovery by the intelligent wife of a Manhattan millionaire that she too is oppressed, first because she went to an oppressive prep school that was not like Summerhill, second because she is a woman and cannot go down to Wall Street like her husband, leads her to the final step of equating her oppression with that of the slum victim. Not only is this a vicious and dishonorable equation (her children are not born brain-injured in unsterile delivery rooms; she is not starving; her children do not chew lead-infested paint; her sickness, cancer, epilepsy, heart disease, does not go unexamined and untreated) but also such an equation insures that neither form of oppression will ever be dealt with in a conscientious way. Each will produce literature, controversy, talk shows, a new thing to be into, a special issue of *Transaction (Society* now) or the *Partisan Review*. Nobody who is now in pain will be in less pain when it is all over.[31]

A kind of "oppressed interest group competition" develops with each oppressed group making its claim to being the most oppressed, each jockeying for a better position within the existing system rather than joining together against it. The group's middle-class leadership pushes a set of demands, often treating the injustices suffered by other groups as something of lesser urgency, and sometimes unaware of the unarticulated oppressions of the group's own lower-class members.

POWER AND POWERLESSNESS AS CUMULATIVE CONDITIONS

As stated earlier, the unequal distribution of social desiderata under modern capitalism is due largely to the unequal distribution of power resources in a society where power rather than need is the determinant of who gets what. The conditions of powerlessness and want tend to reinforce each other and those most in need are most likely to have their claims neglected or suppressed.

Inequities tend to be compounded for the haves as well as the have-nots. The possession of one power resource often creates opportunities to gain access to other resources, as when celebrity and money bring opportunities for political leadership. Thus we have instances of the rich using their wealth to gain access to public office, and of politicians using public office to gain access to wealth; generals and college presidents become corporate executives, and corporate executives become administrative leaders in state and federal governments; movie actors of fame and fortune become governors and senators, and senators have been known to become millionaires.[32]

Because there are varied resources and varied avenues for accumulating power some observers mistakenly conclude that resources are more or less widely distributed. If "inequities in political resources remain, they tend to be noncumulative," Robert Dahl writes; thus no one group either monopolizes or is totally deprived of the attributes of power.[33] Almost any group, Dahl concludes, has access to *some* resources which it can exploit to gain influence. But the enormous inequities existing among various groups and classes would suggest just the opposite: if indeed resources can be compounded, then they tend to be *cumulative* rather than noncumulative. Power resources are accumulated over time and are not up for grabs with each new issue. As already noted, those who enjoy access to resources are best able to parlay such advantages into greater advantages, using the resources they already possess to accumulate still more. While those who are most needful of reallocations of goods and services are, by that very fact, farthest removed from the resources necessary to command reallocations and least able to make effective use of whatever limited resources they do possess.

That there are great inequities in American society should come as no surprise to anyone who has moved beyond the conventional wisdom of the 1950s. Far from being distributed randomly, the allocation of resources is heavily skewed in favor of the materially better-off individuals, social groups, institutions, and classes. All other things being equal, a group with good organization, or social legitimacy, or special knowledgeability, or skill in using legal channels, or skill in manipulating symbols will be more effective than a group lacking such attributes. But all other things are rarely equal and more often than not the very ability to utilize such resources depends on the availability of still other resources which are most closely associated with class and wealth. Those groups endowed with large amounts of money, as opposed to those with limited money, are best able to command the time, energy, skills, technology, and visibility needed for durable and effective organization. Even a pluralist like Dahl seems to recognize this when he notes that there are important "objective" differences among people which limit their potential power: "Being poor or rich, well-educated or uneducated, a professional man or an unskilled laborer, living in a slum area or a middle-class neighborhood—these are differences in objective situations of a most persistent and general sort that are likely to show up in a variety of different ways over a long period of time."[34] These are differences of a *class* sort which have lasting effects on the accumulation and use of power resources.

One need not conclude that the resources of power are exclusively the derivatives of wealth, nor that only the rich have access to them, but corporate wealth enjoys a superior initiative in making favorable things happen, an initiative which inheres in the ability to procure the talent, technology, loyalty, legitimacy, cultural prestige, and organized efforts of public and private institutions.[35] Pluralists to the contrary, I am arguing here that the resources of power tend to be cumulative and therefore the conditions of power and powerlessness also tend to be cumulative.

By drawing a direct link between the use of power and access to power resources, and by speaking of power conditions as "objective situations of a most persistent and general sort," I am introducing the idea that power can be delineated by means other than observing actors engaged in specific policy conflicts. The structured distribution of power resources prefigures the agenda of social decisions. Thus we can speak of someone as *having* power as well as using it. The mere possession of resources has an empowering effect by limiting the possibilities of action for others and evoking a series of anticipatory reactions from them.

Objections to this position have been raised by those who argue that access to resources is no guarantee the resources will be used properly or used at all.[36] One cannot always anticipate the specific situations in which resources will be utilized; one cannot claim that there is a predictable one-to-one relation between, say, the possession of money and the uses to which it is put. Thus, it is argued, "the distribution of [power] resources in a system tells us very little about who will *attempt influence*," or how influence is actually perceived and used.[37]

By that view, power resources are likened to commodities sitting in a warehouse, of no influence whatever unless put to use. But we might remind ourselves that the resources of power are not of that simple nature and *the existing distribution of resources frequently exercises an influence even without being actually mobilized*. Arguing that the possession of resources does not necessarily lead to the exercise of influence, Gamson cites the case of the individual who "may feel that his resources will be inadequate to meet those that are countervailing. Existing competition may raise the costs above the amount he is prepared to pay."[38] But this example more readily illustrates how the distribution of resources *does* exercise an influence of its own. The individual was deterred because he discerned the superior resources of another, the *possession* (rather than the use) of which was sufficiently persuasive to stop him.

Plainly, what makes the possession of resources so formidable is one's anticipation that they might be used. Anticipatory reaction is the mainstay of power. All ruling groups rely on it to govern. Nations rely on it for their security. It is the means whereby the possessor of power resources can enjoy the effects of such resources without having to expend them. To win a struggle is one thing, but to have your way by impressing others that struggle would be futile, that is power at its most economical and most secure. It follows that the greater one's resources, the more one is able to make efficient use of them, that is, the less one actually has to use them. The fewer one's resources, the less able is one to make efficient use of what little one has. Power is positional as well as decisional.

NOTES

1. Robert Dahl, in *Who Governs?* (New Haven: Yale University Press, 1961), p. 226, suggests a list of power resources for "the American political system" as including time; access to money; credit and wealth; control over jobs; control over information; esteem or social standing; the possession of charisma, popularity, legitimacy,

legality, and the rights pertaining to public office. Pluralists do not mention the use of force and violence as a political resource.

2. Dahl, *Who Governs?*, p. 271.

3. See Gerhard Lenski's discussion of wants and needs in his *Power and Privilege* (New York: McGraw-Hill, 1966), pp. 37–39.

4. There has been a flood of literature on the American poor and the working class documenting these propositions. See for instance Dorothy B. James, *Poverty, Politics and Change* (Englewood Cliffs, N.J.: Prentice-Hall, 1972); Paul Jacobs, *Prelude to Riot* (New York: Random House, 1966); Kenneth Clark, *Dark Ghetto* (New York: Harper & Row, 1965); Marc and Phyllis Pilisuk (eds.), *Poor Americans: How the White Poor Live* (New Brunswick, N.J.: Transaction Books, 1971). A classic article is Harvey Swados, "The Myth of the Happy Worker," *The Nation*, 185, no. 4 (1957), 65–68.

5. Ralph Miliband, *The State in Capitalist Society* (New York: Basic Books, 1969), p. 16.

6. Andrew Levison, *The Working Class Majority* (New York: Penguin, 1975).

7. David Steinberg, "An Uncertain Theory of Poverty: Life Under the Plague," *The Activist*, Fall 1966, pp. 19–20.

8. Mary Kohler, "The Rights of Children—an Unexplored Constituency," *Social Policy*, 1 (March/April 1971), 36.

9. Cited in William Dankenbring, "The Growing Tragedy of Battered Children," *The Plain Truth*, 36 (July 1971), 37.

10. Dr. Ray E. Helfer, quoted in ibid.; see also Ray E. Helfer and C. Henry Kempe, *The Battered Child* (Chicago: University of Chicago Press, 1969); David G. Gil, *Violence Against Children* (Cambridge, Mass.: Harvard University Press, 1970); also articles by Serapio Zalba, Paul Lerman, and Norman Denzin in *Transaction*, 8 (July/August 1971).

11. Kohler, "The Rights of Children," p. 37.

12. See Nick Kotz, *Let Them Eat Promises: The Politics of Hunger in America* (Englewood Cliffs, N.J.: Prentice-Hall, 1969). In areas most afflicted by economic recession, instances of child abuse caused by demoralized unemployed fathers have been known to increase dramatically. See Saul Friedman, "Falling Apart," *The Progressive*, February 1976, pp. 38–40.

13. Quoted in Jonathan Spence, *To Change China* (Boston: Little, Brown, 1969). Bethune served as a doctor in China but the observation is drawn from his experiences in Western Europe, Canada, and the United States. See also Ellen Frankfort, "Making of a Surgeon: Practicing on the Poor," *Village Voice*, April 22, 1971, pp. 44, 48.

14. Simone de Beauvoir, "On Aging," *Ramparts*, September 1970, pp. 22–23. This selection appeared later in a larger work by de Beauvoir, *The Coming of Age* (New York: Putnam, 1972).

15. Margaret Benson, "The Political Economy of Women's Liberation," *Monthly Review*, 21 (September 1969), 15–16.

16. An attempt to focus on the historical class dimensions of women's oppression is found in Rosalyn Boxandall, Linda Gordon, and Susan Reveryby (eds.), *America's Working Women* (New York: Random House, 1976); also Nancy Seifer, *Nobody Speaks for Me!* (New York: Simon and Schuster, 1976); Lilian Breslow Rubin, *Worlds of Pain* (New York: Basic Books, 1976); Ann Gordon, Marie Jo Buhle, and Nancy Schrom, "Women in American Society," *Radical America*, 5 (July–August 1971). For a criticism by middle-class feminists of how women of their class relate to working-class women in oppressive ways, see C. Reid and C. Bunch, "Your Class Is Showing," *Liberation*, December 1975, pp. 19–22; see also "Ms. Blue Collar," *Time*, May 6, 1974, p. 80

17. Ruth Sidel, *Women and Child Care in China* (Baltimore: Penguin, 1973), p. 6.

18. Urban lower-class Black youth have the highest rate of unemployment of any category in the United States and show a strikingly high rate of suicide. For an extensive study, see Herbert Hendin, *Black Suicide* (New York: Basic Books, 1969).

19. For a discussion of the control characteristics of total institutions see Erving Goffman, "Characteristics of Total Institutions," in Maurice Stein, Arthur Vidich, and David M. White (eds.), *Identity and Anxiety* (Glencoe, Ill.: Free Press, 1960), pp. 449–479.

20. Detailed accounts have appeared in recent years documenting the shocking conditions in such places as the Arkansas State Penitentiary, the Cook County Jail in Chicago, the Women's House of Detention in New York, and the Soledad Correctional Facility in California. For a general discussion of prison conditions see Bruce Jackson, "Our Prisons Are Criminal," *New York Times Magazine,* 7, September 22, 1968, p. 44 ff. Testimony on the conditions of prisons and juvenile detention institutions was collected by the Dodd Senate Subcommittee and reported in the *New York Times,* March 4, March 5, and March 6, 1969; June 19, 1969; July 8, July 9, and July 29, 1969. The report of the National Commission on Causes and Prevention of Violence offers similar findings; see the *New York Times,* November 2, 1969. Conditions within most mental hospitals are no better and often worse than in penal institutions; see G. B. Jenkins, "Insanity's Victims: 60 Days on Ward Two," *Village Voice,* April 1, 1971. The remarkable documentary by Frederic Wiseman, "Titicut Follies," exposes the inhumane conditions at the State Mental Hospital in Bridgewater, Massachusetts, a film that has been banned in Massachusetts by state authorities.

21. For a study of the class, racial, and legal injustices of mental hospitals, see Bruce J. Ennis, "Mental Commitment," *Civil Liberties* (publication of the American Civil Liberties Union), October, 1969, p. 3.

22. An anonymous hospital worker, "Mental Hospitals and the Poor," *Workers World*, December 25, 1970, p. 7.

23. Thomas Szasz, *Ideology and Insanity* (Garden City, N.Y.: Doubleday, 1970), pp. 83, 213.

24. For two representative samples, see John Kenneth Galbraith, *American Capitalism* (Boston: Houghton Mifflin, 1952); and Daniel Bell, *The End of Ideology* (Glencoe, Ill., Free Press, 1960); also the writings of Seymour Martin Lipset, Earl Latham, David Riesman, Nathan Glazer, Edward Banfield, and others too numerous to mention. For a good critique, see J. H. Westergaard, "Sociology: the Myth of Classlessness," in Robin Blackburn (ed.), *Ideology in Social Science* (New York: Vintage, 1973), pp. 119–163.

25. G. William Domhoff, *Who Rules America?* (Englewood Cliffs, N.J.: Prentice-Hall, 1967), pp. 23, 12–37 for an analysis of upper-class consciousness.

26. Andrew Hacker in the *New York Review of Books*, May 1, 1975, p. 9.

27. Louis Banks, "The Mission of Our Business Society," *Harvard Business Review*, May/June 1975, reprinted in Henry Etzkowitz and Peter Schwab, *Is America Necessary?* (St. Paul, Minn.: West Publishing, 1976), p. 569.

28. C. Wright Mills, *Power, Politics and People*, ed. Irving Louis Horowitz (New York: Oxford University Press, 1963), p. 317.

29. See Domhoff, *Who Rules America?*, and E. Digby Baltzell, *The Protestant Establishment* (New York: Random House, 1964); and *An American Business Aristocracy* (New York: Collier, 1962).

30. Joseph Schumpeter, "The Problem of Classes," in *Two Essays by Joseph Schumpeter* (New York: Meridian Books, 1955), pp. 107–108.

31. Jonathan Kozol, "How Schools Train Children for Political Impotence," *Social Policy*, 3 (July/August 1973), 20.

32. For instance, "the richest man in the Senate," the late Robert Kerr of Oklahoma, was a multimillionaire who made his fortune *after* he had been elected to the Senate. G. William Domhoff in *Who Rules America?* (Englewood Cliffs, N.J.: Prentice-Hall, 1967) documents the interrelatedness of various elites.

33. Dahl, *Who Governs?*, p. 85.

34. Ibid., p. 97. Unfortunately Dahl never explored the implications this observation might have for pluralism.

35. For ample documentation of this point, see my *Democracy for the Few*, 2nd ed. (New York: St. Martin's, 1977) and the sources cited therein.

36. This position is expressed in various ways by Robert Dahl, *Who Governs?* (New Haven: Yale University Press, 1961), and Nelson Polsby, *Community Power and Political Theory* (New Haven: Yale University Press, 1963).

37. William Gamson, *Power and Discontent* (Homewood, Ill.: Dorsey Press, 1968), p. 97.

38. Ibid., p. 96.

7

The Legitimation of Class Dominance

It is said with good cause that wealthy classes always seek to secure their social legitimacy. Legitimacy is achieved when a social relationship (or value, symbol, personage, or idea) gains popular acceptance and esteem. Here I will consider some of the ways the dominant class attempts to legitimate its position in society.

SANCTIFYING CLASS PRIVILEGES

Every privileged class propagates the notion that the existing social system constitutes the natural order of things. In this way, those on top try to give legitimacy and permanence to their position. Max Weber commented on the ability of privileged groups "to have their social and economic positions 'legitimized.' They wish to see their positions transformed from a purely factual power relation into a cosmos of acquired rights, and to know that they are thus sanctified."[1] Elsewhere, Weber points out that the man of fortune "is seldom satisfied with the fact of being fortunate."

Beyond this, he needs to know that he has a *right* to his good fortune. He wants to be convinced that he "deserves" it, and above all, that he deserves it in comparison with others. He wishes to be allowed the belief that the less fortunate also merely experience their due. Good fortune thus wants to be "legitimate" fortune.

Strata in solid possession of social honor and power usually tend to fashion their status-legend in such a way as to claim a special and intrinsic quality of their own, usually a quality of blood.[2]

The legitimating myths, or "status-legends" as Weber calls them, serve not only to bolster the self-esteem and soothe the conscience of the rich but help fulfill the important function of sanctifying class dominance. "The strongest," Rousseau writes, "is never strong enough to be always master, unless he transforms his strength into right, and obedience into duty."[3] For property to be secure it must have social legitimacy. At the same time, it is itself a source of that legitimacy. "Property as such is not always recognized as a status qualification, but in the long run it is, and with extraordinary regularity"[4] With property comes power and, in time, power itself enhances the legitimacy of the holders of power. Speaking of the emerging capitalism of nineteenth-century America, Matthew Josephson wrote:

In olden days, mercenary captains, hereditary princes, landed nobles or mighty prelates of the church would have preyed on the tradesman, held him down with their contempt; now all society protected him, government policed his property, paid him homage—and tomorrow in the sequel to the national crisis the country would change its laws, its Constitution, sacrifice a million lives for him and the economic force he represented.[5]

In every society, the dominant class, be it composed of warriors, priests, landed gentry, merchants, or industrial entrepreneurs, asserts "its existence through claiming to be identical with, as well as representative and advocate of, the whole people to which it furnishes guidance."[6] In present-day capitalist societies, profit and property are represented as serving not only the owning class but all citizens. What corporations do for themselves is said to benefit all of America, and what American capital investments do abroad is said to benefit all the "Free World." Every group, Marx observed, seeks to give "its ideas the form of universality and [attempts] to represent them as the only rational and universally valid ones."'' (This is not to say that the standard beliefs of a society operate with single-minded effects, free of contradictions, ambiguities, and unexpected claims. Ruling-class ideologies are not known for their logical rigor but for their injunctive qualities.)'

A basic objective of any owning class is to represent itself as "the keeper of the National Integrity" (Veblen's phrase) by identifying its prerogatives with the *sacranda*, that is, the sacrosanct beliefs of society. The interests of an economically dominant class never stand naked. They are enshrouded in the flag, fortified by the law, protected by the police, nurtured by the media, taught by the schools, and blessed by the church. "The freedom of business enterprise," Sutton and his associates note after an exhaustive study of the American business creed, "tends to be fused with other freedoms and the simple, unqualified symbols of freedom and liberty are set before us in all the available media."' Private enterprise is represented as the very mainstay of liberty, prosperity, and social order, a necessary condition and sometimes even a sufficient cause of all the special blessings the populace is said to enjoy.

Among the sacrosanct configurations of the social order, the nation-state occupies a special place. The object of highly impassioned dedications, the nation represents the pride, honor, worth, and security of "an entire people." "The art of government," George Bernard Shaw once said, "is the organization of idolatry." Of interest to us is the way such patriotic idolatry tends to sanctify the socio-economic status quo. The slogan "America, love it or leave it" connotes an acceptance of prevailing institutional arrangements which might best be translated as "America, love it *as it is*, or leave it." With private enterprise identified as an essential component of "the American Way of Life," socialist attacks on capitalism are denounced as preachments of "class hatred," the infection of "alien faiths," equated with un-Americanism. Military ventures, often undertaken at substantial public cost to protect private overseas holdings, are portrayed as defenses of "the national honor" or "national security," and protective of everyone's well-being.

All upper-strata groups have sought in one guise or another to cultivate those beliefs which would leave their interests above debate or, if challenged, would force the challenger to appear as something of a blasphemer. The orthodox notions ensure the "iconization" of the social order and the class relations within that order. The worth of certain social arrangements is not to be debated or tampered with, and *instrumental* values are no longer critically examined for their performance and payoff but are treated as *end* values. Indeed, the tendency in any dominant ideational system, as noted in our earlier discussion of orthodoxy, is to transform the credenda (the accepted but still debatable beliefs) into the sacranda (the sanctified dogma.)

Those who support the ongoing social order seem convinced of their claims, nor should it surprise us that persons, classes, and nations believe in their own virtue. To presume that a belief gains or loses merit depending on whether or not its advocates are "sincere" is to miss the point. Even fascists are sincerely convinced of the virtue of their goals. What is significant is not whether the propagators of a dominant ideology believe in their own virtue—we may presume they do—but that others do, including many who, not sharing directly in the dominant interests and perhaps even being victimized by such interests, are so deeply imbued with the prevailing sacranda as to be deaf or hostile to dissenters.[10]

The dominant classes treat their position as evidence of the justice of the natural order of things, frequently going so far as to ascribe their advantages to some supernatural origin. "They have had a care," Hobbes wrote in *Leviathan,* "to make it believed that the same things were displeasing to the Gods, which were forbidden by the Lawes." Centuries later John D. Rockefeller, Sr., informed the world: "I believe the power to make money is a gift of God . . . Having been endowed with the gift I possess, I believe it is my duty to make money and still more money, and to use the money I make for the good of my fellow man according to the dictates of my conscience."[11] The results of such arrangements—as seen by those closest to the Deity's selective generosity—are, of course, declared to be socially beneficial for all.

Today, with less religiosity and more sophistication, the public is bombarded with media advertisements that treat the free-enterprise system as a providential force and a natural ordering of human life. Special endowments are treated as evidence of individual virtue, the promise of success and mobility being held out to any person with the right amount of talent, pluck, and diligence. Upper-class privileges are thought to be earned by capable persons or by their forebears who then exercise the right to pass on the fruits of their labor to their progeny. The inheritance of wealth ensures the inheritance of widely differing life chances, but this fact seems not to diminish the belief held by many that the system is open to talent, rewarding the energetic while relegating the slothful and incompetent to a deservedly lowly place.[12] The privileges of the rich, to the extent they are recognized as such, are treated as visible corroborations of superior accomplishment, while the deprivations of the less fortunate are taken as evidence of their inferior abilities. By that view, systemic payoffs can be accepted as the outcome of individual rather than systemic forces, of achieved rather than ascribed statuses.[13]

In time, the owners of wealth claim to be the *source* of society's productive capacity, thus turning reality on its head. Being well-provided for by the labor of many, corporate elites reverse roles and portray *themselves* as the providers of many. In the late eighteenth century, "manufacturer" meant *worker*, literally he who makes things with his hands; today the title is given to the *owner* of the manufactured goods. In the earlier days of handicraft industry it was understood that he who produced the property was the owner. In the modern business age it is assumed that he who owns the property is the producer. Creation used to denote ownership, now ownership implies creation. Thus today we speak of corporations as "producer interests."

The public, too, is educated into believing that the *acquisition* of property is evidence of the *production* of wealth.[14] And those who profit from ownership of the means of production are hailed as the source of that production. The special rewards enjoyed by the owning class are considered justifiable recompense for the special responsibilities they assume in regard to the nurturance of society itself.[15] The corporations are viewed not as the expropriators of labor and wealth but as the providers of the jobs, goods, and services which make prosperity and survival itself possible.

In a certain respect, it is understandable how the working populace might sometimes see its interests aligned with those of business. Just as a serf's survival is tied to the fortunes of his lord or just as any subordinate finds his own meager and dependent opportunities secured in the shadows of superordinate interests, so do the wage and salaried workers of an industrial society, given their limited resources and vulnerable occupational statuses on a "free labor" market, experience their employers' ill fortune with telling effect. The conditions of exploitation, then, help create the conditions of dependency which lend legitimacy and support to the exploitative relationship.

DENYING THE EXISTENCE OF CLASS INJUSTICE

When the privileges of the owning class are not being justified, their existence is being denied. "All establishments have vested interest in hiding some of the sources of their privileged position," Barrington Moore, Jr., observes.[16] As noted earlier, the orthodox creed encourages the view that the rich have no greater power than the poor and that they actually contribute more to, and receive less from, economic and political life than do the lower classes. Institutional authority, whether public or private, is seen as voluntaristic rather than coercive, neutral rather than of vested interest, and responsive to popular need rather than to private gain. The loci of power are said to be in every group, even in every citizen, and social relations are portrayed as mutually beneficial rather than asymmetrical and exploitative. It is presumed that a community of interests exists between haves and have-nots, one that would be more evident were the masses less excessive in their demands and less susceptible to exaggerated expectations and the agitations of wrongful leaders.

A way of denying the existence of privilege is to deny the reality of its abuses. Thus for many years it was announced that almost all Americans shared in a middle-class affluence. When it was no longer possible to deny the unhappy effects of privilege, as when a large poverty-stricken class was rediscovered in the early 1960s and recession struck in the 1970s, the effects then were ascribed to supposedly innocent causes such as "hard times," "market problems," and "modern industrial life." Since the economic system is seen as inherently good, then one cannot ascribe the system's ill effects to the system itself.

When the *economy* is blamed for the "hard times," it is in an unspecified way, with no indictment made against the *capitalist* economy as such. Rather "the economy" is spoken of as almost a natural force, like the weather. Recessions and depressions, then, are but the economy's hurricanes and typhoons that catch us all in the same boat together. When *human* causes are found, the blame is usually placed on the entire populace. Thus President Nixon and various business spokesmen argued that inflation was caused by people buying too much; the environmental crisis was due to "our" general neglect; and unemployment could be ascribed in large part, if not entirely, to people having switched from a "work ethic" to a "welfare ethic."

For generations reform-minded upper-class persons have proposed policies resting on integrative, cooptive, nonconflict strategies which denied the existence of antagonistic class interests. "Improving the lot of the poor," Susan and Norman Fainstein write, "was not interpreted to mean increasing their power or wealth at the expense of the power and wealth of other members of society. The idea that improvements in social welfare could lead to measures antagonistic to the interests of the bourgeoisie was either inconceivable to or not countenanced by the Progressives."[17] So today, "reform" means increasing the opportunities for economic mobility for some select few low-income persons, "integrating" the poor into the "mainstream" values of the society by teaching them better life-styles, and giving them enough public assistance to take the edge off their discontent.

The poor are to be "bettered" not by a collective advance in their class conditions through fundamental economic transformation, but by the power of moral example, by exposure to middle-class values and the efforts of middle-class missionaries who descend upon them in the guise of social workers, community workers, settlement-house counselors, and the like, it being presumed that with the right kind of guidance, education, social skills, and opportunities for *individual* self-improvement, the poor will become "a part of society" like the rich and the rest of us. An official brochure distributed in 1975 for "University Year for Action," a federally sponsored program for college students who are to work among the poor, explains it this way:

> How does UYA benefit the poor community? The primary objective of UYA is service to the poor. UYA provides poor communities with manpower and services which would not otherwise be available, and puts

those who need help in direct contact with resources previously unavailable or unknown to them. UYA brings people and institutions together to create a greater understanding and *to foster an integration in our society between rich and poor*. [Italics added.]

Implicit in this statement is the dubious notion that the rich and poor have a common interest and that by "better understanding" they can be brought closer together in ways beneficial to both.

The dominant class also propagates the elitist notion that the mass of ordinary people are incapable of controlling their own destiny. One might recall former Vice-President Spiro Agnew's comments that poor people must not presume to know what is best for themselves but must follow the dictates of public leaders and other "experts," just as the sick cannot diagnose and treat themselves but must look to medical specialists. One eager spokesman for the powers that be, Daniel Patrick Moynihan, put it this way: "It may be that the poor are never 'ready' to assume power in an advanced society: the exercise of power in an effective manner is an ability acquired through apprenticeship and seasoning."[18]

Those who enjoy positions of dominance have frequently denied the existence of oppression by cultivating an image of the "happy have-nots," the plebs, commoners, peasants, laborers, colonized natives, servants, women, and slaves who, along with their reputed mental and moral deficiencies, are said to be endowed with a childlike cheeriness and oblivion to the problems of the world. Those burdened with the cares of power and property have felt amused, charmed, and even envious of the happiness of their underlings, although never enough to want to change places with them. Seldom have they considered whether there might be something feigned or compensatory in the demeanor which the oppressed present to the oppressor, or something selectively self-serving in their own perceptions of those below.

It was de Tocqueville who observed: "The cheerfulness the Frenchman often displays under even the most untoward circumstances can be misleading. It merely shows that feeling there is nothing to be done about it, he tries to forget his troubles and refuses to brood over them; it does not mean that he is unconscious of them."[19] In his discussion of the oppressions suffered by seamen during the eighteenth century, Jesse Lemisch notes that "Jack Tar" could be seen as jolly, childlike, irresponsible, and in many ways surprisingly like the Negro stereotype, because he was treated so much like a child, a servant, and a slave. What the employer saw as the necessities of an authoritarian profession were written into law and culture: the society that wanted Jack dependent made him that way and then concluded that that was the way he really was.[20]

By forcing oppressed groups to resort to various survival mechanisms, including ostensibly devious, dependent, and shiftless modes of behavior, oppression creates the conditions for its own justification.[21] Even as they bemoan the existence of such unfortunate traits in their "wards," oppressors do all they can to reinforce the patterns of dependency, apathy, profligacy, and sloth which supposedly represent the inevitable nature of the oppressed, going so far as to inflict a wide range of punishments on those who depart from the established models of submission and ineptitude.

Frequently the roles of victim and victimizer are reversed—in the minds of the latter—and the dominators will complain of being disadvantaged and put upon by the dominated. Thus for many generations, imperialism was portrayed as the "white man's burden," a sacrifice made by the colonizer on behalf of the colonized. Management often views itself as oppressed by the coercive and greedy demands of labor. Whites, including many in the more privileged income brackets, complain that "Blacks are getting everything handed to them on a platter while we have to work for it." During the 1950s a number of popular books and articles portrayed American males as oppressed by "Momism" and driven by female-created values.[22] And in the 1970s some persons went so far as to claim that the White male was the particular victim of "reverse discrimination."

TO HAVE AND HAVE NOT

The history of class societies offers little reassurance that those who do not share in the available prosperity can place their faith in those who do. "In the absence of its natural defenders," John Stuart Mill said, "the interest of the excluded is always in danger of being overlooked." In a competitive, acquisitive society people do not readily sacrifice their own class advantages out of regard for the needs of others, and their dedication to justice is not likely to compel them to cast aside their own privatized pursuits. "History," wrote Martin Luther King from the Birmingham city jail in 1963, "is the long and tragic story of the fact that privileged groups seldom give up their privileges voluntarily."

The threatened loss of their wealth is treated by the owning class as a fate worse than death. The tendency toward a more equal distribution of the social desiderata, a "leveling" of status, wealth, and privilege, even one that would allow modest but ample material abundance for those who now possess vast fortunes, is seen not merely as a material loss but as the cataclysmic undoing of all social order, a destruction of one's identity and special value, an end to what makes life worth living. Operating on the assumption that all distribution must be competitive rather than communal, the haves fearfully anticipate that more for the have-nots will only mean less for themselves—and in a sense they are correct, since a fundamental reordering of social priorities would entail a marked diminution of their class privileges.

A harsh judgment was delivered by Rousseau, who argued that the rich enjoy their fortune "only in so far as others are destitute of it; and because, without changing their condition, they would cease to be happy the moment the people ceased to be wretched."[23] But something more than sadistic glee lies behind this feeling of the rich. As Rousseau himself adds: "We find our advantage in the misfortune of our fellow-creatures, and the loss of one man almost always constitutes the prosperity of another."[24] Let us develop this idea further: the haves sense that their privileges exist at the expense of the have-nots. They are possessed of a scarcity psychology, arising from their objective class position, which leads them not only to treat their acquisitions as an enjoyment but enjoyment itself as an acquisition, a limited commodity which not everyone can hope to possess. Privilege, of course, denotes a social relation, one in which scarcity is preserved. One cannot be privileged except in relation to others and in ways that assume a condition of relative deprivation for others. To be able to enjoy what few others can hope to have adds a special social meaning to the acquisition, a special sense of self-status and self-worth. Behind such concepts as "privacy," "property," "privilege," "exclusiveness," "opportunity," "reward," "top value," "special," and so forth, is the presumption of a scarcity of valued things and a distribution that is select rather than universal.

Along with the desire for relative status and worth there is the simple desire to have what is worth having. If it is assumed that there is not enough to go around, then one tries to keep a tight hold on what there is. In the minds of the haves, the equalization of life conditions means not only the end of the enjoyment of class privileges but a loss of the good things, the special things, that make life worth living. The owning class is committed, with all the ferocity of self-interest, to the principle of socio-economic inequality. This commitment is not merely a matter of greed or malice but a manifestation of a class defending its privileges, that is, a class defending its life.

NOTES

1. Max Weber, "The Meaning of Discipline," in Hans Gerth and C. Wright Mills (eds.), *From Max Weber: Essays in Sociology* (New York: Oxford University Press, 1958), p. 262.

2. Weber, "Social Psychology of World Religions," in ibid., p. 271.

3. Jean-Jacques Rousseau, *The Social Contract* (New York: Harper, 1947).

4. Weber, "Class, Status, Party," in ibid., p. 187; also Gerhard Lenski, *Power and Privilege, A Theory of Social Stratification* (New York: McGraw-Hill, 1966), p. 431.

5. Matthew Josephson, *The Robber Barons* (New York: Harcourt, Brace and World, 1934), p. 30.

6. Ferdinand Toennies, *Community and Society* (East Lansing: Michigan State University Press, 1957), p. 259.

7. Karl Marx, *Selected Writings in Sociology and Social Philosophy*, ed. by T. B. Bottomore and Maximilian Rubel (London: Watts, 1956), p. 80.

8. See Francis X. Sutton et al., *The American Business Creed* (New York: Schocken, 1962), p. 264.

9. Ibid., p. 253.

10. See the next chapter for a further exploration of this theme.

11. Quoted in Josephson, *The Robber Barons*, p. 325.

12. See Sutton et al., *American Business Creed*, for a comprehensive treatment of this ideology.

13. In the United States the durability of such beliefs is rather impressive. In 1939, during the Depression, the great majority of Gallup poll respondents said "ability" rather than "luck" was the key to advancement. Three decades later, in April 1970, 86 percent of all persons interviewed continued to ascribe success to personal "ability," compared with only 8 percent who said "luck." Gallup poll report, *Boston Globe*, April 30, 1970.

14. Thorstein Veblen, *The Theory of Business Enterprise* (New York: New American Library, n.d.), p. 138.

15. See Robert E. Lane, *Political Ideology: Why the American Common Man Believes What He Does* (New York: Free Press, 1962), pp. 52–81.

16. Barrington Moore, Jr., "Tolerance and the Scientific Outlook," in Herbert Marcuse, Barrington Moore, Jr., and Robert Paul Wolff, *A Critique of Pure Tolerance* (Boston: Beacon Press, 1965), p. 61.

17. Susan S. Fainstein and Norman J. Fainstein, "American Social Policy: Beyond Progressive Analysis," in Dorothy Buckton James (ed.), *Outside Looking In: Critiques of American Policies and Institutions, Left and Right* (New York: Harper & Row, 1972), p. 214.

18. Daniel Patrick Moynihan, *Maximum Feasible Misunderstanding* (New York: Free Press, 1969).

19. Alexis de Tocqueville, *The Old Regime and the French Revolution* (Garden City, N.Y.: Doubleday, 1955), p. 134.

20. Jesse Lemisch, "Jack Tar in the Streets: Merchant Seamen in the Politics of Revolutionary America," in Irwin Unger (ed.), *Beyond Liberalism: The New Left Views American History* (Waltham, Mass.: Xerox College Publishing, 1971), p. 5; originally appeared in *William and Mary Quarterly*, 3rd ser. (July 1968), 371–407.

21. Charles H. Nichols, *Many Thousand Gone: The Ex-Slaves' Account of Their Bondage and Freedom* (Bloomington: Indiana University Press, 1969), provides an interesting treatment of how the varieties of "typical" slave behavior were survival mechanisms.

22. Kay F. Reinartz, "The Paper Doll: Woman in Popular Songs," in Jo Freeman (ed.), *Women: A Feminist Perspective* (Palo Alto, Calif.: Mayfield, 1975), p. 295.

23. Jean Jacques Rousseau, "A Discourse on the Origins of Inequality," in *The Social Contract and Discourses* (New York: Dutton, 1950), p. 266.

24. Rousseau, *The Social Contract and Discourses*, p. 2 of the Appendix.

8

Class Consciousness
and Individualized
Consciousness

The awareness people have of their common class interest is what is usually meant by "class consciousness." Despite its internal fissures, the owning class possesses a more developed consciousness than the working class. After an extensive study of pressure groups, Schattschneider concluded: "Business men collectively constitute the most class conscious group in American society. As a class they are more highly organized, more easily mobilized, have more facilities for communication, are more like-minded, and are more accustomed to stand together in defense of their privileges than any other group."[1]

Whatever their differences, members of the business community share remarkably like-minded perspectives regarding the virtues of the capitalist order, the evils of alternative systems, and the use of the state to maintain corporate dominance against the demands of working classes at home and abroad. "Beyond all their . . . disagreements, men of wealth and property have always been fundamentally united, not at all surprisingly, in defense of the social order which afforded them their privileges."[2]

THE ABSENCE OF WORKING-CLASS CONSCIOUSNESS

The same cannot be said of the great mass of salaried and wage workers, who live on what they earn from their physical and mental labor. Given their limited resources and their vast but unorganized numbers, unity of action remains an exceptional accomplishment. It was Weber who noted that no matter how unequal individual life chances may be, "this fact in itself, according to all experience, by no means gives birth to 'class action' (communal action by the members of a class)." Class action "is linked to the transparency of the connections between the causes and the consequences of the 'class situation.'"[3] Class exploitation, being a condition that existed all along, is not a sufficient cause for class action. Only when large numbers of people grasp the relationship between life deprivations and class relations, when existing social injustices are linked to the abuses of the class situation rather than accepted as some natural ordering of life, does class consciousness begin to emerge.

Along with the superior propaganda and educational resources of the business community, other conditions within the social system itself discourage the development of class consciousness. For one thing, class conflicts of interest are sometimes difficult to detect, requiring an understanding of exploitative forces that are frequently complex and removed. The corporate thieves who steal millions of dollars through pricing and speculating are less likely to be seen as criminals, let alone brought to justice, than more ordinary thieves. But *intra*class differences in income, occupation, education, life-style, locale, and neighborhood are highly visible and readily become a focus of personalized attention and competition among ordinary people.

Likewise, the deprivations suffered as a result of a vast hierarchical chain of exploitative social relations are usually mistakenly perceived as coming from more immediate sources. People frequently feel a greater antagonism toward those directly above them than they do toward the seemingly remote loci of institutional control.[4] A worker is apt to resent the constraints imposed by the foreman (who is of the same class as he) but has a less clear opinion of that unseen, far-off unit known as the board of directors. Soldiers often will dislike their noncommissioned officers more than the distant chiefs of staff who set the strategy which brings them to their unsavory tasks. Low-income consumers might show more resentment toward shopowners who deal directly with them than toward the more removed whole-salers and large producers who play such a powerful role in determining prices and quality. Furthermore, by dividing people vertically into many specialized tasks and statuses, big organizations often leave them more closely identified with the organization than with each other. A postman may feel a greater unity with his postmaster on the basis of their common work ties than with an automotive worker, secretary, or farm laborer on the basis of their common class interest.[5]

In general, intraclass fissures foster *vertical* social perceptions rather than lateral ones. When one looks horizontally, that is, towards one's own peers and coworkers, it is usually not for solidarity but for cues as to how one's intraclass competitors are doing. Most often one's gaze is fixed vertically on those above and the goal is to fight one's way up the greasy pole. In contrast, class consciousness is essentially a lateral perception, the ability to make common cause with others who are normally defined as one's competitors.

In normal as opposed to revolutionary situations, most competition is not between the propertied and the propertyless *but among the propertyless themselves* for earnings and positions within institutionalized structures. "Of all the many reactions to the exercise of power and privilege in societies, the one most valued by elites themselves is that of competition among nonelites for positions in their employ," Lenski notes. There ensues what he calls the "deadly struggle for survival among the offspring of the common people."[6] The competitive isolation that the struggle forces upon working people makes the notion of shared class interests difficult to entertain. The energies of people are so absorbed by the demands of economic survival, by family responsibilities, and by the many ordinary life-maintenance tasks as to leave little time for questioning the terms of social existence. Everyday life allows few opportunities for organizing mass efforts around common class interests. Rather than making history, people must worry about making a living.[7]

Along with the competition of all against all is the competition of some against some. Within the working class there are regional, religious, ethnic, and racial differences that play a part in dividing working people against each other. Ethnic and racial characteristics, superficial as they may seem on close examination, often have a higher visibility than class interests and are rarely taken lightly. Common cause is more readily made with "our own kind" than with those out-groups sharing a common working-class situation. If anything, the out-groups become the objects of the frustrations and status anxieties that result from the intraclass struggle. Many a working-class movement at home and abroad has wrecked itself on its internal religious, racial, and national differences. The history of the American labor movement is replete with instances of nativist workers opposing immigrants and immigrants opposing other immigrants. In the South, a region relatively free of late immigration, racial animosities were crucial in destroying southern populism and other working-class protests.[8]

By focusing on the particularities of ethnic culture, people avoid, intentionally or otherwise, the commonalities of class oppression. The oppressed conditions of the most exploited minority groups are thereby more easily treated as peculiarities of the groups themselves, manifestations of "cultural deprivation," "ante-bellum demoralization," or whatever, which are supposedly idiosyncratic to a particular racial or national experience. So argue the defenders of the existing American social order,[9] especially when they realize that the demands for equality are no longer demands for piecemeal, individuated, competitive advancement but for a sweeping reallocation of resources aimed at bettering the mass of the group's impoverished members, a kind of transformation impossible to effect within the existing class order.

Racism is functional to capitalism, then, not only because it divides Black and White working people from each other, but because it provides a system-sustaining explanation for existing inequalities. It is another instance of blaming the victim. The oppression is seen as being caused by the victims rather than by the system which victimizes them.

Sex differences play a role similar to racial ones. When male workers treat women as competitors rather than companions, attention is diverted from the interests which male and female workers have in common, and intraclass competition is intensified at the expense of interclass struggle. Having been identified as inferiors, women, like Blacks or other racial minorities, are relegated to the meanest, dullest, dirtiest, lowest-paying jobs available, or are paid inferior wages when doing the same work as men. As with racist labor practices the effect is to deflate the wage scales of all workers. The poorly paid White males can always point to worse-paid Blacks and women. As has been frequently pointed out, women perform not only many of the poorest-paying jobs but also the nonpaying jobs, carrying out the life-maintenance tasks of housework and child care which, while socially necessary for the everyday functioning of workers and the generational continuation of the working class, are relegated to the lowest status, indeed, in regard to the labor market itself, to a nonstatus.

The phenomenon of trade unionism, at first glance, appears as something of an exception to this discussion. Unions are an effort to improve an entire group of workers rather than specific individuals, and these workers include many women and members of racial minorities. Yet the collective actions of trade unions usually do not go beyond the immediate bread-and-butter concerns of particular members at a particular workplace, sometimes pitting one union against another and seldom resulting in class-wide or even community-wide political actions. Unions frequently do not honor the picket lines of other unions, engage in jurisdictional fights and membership raids against each other, and are sometimes riddled with racist and sexist divisions. Far from developing a class-wide consciousness, as do certain of the European Communist unions, American unions seem to engage in individualistic intraclass competition carried to an immediate group level.[10]

People who suffer the class oppressions of this society often come to believe in the intrinsic superiority of those occupying positions of command and responsibility. As one psychologist puts it:

> The actual power relationship in our society gives continual reinforcement to our ideology of the inferiority of the oppressed . . .
> The oppressed person not only will learn that he is an inferior specimen but also will understand and come to respect these standards that

judge him. He will, in other words, learn why he is inferior. He will see that he does not look or talk the way he "should," that he is not "educated," that he has a low IQ, that he is not a "success," and that he has very little in the way of "achievements" . . . He will not necessarily feel that his situation is hopeless. Though he cannot hope to be the best, he may be able to avoid being the least . . .

The plain fact is that people acquire attitudes that by no means necessarily reflect their objective class interests, but that cannot be changed by political education alone simply because these attitudes tend to blunt or transform the meaning of that education. It is exceedingly difficult to educate a workingman to his class interests when he is ashamed of belonging to that class and interested not in advancing it but in distinguishing himself from it.[11]

For many persons, "apathy" becomes an unconscious adjustment to powerlessness. Escapes into hedonism, alcoholism, crime, and drug addiction also provide ways of dealing with one's powerlessness and one's damaged self-esteem. In addition, the oppressed are driven to oppress each other. Backbiting, bad-mouthing, betrayal, and belligerency become common behavioral patterns. It is less a war of all against all than a war of one against oneself, for in one's peers one sees what one has been taught to doubt and hate in oneself. Self-hate becomes a valuable asset for the powers that be, directing the antagonisms of racial minorities, women, workers, children, and other oppressed groups in on themselves.[12] Prison authorities, aware of the value of racism in preventing unified actions by inmates, have been known to encourage Black-White antagonisms and even punish attempts at racial unity. Military authorities have reacted in a similar manner, harassing groups of Black and White enlisted men who join together to fight racism, and protect their common interests.[13]

CONSUMERS AND SPECTATORS

While some of the more fortunate and ambitious members of the working populace might achieve occupational advancement, this has little effect on the realities of class power. Studies show that in the United States there has been an expansion in the intermediary occupations between laborer and manager, a growth in the clerical and service labor force. "Empirical studies do not, however, justify the conclusion that these trends constitute a change in class structure."[14] Owning and nonowning classes have experienced little change in relative income distribution. A large poverty-stricken stratum shows no sign of shrinkage. The increase in "white-collar" clerical and service employments largely represents a growth in low-paying, low-skilled jobs and in no way changes long-standing conditions of class inequality.[15]

While commonly designated as the "middle class," professional groups lack certain characteristics of the middle class in earlier America. Usually they are dependent upon corporate organizations for their livelihood, and are composed of employees rather than small employers. Opportunities for self-employment are declining with the growing concentration of business enterprise. In the last two generations the self-employed middle class has shrunk from 33 to 20 percent of the labor force while the number of salaried employees of various levels of skill who work for organizations has bounded from 6 to 25 percent. "In terms of property," conclude Gerth and Mills, "the white-collar people are *not* 'in between' capital and labor; they are in exactly the same property-class position as the wage workers. They have no direct financial ties to the means of work, much less any legal claims upon the proceeds from property."[16] Similarly, "the new middle class has many attributes in common with the traditional conception of a proletariat. And it is possible to argue that those who were once known as the working class have simply put on white collars."[17]

Many are called to lend their occupational service to capitalist interests but few are chosen for entrance into capitalist ranks. Upward mobility is dictated less by the dreams of the lowly than by the needs of the mighty. Our fondness for rags-to-riches tales should not obscure the fact that for the key managerial posts in the corporate structure, and for the actual ownership positions, the upper class in American society is still largely self-recruiting.[18]

Be that as it may, there are many employees who make a positive identification with capitalism. Controlling no portion of the means of production and enjoying none of the profits of ownership (aside from an occasional small stock holding), better-paid salaried employees and professionals frequently identify themselves with the owning class by virtue of their higher income and possession of expensive durable-use consumer goods, a misconception readily encouraged by the popular habit of referring to consumer commodities as "property," and by the popular ignorance concerning the magnitude and impact of *corporate* property.

Personal possessions such as homes and automobiles, of course, do not qualify one as a member of the owning class. "Owning class" refers to those who possess income-producing corporate property rather than income-consuming personal-use property. But owners of personal-use property will often mistakenly see themselves as having a common interest with those who expropriate labor and land for profit. Having achieved an "affluent" if sometimes heavily mortgaged and precarious middle-class consumer status, these employees discover the same moral virtue in their "holdings" that owning-class persons find in theirs, and often manifest the same hostility toward their less affluent brethren.

Devoting much of their life energies to personal acquisition, many working people become as committed to property as any of the corporate rich. Any system which promises a more equitable distribution of goods is seen as robbing them of the fruits of their labor. They become stricken by "the fear of equality," and remain dedicated to the idea that possessions, no matter how vast, are to remain with the possessor, an attitude that best serves the interests of the owning class. Having given the better portion of their life's labor to privatized accumulation, people are not ready to declare as morally bankrupt the economic system that has consumed their past and mortgaged their future. To do so would be to admit that they have been living by false values and have wasted their lives, a notion too staggering to embrace.

The socialization of people into consumerism serves to retard class consciousness. By "consumerism" I am referring to the tendency to treat the consumption and accumulation of goods and services as a central purpose of life. People have always had to consume in order to live, and consumption styles have long been a measure of one's class status, but consumerism is, historically speaking, a relatively recent development in which masses of people seek to accumulate more than they need and often more than they can enjoy. The feelings of accomplishment and personal worth seldom found in work are sought in commodity accumulation. And consumption is no longer just a means to life but a meaning for life.

Consumerism is more than an attitude arising from personal greed. It is a mode of social behavior functional to capitalist society. The corporate need is to produce more to sell more to profit more to produce more, and so on endlessly. Rising consumer demand provides new opportunities for investments, which in turn create new profits that must find new opportunities for investment. The ceaseless search for markets causes producers to devote a good portion of their wealth to generating new consumer demand. Mass-market advertisements also serve to standardize tastes and legitimize both the products of the system and the system itself, representing the consumer-obsessed, commodity-ridden life as "the good life" and "the American Way."[19]

From the standpoint of the worker, the need is to earn more to spend more to have more. Under capitalism, the acquisitive impulse is not merely indulged, it is constantly instigated and developed into a life imperative that cannot easily be put to rest, a psychology of "moreness" knowing no end. As people seek to acquire more than enough, they are plagued with the feeling of never having enough, so that as material abundance increases so does the sense of scarcity.

As they become possessed by increasingly greater demands for the goods and services of the system the propertyless also become more beholden to those who control the "satisfying" resources, that is, those who control jobs and markets. "Emergent needs serve [to strengthen] the dependence of people on those who can supply the resources required to meet these needs, notably employers."[20] One might recall Marcuse's observation about capitalism's

increasing necessity to produce and consume the non-necessary . . . Former luxuries become basic needs, a normal development which, under corporate capitalism, extends the competitive business of living to newly created needs and satisfactions. The fantastic output of all sorts of things and services defies the imagination, while restricting and distorting it in the commodity form, through which capitalist production enlarges its hold over human existence.[21]

Capitalist production also enlarges its hold over human consciousness and self-definition. Consumerism pits workers against each other, each striving to maintain a standard of living defined by a process of invidious comparison and conspicuous consumption, popularly described as "keeping up with the Joneses," in which one's neighbors, friends, and coworkers become one's consuming competitors.

Not all consumer anxiety is a matter of competitive acquisitiveness, however, especially when income is the main determinant of one's life chances. Increasingly more income is required for our essential needs as well as our newly fabricated wants. Having achieved a level of consumption comparing favorably to that of an earlier generation, working people still find themselves in serious need of such essentials as food, housing, heat, medical service, and transportation, essentials which devour large portions of their earnings. It is true that new wants and expectations have arisen, but so have the costs of old necessities. Not only has capitalism developed a "higher standard of living" but a far more costly way of living.

The attention and energies of people in capitalist society become decidedly privatized. One's own income, gain, satisfaction, and success become the central devotion of one's life. Social goals receive few considerations and those who seek collective betterment incur the hostility rather than the admiration of the privately advantaged. Speaking of the materialistic bourgeois society of the mid-nineteenth century which he felt had come to exercise such a uniform and despotic hold over individuals, de Tocqueville offered some pertinent thoughts:

> Far from trying to counteract . . . [self-seeking] tendencies despotism encourages them, depriving the governed of any sense of solidarity and interdependence; of good neighborly feelings and a desire to further the welfare of the community at large. It immures them, so to speak, each in his private life and taking advantage of the tendency they already have to keep apart, it estranges them still more. . . .
>
> Since in such communities nothing is stable, each man is haunted by a fear of sinking to a lower social level and by a restless urge to better his condition. . . . [E]verybody is feverishly intent on making money or, if already rich, on keeping his wealth intact. Love of gain, a fondness for business careers, the desire to get rich at all costs, a craving for material comfort and easy living quickly become ruling passions. . . . It is in the nature of despotism that it should foster such desires and propagate their havoc. Lowering as they do the national morale, they are despotism's safeguard, since they divert man's attention from public affairs and make them shudder at the mere thought of a revolution.[22]

The consumer society is also the spectator society. Both consumerism and spectatorism feed off powerlessness. Having little say over the conditions of their labor and lives, people seek satisfaction in their buying power and their alleged "consumer sovereignty." The world and its happenings are the creations of others and one becomes a mere spectator to it all. Activity is replaced by audience, participation gives way to passivity, and communal involvement is replaced by mass voyeurism. Individuals threaten suicide in public places or are assaulted in broad daylight and crowds gather to gape. The personal doings of celebrities become items of popular Peeping Tomism. The sexual act is recorded on film and draws large audiences who seemingly would rather view it than do it. Home life falls under the stupefaction of the television set. Public affairs are presented as a succession of far-off events that sometimes catch our attention. Even the "interested citizen" usually remains little more than the spectator citizen.

Human experience is compressed into a narrow routinized sphere of passivity and privatism, allowing little opportunity for active engagement in the social environment. The end result is commodity overdevelopment and human underdevelopment.

> How curiously limited is the vision of human excellence that has got built into our society . . . It is a vision that is inextricably linked with the market society. And the sad truth is that it is a vision of inertia. It is almost incredible, until you come to think of it, that a society whose keyword is *enterprise*, which certainly sounds active, is in fact based on the assumption that human beings are so inert, so averse to activity, that is, to expenditure of energy, that every expenditure of energy is considered to be painful, to be, in the economist's term, a disutility. This assumption, which is a travesty of the human condition, is built right into the justifying theory of the market society . . . The market society . . . is commonly justified on the grounds that it maximizes utilities, i.e., that it is the arrangement by which people can get the satisfaction they want with the least effort. The notion that activity itself is pleasurable, is a utility, has sunk almost without a trace under this utilitarian vision of life. This is not surprising, since the economists, and the liberal theoreticians following them, have taken as given the capitalist market society where no one works except for a reward.[23]

As with economic and political affairs, so with most other social activities, small numbers of professionals monopolize skills for profit while the people are reduced to the dependency of the layperson. The ratio of listeners to speakers, viewers to actors, and laypeople to specialists becomes ever more lopsided. The crafts, skills, music, and recreations of folk culture, once the everyday treasure of the common populace, are expropriated by the commercial market. On this point Harry Braverman is worth quoting at length:

> The industrialization of food and other elementary home provisions is only the first step in a process which eventually leads to the dependence of all social life, and indeed of all the interrelatedness of humankind, upon the marketplace. . . . The population no longer relies upon social organization in the form of family, friends, neighbors, community, elders, children, but with few exceptions must go to market and only to market, not only for food, clothing, and shelter, but also for recreation, amusement, security, for the care of the young, the old, the sick, the handicapped. In time not only the material and service needs but even the emotional patterns of life are channeled through the market.
>
> It thereby comes to pass that while population is packed even more closely together in the urban environment, the atomization of social life proceeds apace. In its most fundamental aspect, this often noticed phenomenon can be explained only by the development of market relations as the substitute for individual and community relations. The social structure, built upon the market, is such that relations between individuals and social groups do not take place directly, as cooperative human encounters, but through the market as relations of purchase and sale. Thus the more social life becomes a dense and close network of interlocked activities in which people are totally interdependent, the more atomized they become and the more their contacts with one another separate them instead of bringing them closer."

ATOMIZED INDIVIDUALISM

Under modern capitalism, society itself becomes little more than an impersonal arena of private interests, of people devoid of strong communal bonds, living for individuated, rather than collective, need. Organic links dissolve before the rationalized, restless demands of the market society. Divested of functional productive tasks and communal relations other than the necessity of having to earn money and consume, the individual often has a difficult time "finding" himself or herself. The need to discover "who am I?", a preoccupation unknown to many earlier societies, is mistakenly treated as an interior personal matter having nothing to do with the way society is organized. Implicit in the quest for one's "individuality" is the dubious notion that the individual exists as something abstracted from a social matrix, apart from the web of tasks, obligations, affections, and collective relationships which give people their identities, their social meaning, and their experience of humanity and of themselves. Thus people search for "autonomy" and seek to free themselves from emotional dependency upon others without questioning whether such an accomplishment is, in the deepest human sense, desirable or possible. Finding so many of their social relations to be loveless, exploitative, and opportunistic, people mistakenly seek to build an individualized autarky, to find "liberation" in a composed isolation.

For many middle-class women socialized into oppressive male-dominated role patterns harmful to their own human development, the move toward reclamation of their own opinions, tastes, time, talents, and productive energies has a truly liberating and worthwhile effect. But here, too, after a while "liberation" if defined primarily as a process of individuation, extrication, and living for oneself *qua* self runs into its own contradictions. Striving for privatized achievement rather than communal unity among commonly oppressed persons, the new woman begins to resemble the old man, as Jean Elshtain put it, a slightly modified rendition of the careerist, competitive, aggressive male, and a more perfectly functional cog of capitalist society. However, some women are attempting to define the struggle for liberation in terms that go beyond personal advancement and individuated experience.

To the extent that women are challenging the sexist culture that taught them self-hate and set them against each other for the favors of men, and to the extent they are developing groups dedicated to mutual help and cooperative efforts, their struggle may have a crucial effect on the dominant ideology of this society. Yet the question remains for all groups and persons: liberation toward what? And how far can any group liberate itself within the prevailing social order?[25]

In most instances, as just noted, liberation within a privatized, atomized capitalist society follows privatized, atomized paths. Not surprisingly, then, people complain of aloneness, alienation, and meaninglessness, of being detached and adrift. Some try to solve the problem by fashioning alternative life-styles in communal settlements that are often difficult to sustain without benefit of a broader cultural and productive base. These counter-culture people spend endless hours getting "in touch with their feelings," exploring personalized relations, and seeking out expressive rather than instrumental activity. Their commitment to group life is counteracted by what Gans calls their "obsession with self."[26] Work is treated by them not as a form of creative activity but as a necessary means of material support. In this sense, they are little different from ordinary working people. In fact, although usually of middle-class background and college educated, they hold mostly menial jobs. Yet many of them manifest an incredible indifference to the struggles and oppressions of working people. They engage in almost no organized political activity and long ago discarded their antiwar activism. Their focus is on their personal wants, expressions, and identities. While having broken with the dominant bourgeois culture, they are in this respect very much a product of it.

Generally speaking, whether people are successful professionals or counter-culture hippies, whether living in fashionable urban apartments or rural communes, their inclination is not to ascribe personal unhappiness to privatized patterns of life but, just the opposite, to an insufficient realization of private experience. Hence they burrow still deeper into the ego's psychic isolation in the hope of easing the pain of their social isolation. Marx himself noted that the individual in capitalist society is "withdrawn into himself, wholly preoccupied with his private interest and acting in accordance with his private caprice."[27]

The search for a privately defined, socially abstracted self may be a false and self-defeating one but it is symptomatic of a real problem of alienation. The complaint of not knowing "who I am," of not feeling alive, of not having satisfying experiences is a real one. People want the opportunity to feel affection, trust, and mutual esteem and engage in socially meaningful and useful activities, thus, indeed, getting in touch with their own feelings and the feelings of others. That the society offers only false solutions to the complaint does not mean that the complaint is false. But in psychological alienation, as in economic exploitation, the blame is usually placed on those who suffer the effects. Since the world is taken as a neutral condition, then the fault must be within ourselves. Collective unhappiness is treated as a collection of unhappy individual problems. Once more, the problem is treated in its symptoms rather than in its systemic causes. Even persons who announce that "we live in a sick society" promptly discard that insight and fall back on individualized diagnoses, it being assumed that a sick society is nothing more than a society of sick individuals. Most of those who deal with the conditions of the soul or psyche, be they faith healers or psychotherapists, organize their practice and their theories around these same individualized premises.[24]

Experienced as psychic isolation, the burden of social atomization becomes unbearable enough for some people to give themselves entirely to occult and religious experiences which promise an escape from the constricted ego, a surrender of self to some all-knowing authority and to a phantasmic vision of the past and future. Today one can be treated to the spectacle of college-educated, secularized youth entering into tightly knit authoritarian cults and adhering to exotic, supernatural doctrines which are treated reverently as "complete wisdom" handed down from one or another "spiritual master." Inner migration and charismatic transcendence occur not only among affluent college youth but also among the working and middle-class followers of television evangelists. Inner migration is a way of resolving some of the pains of atomization, social uselessness, and economic want in immediately personalized ways without having to confront the momentous difficulties of class struggle. The uncertainty and isolation of life in the market society are washed away by a spiritual force that works not unlike magic. Now all problems can be solved by "looking to Jesus." All answers to all things can be found "in Jesus." While offering a "new life with Jesus" or whomever, such movements quite readily accommodate themselves to the existing class structure. The dominant socio-economic system is left uninvestigated and unchallenged. Rather than rebuilding society, the promise is to find a new self in the old society.

The process of salvation is itself individuated, not unlike the pursuit of material success. One seeks one's own way to heaven and happiness, with one's attention fixed vertically on the upward and inward voyage rather than laterally on the social injustices of this world and the oppressions suffered by others. The intent is to advance oneself spiritually rather than help others materially. At the same time, such devotees, accepting the most conventional values of the existing order, are quite capable of attending to their own material interests. As was said of the earlier religious sects: "They intended to do good, and instead did well," so the "spiritual revolutionaries" of today, even with their vision turned to another world, are not indifferent to the rewards of this one. Indeed, some sects explicitly promise that inner spiritual peace will bring more successful economic performance.

Thus does oppression create the conditions for its own perpetuation. The miseries and dissatisfactions of the existing order lead to behavior and attitudes that buttress the status quo and make unified action against it that much more difficult.

To comment on what has been said so far: while the socialization of owning-class members is designed to foster class loyalties and cohesions, the socialization of the propertyless moves with opposite effect. The development of working-class consciousness is retarded by appeals to national and patriotic solidarity which deny the reality of class conflict, by myths which deny the existence of class oppression, and by fissures within the working populace along income, occupational, ethnic, racial, and sexual lines. In addition, the necessities of intraclass competition, the conditions of powerlessness and the socialization into patterns of consumerism, spectatorism, and atomized individualism make class consciousness that much more problematic. What Bertell Ollman says of industrial workers seems true of most Americans: "Their conditions have so limited their conceptions, that their conceptions offer them little opportunity to break out of their conditions."[29]

Of significance is the way the material advantages enjoyed by the owning class enable it to direct the attentions and define the interests of the nonowning class. Those who command the means of production thereby exercise a crucial influence over the organization of society and over the anxieties, energies, aspirations, and imaginations of the populace. In effect they control many of the means of socialization itself.

Since the militancy of class consciousness is partly determined by the possibility of satisfying class demands, as when expectations are heightened by the imminence of fulfillment, then those who control the satisfying resources, to a great extent, control the determination of wants, the range of expectations, the definition of interests, that is, the consciousness of the populace. To control behavior by setting the immediate limits of interest for other people is to shape the day-to-day experiences of their lives and consciousness in ways which formal indoctrination cannot do. Indeed, *the persuasiveness of formal indoctrination rests largely on the fact that it is embedded in and supported by the very social conditions which it seeks to legitimate.* Thus, the class structure itself is a major determinant of the unequal articulation of class consciousness.

Once again we see that power is used not only to pursue interests but to define interests, or the range of interest choice, and therefore the range of class consciousness. Consciousness is influenced not only by manipulating the symbolic environment but also by commanding the substantive activities and experiences available to others. To be able to predetermine what are the imperatives of work, leisure, and competitive survival is to be able to define reality itself and therefore the immediate interests of other people. By adhering to the existing system of production, consumption, and social organization, working people are making a choice of relative deprivation, selecting the course that best assures their immediate survival. Hence, by "doing what is best for themselves," they are sustaining the class structure that exploits them.

The absence of competing images, symbols, and organization from working-class sources, especially evident in the United States, leaves the capitalist culture unchallenged and prevents the emergence of a competing class consciousness, thus further sustaining the impression that class interests are harmonious and the needs of most people are being satisfied, or that the deprivations suffered by many stem from innocent causes and individual deficiencies. Even when new demands arise, they are expressed in a context that accepts as a "realistic" given the exploitative, asymmetrical nature of the ongoing exchange relations between classes.

In time, the ubiquity of elite-controlled conditions leave the mass of the people with no clear sense of the limitations imposed upon them. The legitimacy of substance and practice gives an affirmative value to existing social relations, their coercive and exploitative qualities being blurred by habit, custom, and familiarity. Thus do working people, filled with fear, resentment, and anger about their life conditions, remain essentially supportive of the existing social order.

Yet the quality of that social order should not escape critical comment. What we are left with is a society in which self-gain and self-advancement become the all-consuming goals in life, and self-survival the crying necessity. The competitive compulsions that were once the peculiar mark of the entrepreneurial class now engage the entire populace. Modern capitalism, for Tillich,

> is the manifestation of . . . the war of all against all, accepted as a principle, hence of an activity motivated always by the impulse to seek one's own interests at the expense of others. The peculiarly demonic element in the situation of capitalist society is this, that the conflict is not the expression of individual arbitrariness or of chaotic anarchy but is necessarily bound up with the maintenance of the capitalist economic system and is the result of that system itself.[30]

Or as Weber put it: "The Puritan wanted to work in a calling; we are forced to do so."

The dedication to relentless work and self-advantage, the inclination, nay, the necessity to treat other human beings as instrumental rather than end values, as competitors and potential enemies, the tendency to measure one's personal worth by one's material and hierarchical status, to experience other people's failures as our successes and their successes as our failures, such value orientations are propagated at substantial expense to the sensibilities associated with creative leisure, love, play, companionship, work, and communal endeavor. "Specialists without spirit, sensualists without heart," were Weber's memorable words, "this nullity imagines that it has attained a level of civilization never before achieved."[31] The compulsions of a modern capitalist economic order become our dedications, and the dedications socialize people into maintaining the very order which creates the compulsions. Thus do our virtues become our necessities long after they have ceased to be virtues—if ever they were that.

NOTES

1. E. E. Schattschneider, *Politics, Pressures and the Tariff* (Hamden, Conn.: Archon, 1963), p. 47.

2. Ralph Miliband, *The State in Capitalist Society* (New York: Basic Books, 1969), p. 47.

3. Max Weber, "Class, Status, Party," in Hans Gerth and C. Wright Mills (eds.), *From Max Weber: Essays in Sociology* (New York: Oxford University Press, 1958), p. 184 (italics in the original).

4. A point well developed by Morris Rosenberg, "Perceptual Obstacles to Class Consciousness," *Social Forces*, 32 (October 1953), 22–27.

5. Ibid., p. 23. See also the discussion in the next chapter.

6. Gerhard Lenski, *Power and Privilege, A Theory of Social Stratification* (New York: McGraw-Hill, 1966), p. 64.

7. Richard Flacks, "Making History vs. Making Life: Dilemmas of an American Left," *Working Papers for a New Society*, 2 (Summer 1974), 58.

8. C. Vann Woodward, *The Strange Career of Jim Crow* (New York: Oxford University Press, 1957), and Stanley Aronowitz discusses the conservative effect of southern and eastern European immigrant workers on the U.S. labor force in his *False Promises: The Shaping of American Working Class Consciousness* (New York: McGraw-Hill, 1973), chapter 3.

9. For instance, establishment apologists like Daniel Patrick Moynihan; see his *Maximum Feasible Misunderstanding* (New York: Free Press, 1969).

10. In chapter 11 I provide a more detailed criticism of unions.

11. David Shapiro, "On Psychological Liberation," *Social Policy* (July/August 1972), 10, 12.

12. See Michael Parenti, "The Politics of the Classroom," *Social Policy* (July/August 1973), 67–70; also Nancy Henley and Jo Freeman, "The Sexual Politics of Interpersonal Behavior," in Jo Freeman (ed.), *Women: A Feminist Perspective* (Palo Alto, Calif.: Mayfield, 1975), p. 399.

13. See *GI Project Alliance News Bulletin*, January 1976, for one such instance at an American military base in South Korea. For the use of racism by prison authorities, see Robert Minton and Stephen Rice, "Using Racism at San Quentin," *Ramparts*, January 1970, pp. 19–24.

14. Frank E. Myers, "Social Class and Political Change in Western Industrial Systems," *Comparative Politics*, 2 (April 1970), 395.

15. Harry Braverman, *Labor and Monopoly Capital* (New York: Monthly Review Press, 1974), p. 293ff.

16. Hans Gerth and C. Wright Mills, *Character and Social Structure* (New York: Harcourt, Brace and World, 1953), p. 312; also Braverman, *Labor and Monopoly Capital*, p. 377ff.

17. Andrew Hacker, *The End of the American Era* (New York: Atheneum, 1970), p. 37.

18. Miliband, *State in Capitalist Society*, pp. 39–45, and the studies cited therein; also G. William Domhoff, *Who Rules America?* (Englewood Cliffs, N.J.: Prentice-Hall, 1967).

19. An excellent work on this subject is Stuart Ewen, *Captains of Consciousness: Advertising and the Social Roots of the Consumer Culture* (New York: McGraw-Hill, 1976).

20. Peter Blau, *Exchange and Power in Social Life* (New York: Wiley, 1964), p. 121.

21. Herbert Marcuse, "Repressive Tolerance," in Herbert Marcuse, Barrington Moore, Jr., and Robert Paul Wolff, *A Critique of Pure Tolerance* (Boston: Beacon Press, 1965), p. 50.

22. Alexis de Tocqueville, *The Old Regime and the French Revolution* (Garden City, N.Y.: Doubleday, 1955), p. xiii.

23. C. B. Macpherson, *The Real World of Democracy* (London: Oxford University Press, 1965), p. 38.

24. Braverman, *Labor and Monopoly Capital*, pp. 276–277.

25. For a study of the women's struggle which concludes that the liberation of women requires the economic and political liberation of men and women, see Kathy Kahn, *Hillbilly Women* (Garden City, N.Y.: Doubleday, 1973).

26. See Herbert J. Gans, "'Milestones': The Counterculture Revisited," *Social Policy*, March/April 1976, pp. 57–58; a good review of a lengthy film about counterculture people.

27. Karl Marx, "Zur Jüdenfrage," quoted in Bertell Ollman, "Toward Class Consciousness Next Time: Marx and the Working Class," *Politics and Society*, 3 (Fall 1972), 10.

28. For an excellent critique, see Jeffry Galper, "Personal Politics and Psychoanalysis," *Social Policy*, November/December 1973, pp. 35–44.

29. Ollman, "Toward Class Consciousness," p. 10.

30. Paul Tillich, *The Religious Situation* (New York: Meridian Books, 1956), p. 109.

31. Max Weber, *The Protestant Ethic and the Spirit of Capitalism* (New York: Scribner's, 1958), p. 182.

9

Social Role
and Control

If we move away from the classical liberal view of society as a free-flowing collection of individuals and groups, and consider how people are, among other things, carriers of *socially defined* identities arising from *institutionally defined* roles, then we can begin to treat the subject of power in its systemic dimensions, as something more than a scatter of issues and personalities. Then, too, we can treat institutions not as neutral entities standing amidst us with all the natural innocence of mountains, but as organizations commanding the resources of society on behalf of special, partial interests.

In this chapter and the two following, three basic questions are treated: (1) How do the influences within major institutions shape individual consciousness and socialization? (2) What interests, if any, exercise ultimate control within institutions? (3) Are institutions themselves tied to each other by any particular preponderance of power and interest? The momentous scope of such questions should not deter us from attempting to develop some essential propositions. Again it should be noted that the focus is on institutions in American capitalist society, although much said here may apply to organizations in other countries.

ROLE, INSTITUTION, AND
SOCIAL SYSTEM

The individual's socialization is a process that does not end with the "formative years" but continues until his or her demise. Throughout life, one's actions and choices are shaped by social roles and statuses. By "role" and "status" I am referring to the repeatable and modal components of social behavior, the expected, predetermined privileges and responsibilities of any social position. Some sociologists think of the socially defined position as the status; the role, then, would be the enactment of the status.[1] The fulfillment of a role's irreducible demands does not prevent individuals from bringing personalized elements into their role performances. But the idiosyncratic element cannot obliterate the minimal role demand if the role is to be fulfilled. Thus teachers of widely differing classroom approaches, personalities and scholarly interests must all carry out certain minimal institutionally defined functions in order to be considered as fulfilling their obligations as teachers, or fulfilling the *role* of teacher.

In every society certain traits such as age, sex, ethnic origin, physical appearance, kinship, division of labor, and control of wealth influence the allocation of roles among individuals. These traits themselves are enshrouded in culturally defined values. But these values, in turn, do not persist purely by happenstance; they are largely the outgrowth of long-standing institutionalized interests and power relations (a point we shall return to later on). Status can be either *ascribed*, that is, assigned by tradition regardless of individual performance—as with an hereditary nobility—or *achieved*, that is, requiring specially cultivated accomplishments—as with the training of artisans and professionals. In most societies the number of purely achieved statuses are less than is commonly supposed since achievement itself is almost always dependent upon antecedent conditions ascribed by custom and class.

The mobilization of individuals into roles and statuses dedicated to the performance of a collective endeavor over durable periods of time usually earns the name of "institution." Hence, we speak of the "institution of the family" to describe one established subsocietal pattern of differentiated but interrelated roles and statuses. The term "institution" also designates the highly articulated structures of group authority, such as the church, the army, the school, the business corporation, the government agency, and the political party. It might be noted that we do not normally speak of the class structure as an institution; but the class structure, composed of aggregations of people of differing wealth and social prestige, serves and is served by the various institutions.[2]

The networks of communication, interest, and power that link the various groups, institutions, and classes are what is meant here by the "social system" or "social structure." The distinction between "structure" and "system," as these terms are employed both by social scientists and laymen, is not always clear. Perhaps it is roughly the difference between the "morphology" and the "physiology" of the "social organism." But generally it is difficult to talk of structure without system or system without structure. Thus Dahrendorf speaks of "social structure in terms of a functionally integrated system."[3] Here I use the terms interchangeably.

The way individuals become socialized into their world is determined in part by the institutional roles they come to occupy. *These roles for the most part are not individually determined but are shaped by the institutions themselves.* And in determining the minimal requisites of role performance, the institutions are guided by their own essential interests, or more specifically the essential interests of those who control them.

AGENTS OF SOCIALIZATION

To develop this idea of socialization by institutional role we might turn our attention to specific institutions in contemporary America, starting with some brief observations about the family. The shaping of an individual's behavior begins with the controls imposed in infancy on feeding, elimination, body motion, and verbal and emotive expression. At an early age children learn competitive performance, exclusive possession of material objects, and submission to parental authority. Long before entering any direct relationship with an employing institution, children are taught to develop marketable skills and attitudes, as adults attempt to instill in them the importance of cultivating correct and pleasing responses toward "superiors." Eventually children learn to treat other people as so many instrumental values in the service of their own ambitions; similarly they will treat themselves as a marketable value, learning to sell their personalities to adults and, someday, to interested employers. "The same family that teaches a child social usage passes on a sense of what occupational achievements and political principles are expected."[4]

Parents search for the right elementary school for their children in the hope that this will give them access to the secondary school that might lead to the kind of college that would bring them to profitable careers. Thus life-styles, values, and efforts seemingly having little to do with economic factors may be shaped largely by implicit but strong economic considerations without the need for any direct oversight by the managers and owners of industry.[5] What is compartmentalized as "economic" is often social and personal in its everyday ramifications and is not to be treated as something distinctly apart from its sociopsychological dimensions.

Of the various socializing agents, school is one of the most powerful, subjecting the individual to an intensive indoctrination that begins in the early years and continues well into maturity. Schools "have grown, in industrial societies, into the place of agents of role allocation,"[6] it being their task to recruit, train, and indoctrinate the personnel needed for role performance in other institutions within the social system.

The objective of primary and secondary education, as enunciated by the legislators, educators, and community leaders who control it, is to propagate a devotion to the dominant values of the American system. The endeavor might be judged a success, so much so that many education critics agree that most schools in America, regardless of their racial and class composition, are transmitters of conventionality, doing little to cultivate the more critical and creative potentials of children. A Carnegie Corporation study group, spending $300,000 and three and a half years time, discovered that the American public school system is "intolerable, oppressive and joyless" and that "the most important characteristic the schools share in common is a preoccupation with order and control," as evinced by "the stultifying rules, the lack of privacy, the authoritarianism, the abuse of power.'' The report concluded: "It is not the children who are disruptive, it is the formal classroom that is disruptive—of childhood itself.''' Students live under threat of suspension or after-hour detention for minor infractions of the rules. There is, one expert observes, an almost universal usurpation "of any possible area of student initiative, physical or mental." Even in the less restrictive schools "the fundamental pattern is still one of control, distrust and punishment."⁸

The real goal of education is not to produce the critical, independent-minded individual whom many Americans glorify in the abstract and distrust in the flesh, but a person conditioned to working at compulsive and mindless tasks, able to suspend autonomous judgments, to submit to the regulations of superordinates, and to assume his or her place in the elite-controlled institutions. Johathan Kozol takes belated note of the mistaken assumptions held by many education critics:

> We would point out that schools contained and silenced, muted and anesthetized our children. We would point out that this was not the way to turn out honest souls like Thoreau or good men like Gandhi or brave men like Malcolm X or Martin Luther King. . . . "Look," we would say, "this system is not working."
>
> The innocence of this approach now seems quite overwhelming. Public school was never in business to produce Thoreau. It is in business to produce a man like Richard Nixon and, even more, a population like the one which could elect him. It does not require the attribution of sinister motives, but only of the bare survival instincts to know that an interlocking network of industrial, political and academic interests does not exist to subsidize the demolition of its methods.⁹

The grade-school student is persistently exposed to the rituals and dedications of the nation-state. He will learn to salute the flag, pledge his allegiance, sing the national anthem. He will read stories of his nation's exploits which might be more valued for their inspirational quality than for their accuracy. And he will be encouraged to believe in America's global benevolence and moral superiority, and to accept a rather uncritical view of American political and economic institutions. A survey of the political views of 12,000 school children (grades two to eight) from every major region of America found that "most young children believe that the Government and its representatives are wise, benevolent and infallible, that whatever the Government does is for the best. . . ." America is seen as "the best country in the world" and the American flag as "the best flag in the world" by almost all children. Even in the more advanced grades the topics of wealth and power are rarely, if ever, discussed. Teachers concentrate on the formal aspects of government and do not give attention to the influence of powerful, organized groups that might work for something less than the good of all.[10]

After studying the printed materials and films used in classrooms and educational guidance offices, one investigator concludes: "Our schools are cluttered with militaristic indoctrination created by the Pentagon and with conservative propaganda produced by giant corporations—all made available free, or at nominal cost, and all masquerading as pedagogically proper teaching material."[11] Another writer found that American history textbooks used widely in public high schools explicitly propagated a loyalty to the private-enterprise system and depicted the United States as the best nation in the world, well-governed, dedicated to equality and freedom, and committed to its "world responsibility" of fighting Communist aggression and protecting democracy at home and abroad. In almost every instance the viewpoint taken was identical to the one fostered by government and corporate elites.[12]

Teachers who have the temerity to introduce innovative methods, controversial materials, and taboo subjects, especially radical criticisms of American institutions, often face reprimands, threats, or actual loss of jobs. Equally precarious is the position of students who involve themselves in starting student newspapers independent of school censorship, sponsoring unpopular speakers and unpopular causes, or participating in peaceful demonstrations against what are felt to be the unjust policies of the school or the government. To cite just one of many occurrences: in a Milwaukee high school in the autumn of 1969, three students were suspended and threatened with expulsion and vice-squad investigation for handing out leaflets that criticized outdated textbooks, lack of Black history courses, locked lavatories, and newspaper censorship. Their suspension notices formally charged them with "expressions of dissatisfaction."[13]

Institutions of higher education offer more sophisticated extensions of the same socialization. Students and faculty have less say than they think in the uses of the university's immense resources and little control over decisions which affect them deeply.[14] Radical teachers frequently have been subjected to suspension, loss of jobs, loss of financial support, surveillance by government security agencies, and other forms of coercion.

ROLE AND OBEDIENCE

Most professionals are not repressed rebels, waiting only to be unleashed from the tyranny of their employers. As faithful products of their education and society, they define their own betterment in privatized ways, their intent being to avoid conflict and secure a place for themselves within the system, on the system's own terms. Their understanding is that the path to success lies in conforming to "the values, prejudices and modes of thought of the world to which entry is sought."[15] As Miliband noted when describing employees of the mass media, most of them

> can accommodate themselves fairly easily to the requirements of their employers. . . . They mostly "say what they like"; but this is mainly because their employers mostly like what they say, or at least find little in what they say which is objectionable. These "cultural workmen" are unlikely to be greatly troubled by the limitations and constrictions imposed upon the mass media by the prevailing economic and political system, because their ideological and political make-up does not normally bring them up against these limitations. The leash they wear is sufficiently long to allow them as much freedom of movement as they themselves wish to have; and they therefore do not feel the strain; or not so as to make life impossible.[16]

Even those who remain skeptical of the virtues of the employing institution discover that they must adjust to minimal role demands or lose their posts. At the point where the choice is between an untroubled mind and a loss of livelihood (or loss of life or liberty, as in the case of failure to fulfill the role obligations imposed by institutions like the military), necessity becomes the mother of convention and one's principles usually prove more malleable than one's institutional superiors. Whatever the worthy causes one espoused during one's school days,

> the stern expectations of the "outside world" after graduation are such as to induce in many graduates a sense that rebelliousness and nonconformity are expensive luxuries with which it may be prudent to dispense until some future date. But very often, somehow, the future in this sense never comes; instead, erstwhile rebels, safely ensconced in one part or other of the "real world," look back with a mixture of amusement and nostalgia at what they have come to see as youthful aberrations.[17]

The erstwhile rebels come to consider themselves not conservatives but "realists," insisting they are more effective when operating in a spirit of accommodation than in a spirit of confrontation. They "understand how things work" and know that the wisest course is to learn the ropes and "make the system work for you." In time they learn to say, "How much will it cost?", "Who supports it?", and "Let's avoid unnecessary headaches," rather than "Is it fair?", "Is it just?", "Will it help those less fortunate than I?" They become adept at seeing all sorts of difficulties and impracticalities in dissenting approaches. While they give assurances that they are "not against change as such," they show hostility toward specific progressive transformations that might directly affect the ongoing arrangements to which they have so successfully accommodated themselves. Without realizing it they become the thing they say they oppose. More important to them than the fulfillment of their liberal principles is their survival and professional advancement.

The social role one plays is given its fundamental obligations by the interests it serves; the role is fulfilled not when one is uttering laudable sentiments in the privacy of one's home but when one is engaged in the observable performance of institutional duty. Roles get their definitions from their interrelationships with other roles in an institutional structure rather than from the private predilections of those engaged in them. Contrary to the brainwashing fantasy described in George Orwell's *1984*, the modern organization does not demand of its employees that they bring an intrapsychic heartfelt love to their institutional roles but merely that they fulfill those roles with the requisite skill and with no overt opposition or disaffection. There is no requirement for total conformity; general conformity is sufficient. In this way liberal journalists and news editors have performed most proficiently for conservative publications (as the history of *Time* and *Fortune* demonstrate); socially concerned lawyers have worked effectively, if sometimes joylessly, for corporations devoid of any commitment beyond the cash nexus; artists, actors, and writers have trimmed their creative talents to fit specifications set by advertising firms and media networks; scientists and technicians—including some of the few who are assailed by occasional qualms over the uses to which their research might be put—have continued to lend their skills to war-related industries; and entire armies of conscripts have fought in wars which were, to say the least, not at all to their liking.

As in the case of some universities, the institution may even tolerate opinions which run counter to its interests if these opinions are enunciated with enough circumspection so as to maintain a low visibility and not induce sentiments that challenge prevailing institutional arrangements. This measure of tolerance allows individuals to feel they are retaining their critical independence and are not entirely creatures of the organization that materially supports them. There is the interesting but not atypical case of one young dean at Yale University who, at a teach-in during the spring of 1968, made an eloquent and moving statement on the profound immorality of the Vietnam War and the collective guilt of all who cooperated in any way with that war. On a later occasion, the same dean threatened students with expulsion for staging a "mill-in" in an administrative building in protest of ROTC on campus. His belief that all who cooperated with the war machine shared in the war guilt was not meant to induce actions that might have even mildly disrupted the everyday business of the institution which supported both the military and him. Nor was his own sense of moral outrage about the war allowed to threaten his job by interfering with his role performance as dean. All of which might suggest that the power in any institution is not to be found in the opinions of its servants but in the dictates of its masters.

Having taken note of how covert sentiments are tolerated as long as overt role performance is maintained, we might remember that even the most private "off-duty" attitudes of subordinates sometimes come under institutional scrutiny. Deviations in life-styles and personal morals may endanger an employee's status if brought to public attention. Role performance itself usually entails, along with the fulfillment of work tasks, some control over dress, deportment, and demeanor. In some occupations there is an unwritten residual category of evaluation designated as "attitude," or as it is called in the army, "insubordination through manner" or more pointedly "bad attitude," which gives superiors nearly limitless opportunities to fault subordinates without having to establish specific complaints about role performance.

In some professions control over individual political attitudes is quite thorough. In many states, lawyers who have passed the bar examination cannot practice law until they undergo inspection by a "Character and Fitness Committee" consisting of usually conservative jurists and lawyers who are not above questioning the candidate on his or her political opinions. More than one prospective "troublemaker" and political dissenter thereby has been denied the right to practice law.[18] Lawyers like William Kunstler who leap all the hurdles but who subsequently involve themselves in iconoclastic causes, including the hazardous task of defending political dissenters in trials presided over by biased conservative judges, face the threat of contempt and disbarment. In the more security-minded government agencies, surveillance of employees is designed to weed out individuals holding unconventional beliefs no matter how removed from the demands of the particular job these beliefs might appear to be. And in many other occupations, both public and private, persons who make their radical views well known run the risk of unemployment.

Most organizational subordinates emphasize the returns and play down the costs of obedience. People are inclined to make positive identifications with their superiors, it being easier to comply with authority when that authority is seen as benevolent. The use by management of such terms as "team" and "family" to describe work situations is an effort to lend an aura of consensus to the realities of hierarchical control. Rather than being considered coercive, the institutional chain of command is defined as necessary and functional. Obedience in such cases is not felt as a submission to the interests of the powerful but as the proper, constructive behavior of a person who freely accepts responsibilities. It is not uncommon for people to make a virtue of the necessities they face; in that way are their life situations made more bearable for them.

Of interest to us is the function of such propensities for organizational control. This attitude of obedience disseminated among subordinates in any institutional structure or within the entire society becomes a social norm, acting as both an external and internalized force for compliance upon the individual. The pressure to obey comes not only from the superior but from the collectivity of subordinates. Indeed, the directives of superiors are often designated both to police subordinates directly and to reward and reinforce them in their efforts at self-policing. The pressure for role fulfillment, then, can be felt *vertically* from the higher authority that controls the agenda of role performances, but also *horizontally* from similarly situated subordinates who, having internalized the institutional values of obedience, are as critical as any superior of departures in role performance, such departures being seen as an unwillingness to carry one's share of the burden, a violation of essential professional duties, a "letting down" not only of one's superiors but of one's peers, be they ordinary coworkers, professional colleagues, or comrades in arms.[19]

MONOPOLIZING SOCIAL REALITY

To control the fundamental forms of role behavior, as institutions do, is to shape social consciousness in ways that "purely rational" exchanges and isolated polemics cannot do. Roles become habitual and customary, and, as noted in the previous chapter, the coercive, exploitative qualities of social relationships become blurred by habit and custom. Familiarity breeds respect and practice creates its own legitimacy.

For persons socialized into institutional roles, most alternative forms of behavior either violate their sense of propriety or escape their imagination altogether. They do not think of themselves as responding to a *particular* arrangement of social reality but to the *only* social reality there is and—implicit in that fact—the only reality there could be. Since the world as it is, and not as we would imagine it to be, is the one we must deal with, then by that view, present arrangements encompass the sum of our options. To heed the limiting imperatives of the social structure is to accept it on its own terms, never challenging its definition of reality, never exerting the extraordinary efforts needed to transcend that reality. "Realism becomes an unargued and implicit conservatism," as J. Peter Euben points out, and in politics and in all of life, adjustive and incremental goals are considered the only possible and desirable ones.[20] To this might be added Sanford Levinson's observation: "The most subtle form of 'political education' is the treating of events and conditions which are in fact amenable to change as though they were natural events. This is not a question of treating what is as what ought to be but rather as what *has* to be."[21] The result is a failure of imagination to extend beyond the boundaries of acceptable perceptions about ongoing events. Since it takes an exceptional degree of social imagination to transcend the limits of our social imagination, it is small wonder that such limits are recognized only when we are confronted with disruptions of established arrangements, such as when the contentment of an optimal reality ("the best of all possible worlds") is shattered by the angry actions of "malcontents."

Over and above particular systems of reward and punishment for role performances, institutions lend a special persuasiveness to the beliefs they propagate by virtue of their imposing presence. Social institutions are those massive monuments of society which capture and confine the vision of people, and an institution's very existence becomes its own legitimating force. It is a case of supply creating demand. The established ideology has the particular advantage of representing a social order which "whatever its shortcomings, is the best system we have." But again, it is the *only* system we have, and *that* is what is most impressive about it. As a reflection of the prevailing social and economic arrangements, the dominant credo is treated not as just one ideology among many but as a representation of the nature of things.

Those who challenge such arrangements, assuming they ever have the opportunity of getting a fair hearing from any sizable audience, will seem to be espousing views not of this world. The competing vision they raise lacks the legitimacy of substance and practice and therefore is considered suspect, chimerical, a doctrinaire concoction, a social metaphysics which unlike the established metaphysics is considered beyond actualization. More practically, the competing vision, lacking the resources which belong to those who control the material wealth of institutions, cannot, so to speak, "deliver the goods" as does the established ideology; it cannot make a claim to actual performance because it has no means, no supply with which to begin creating a demand.

The dominant institutions in the social system lend the legitimacy of substance and practice to the established norms which in turn teach adherence to the ongoing social system. What should be recognized, at the risk of repeating myself, is that the social norms or values are not self-sustaining, self-adaptive consensual forces working upon us like disembodied Parsonian spirits; rather, they are mediated through institutions, and to the extent that institutions are instruments of power in the service of elitist interests, then the social norms themselves are a product of instutional interests and power relations.

To conclude: social institutions (1) mobilize the forces of indoctrination and formal socialization in the direction of established interests and dominant values (our educational system being only one important example of this mobilization), (2) control the means of material and psychic reward and punishment and institutionally structured behavior (i.e., roles), (3) preempt competing behavioral forms and limit the definition of "reality" to ongoing interest arrangements, (4) lend, by the impact of their very existence, the legitimacy of substance and practice to those arrangements at the expense of ideational systems that challenge the prevailing "reality."

Now we might consider the nature of authority and interest within social institutions and the ways different institutions are related by common interests.

NOTES

1. For instance, Ralph Linton, *The Study of Man* (New York: Appleton-Century, 1936), chapter 8, "Status and Role." For a somewhat different discussion of roles, see Richard Sennett, *The Fall of Public Man* (New York: Knopf, 1977), pp. 33–44.

2. See Peter Blau's comments in his *Exchange and Power in Social Life* (New York: Wiley, 1964), p. 279.

3. Ralf Dahrendorf, *Class and Class Conflict in Industrial Society* (Stanford, Calif.: Stanford University Press, 1959), p. 159.

4. Mancur Olson, Jr., "Economics, Sociology and the Best of All Possible Worlds," *The Public Interest*, Summer 1968, p. 104.

5. For a treatment of how familial and personal identifications are affected by the market society, see Eli Zaretsky, *Capitalism, the Family and Personal Life* (New York: Harper & Row, 1976); also Robert E. Lane, "The Effects of the Market Economy on Political Personality" (paper given at the annual meeting of the American Political Science Association, Chicago, 1976).

6. Dahrendorf, *Class and Class Conflict*, p. 69.

7. As reported in *The New York Times*, September 23, 1970.

8. Edgar Z. Friedenberg, "The Modern High School: A Profile," *Commentary*, November 1963. For other studies of the repressive, conformist, racist, and conventional features of American schools, see Charles E. Silberman, *Crisis in the Classroom* (New York: Random House, 1970); John Holt, *How Children Fail* (New York: Pitman, 1964); Jonathan Kozol, *Death at an Early Age* (Boston: Houghton Mifflin, 1967).

9. Jonathan Kozol, "Look, This System Is Not Working," *New York Times*, April 1, 1971, p. 41. The impressions of one office worker may be to the point: "As far as I can tell, schools are set up so kids will learn a few simple skills like reading and writing and so they'll learn to show up some place every day on time, to do simple jobs over and over, and to obey rules. But what most kids learn is school is how to sneak around rules, how to look stupid. By the time they graduate they're ready to take on a factory or an office." L. Valmeras, "Work in America, II: The Work Community," *Radical America*, 5 (July-August 1971), 84-85. For studies of how schools serve the capitalist class structure as instruments of socialization, inequality, and conformity, see Colin Greer, *The Great School Legend: A Revisionist Interpretation of American Public Education* (New York: Viking, 1973); and Samuel Bowles and Herbert Gintis, *Schooling in Capitalist America* (New York: Basic Books, 1976).

10. Robert Hess, "Political Attitudes in Children," *Psychology Today*, 2 (January 1969), 24-28; also Robert Hess and Judith V. Torney, *The Development of Political Attitudes in Children* (Chicago: Aldine, 1967).

11. Betty Medsger, "The 'Free' Propaganda That Floods the Schools," *Progressive*, December 1976, p. 42.

12. Bob Goodman, "Textbooks Are Bulls—t," *Liberation*, January 1969, pp. 28-30.

13. See Alan Berube, "The Three R's: The Third Is for Repression?", *Resist* (Cambridge, Mass.), Newsletter #22, January 24, 1969; see also the fine collection of articles from the high-school underground press edited by John Birmingham, *Our Time Is Now* (New York: Bantam, 1970); also the report of the Commission of Inquiry into High School Journalism, *Captive Voices: High School Journalism in America* (New York: Schocken Books, 1974). Instances of repression in the schools are sometimes reported in the radical and "underground" press but rarely in the mass media.

14. An interesting essay on the repressive status of the college student is Jerry Farber, *The Student as Nigger* (New York: Pocket Books, 1970). Through 1969-1970 student newspapers on various campuses were censored or shut down because of their radical views or their criticisms of college administrations. According to one report, university officials on some campuses were moving "to gain tighter editorial control." See "Student Press Under Attack," *Daily Illini* (Urbana, Ill.), Sept. 26, 1970. For a survey of conformity and repression in academia during the 1950s, see Paul F. Lazarsfeld and Wagner Thielens, Jr., *The Academic Mind* (Glencoe: University of Illinois Press, 1958). For more recent accounts of protest and repression on campuses, see Sheldon Wolin and John Schaar, "Is a New Politics Possible?", *New York Review of Books*, September 3, 1970, pp. 3-10; E. Z. Friedenberg, "Report from the Niagara Frontier," *New York Review of Books*, May 7, 1970, pp. 29-35; Michael Parenti, "Repression in Academia: A Report from the Field," *Politics and Society*, 1 (August 1971), 527-537; Michael Miles, "The Triumph of Reaction," *Change, The Magazine of Higher Learning*, 4 (Winter 1972-73), 34; J. David Colfax, "Repression and Academic Radicalism," *New Politics*, 10 (Spring 1973), 14-27.

15. Ralph Miliband, *The State in Capitalist Society* (New York: Basic Books, 1969), pp. 263-264.

16. Ibid., pp. 235-236.

17. Ibid., pp. 258-259.

18. To cite a few examples: In Burlington, Vt., one radical lawyer was denied the right to practice for a time because of his involvement in antiwar activities. In Urbana, Ill., a lawyer was kept from the bar because of the troublesome public interest suits he had initiated against several large corporations. In Berkeley, Calif., an outspokenly radical law student was denied entrance to the bar for allegedly "not possessing good moral character."

19. For a study of group cohesion in the military, see Edward Shils and Morris Janowitz, "Cohesion and Disintegration in the Wehrmacht in World War II," *Public Opinion Quarterly*, 12 (1948), 280-315. A well-known study on the internalization of authority is Stanley Milgram, *Obedience to Authority* (New York: Harper & Row, 1974).

20. J. Peter Euben, "Political Science and Political Silence," in Philip Green and Sanford Levinson (eds.), *Power and Community, Dissenting Essays in Political Science* (New York: Random House, 1969), p. 19.

21. Sanford Levinson, "On 'Teaching' Political 'Science'," in Green and Levinson, *Power and Community*, p. 77-78.

10

Who Rules
Institutions?

Enough Western social scientists have no difficulty imagining the omnipresent "totalitarian" controls and the "consensus by terror" said to be at the heart of Communist systems. But our own institutions are assumed to have developed through a process of innocent historical accretion, the result of years of practice and custom, trial and error. Yet the question remains, whose practice and custom? And whose interests have decided what is to be taken as trial and judged as error?

AUTHORITY FROM THE TOP

Those who have ultimate authority in an institution are the ones who have final say over the institution's system of rewards and punishments, its budget and personnel, its policies and property: they are the owners or the trustees or directors. To own the property of an institution is, in effect, to enjoy an enforceable authority to exclude others from control over it. Most private institutions are incorporated by public law, that is, they are corporations even if engaged in such "nonbusiness" endeavors as education, health, and the arts.

To say that institutional proprietors exercise "ultimate authority" is to recognize that they are invested not solely by tradition or sentiment but by *state* charter with the right to deal with the institution's incorporated resources. To have ultimate authority is to own the property, and vice versa. Dahrendorf suggests that "wherever there is property there is authority, but not every form of authority implies property." Since authority is the more general social relation, those who try to define authority by property, define "the general by the particular—an obvious logical fallacy."[1] Dahrendorf's definitions make authority a more inclusive concept than property but this does not mean that the power of property is something less than that of other forms of authority: that question must be determined empirically and not by definition. The authority of property in certain social and cultural contexts assumes a potency that far outstrips other authorities. If property is only one of many forms of authority, in most institutional settings it is the most compelling.

While the daily particulars of institutional decision making involve the interplay of many intricate factors, it is suggested here that in seeking to understand the limits within which decisions are made, one must look to the interests of the persons who control the property and the purse. It is a rough but fairly safe observation that in most institutions those who pay the piper call the tune. They may not be able to exercise perfect control over every note that is played but individuals who stray too far from the score, who create too much cacophony, eventually find themselves without pay or position.

Sometimes the legal owners are too numerous and scattered to exercise control over policies, as is the case with the stockholders of many business firms. But generally the stockholders' interests are well represented by the company's directors, who themselves share the same concern for solvency, growth, and high profits. However, there have been dramatic instances of top managers plundering a firm for their personal gain.[2]

Directors, trustees, and owners exercise power either by occupying the top positions in which ruling decisions are made or by hiring and firing those who do. As Domhoff notes:

> Control is in the hands of the board of directors, a group of men usually numbering between ten and 25 who meet once or twice a month to decide

upon the major policies of the company. In addition . . . the board always includes at least the top two or three officers in charge of day-to-day operations. . . . We consider the boards decisive because, despite the necessity of delegating minor decisions and technical research, they make major decisions, such as those of investment, and select the men who will carry out daily operations. In fact, their power to change management if the performance of the company does not satisfy them is what we . . . mean by "control."[3]

Michael Walzer observes that the directors of most institutions

preside over what are essentially authoritarian regimes with no internal electoral system, no opposition parties, no free press or open communications network, no established judicial procedures, no channels for rank-and-file participation in decision making. When the state acts to protect their authority, it does so through the property system, that is, it recognizes the corporation as the private property of some determinate group of men and it protects their right to do, within legal limits, what they please with their property. When corporate officials defend themselves, they often invoke functional arguments. They claim that the parts they play in society can only be played by such men as they, with their legally confirmed power, their control of resources, their freedom from internal challenge, and their ability to call on the police.[4]

A similar conclusion is drawn by Bruce Berman, who notes how private power is exercised both "in the economy and society" through "organizations whose internal political processes are, with few exceptions, authoritarian, oligarchic and devoid of any democratic procedures or controls."[5]

The boards of directors of most business firms do not exercise a "collegial" power except in the formal, legal sense. That is to say, even among themselves directors seldom operate democratically. Usually one or two of them enjoy a preponderant influence over the corporation. Thus David Rockefeller is not just another "member of the board" of Chase Manhattan Bank but the prevailing voice. Where the board of directors consists of corporate employees dependent on the president for career advancement, "the board is simply a fictional projection of the president himself," whose power is diluted only by the presence on his board of individuals who might have influential links with important creditor or customer interests.[6] Usually the top corporate managers, themselves board members and large stockholders, are the active power within a firm, selecting new members, exercising a daily influence over decisions, and enjoying a degree of independence not to be expected were the board exercising its invested powers over management.[7]

Business corporations are not the only institutions ruled by businessmen. "Nonbusiness" institutions like the churches, universities, newspapers, foundations, and the cultural, medical, entertainment, recreational, artistic, and charity associations, about which more will be said in the next chapter, are either owned outright or directly supervised and controlled by the more active elements of the business class in what amounts to a system of interlocking and often interchanging directorates. Matthew Josephson's description of an earlier era is still pertinent:

> In short order the railroad presidents, the copper barons, the big dry-goods merchants and the steelmasters became Senators, ruling in the highest councils of the national government . . . but they also became in even greater number lay leaders of churches, trustees of universities, partners or owners of newspapers or press services and figures of fashionable, cultured society. And through all these channels they labored to advance their policies and principles, sometimes directly, more often with skillful indirection.[8]

This does not mean that business elites occupy all the top *administrative* positions of "nonbusiness" institutions. Many of these latter slots normally are reserved for persons of specialized professional credentials such as the church minister, university president, news editor, and network director. These administrators are what Gerth and Mills call "the assistants of authority,"[9] the power they hold being either formally delegated to them or informally lent to them. If not all of them thereby become full-time propagandists for the business creed, neither do they emerge as critics of capitalism—not if they wish to retain their positions. More likely they avoid controversial statements and work within the limits set by the socio-economic system that sustains them.

PARTICIPATION WITHOUT POWER

In institutions of any longevity and complexity, practices may evolve from the activities of subordinates and, if offering no challenge to superiors, may be allowed a high visibility and even a ceremonial and quasi-official status. To the extent that they bolster morale and direct subordinate attentions away from substantive grievances, such traditional arrangements may even prove advantageous to those in authority. Furthermore, as noted in the previous chapter, the institutionally controlled roles are themselves so legitimized by practice and familiarity as to disguise their coercive elements.

Certain other characteristics of established institutions foster the image of "neutral" social organizations. For instance, activities at the operational level of any institution may appear highly diffused. Even in the most streamlined organization there are some poorly rationalized conditions that might obscure the loci of power and interest. Furthermore, institutional representatives rarely hesitate to enunciate their dedication to democratic values, the undemocratic nature of their practice in no way interfering with the felt sincerity of their claim. Various institutional representatives may talk of the need for "citizen concern" and "popular involvement," but those who take such mouthings seriously (for instance, in the late 1960s, students, workers, Blacks, political dissenters) to the point of demanding an active role in decisions affecting them soon discover that the call by institutional leaders for constituent "involvement" is implicitly a call for supportive efforts for the policies defined by the institution and not for the mobilization of competing lower-strata demands. As the political scientist Christian Bay once pointed out, every administrator "prefers subjects to citizens," people who live in peace or go to war on cue from their superiors.

Neither the "comfortable" controls of role nor the complexities of operational activities nor the democratic pretensions of organizational representatives should lead us to the conclusion that institutions are innocently shaped by "the forces of culture," devoid of consciously controlling vested interests. To think of institutions as directed by a cultural *deus ex machina* is to overlook the very purpose of modern organizations, namely, the maintenance of articulated structures of authority for mobilizing people and materials in the pursuit of explicitly gainful or otherwise purposeful goals.

The *appearance* of many loci of power in large institutions should not mislead us as to the source of such power. Not every institutional actor can be thought of as exercising power even if all are engaged in carrying out items on the institutional agenda. That many people are making decisions on many different levels does not mean that *power* is widely diffused, nor that the institution is being ruled by consensual decisions. The decisions made at different levels are of varying scope and *are less indicative of a diffusion of power than of a delegation of tasks*. Decisions made by the custodial department regarding heating systems may prove essential to the physical operation of the institution but they are not policy-making decisions, that is, they do not set the priorities and purposes of the institution. Custodial people have areas of discretion in dealing with particular problems and they may be able to persuade superordinates of the advantages in making certain changes in their areas; indeed, good managers would encourage both subordinate discretion on minor particulars and a feedback of suggestions as long as these serve as extensions of, rather than challenges to, the interests of superiors.

The point is, many subordinates who appear to be playing active roles in the decision process are *participants without authority*; their function is to supply opinions, ideas, and tactical suggestions which are supportive of the policies of those in command. The retention of such participants is predicated on their ability to keep their advice in line with the views of those they advise. Should they persist in raising too many objections to the main thrust of things, they run the risk of losing their positions or of no longer being asked for their opinions. Subordinates quickly learn that many superiors who describe themselves as "open to all ideas" really do not wish to hear certain things. Most often what superiors want to hear are schemes which help them implement institutional objectives—as defined by those who command the institution. On occasions when subordinate feedback is negative, the criticism had best be of an instrumental kind, proffered with the assurance that it is designed to strengthen fundamental interests rather than change them.

This may help explain why, in the decision processes of most organizations, exhaustive analysis and discussion are reserved for operational problems while the more encompassing policy premises and institutional objectives are seldom subjected to critical examination. The curious habit of giving the least attention to the most important questions is not a measure of the decision-makers' stupidity but of their implicit dedication to the interests of established power. Quite simply, the fundamental questions are not open for discussion.

In "nonbusiness" institutions, the businesspeople who preside as directors (or regents, or trustees—as they might be called) usually exercise a tight control over matters, lest power slip into the hands of professionals and constituents. In the modern university, to take an institution that claims to be democratic, administrators and sometimes departmental chairmen and other faculty members make important recommendations on hiring, firing, tenure, curriculum, and related matters. This level of decision making is left unchallenged enough so as to leave the appearance that the participants are exercising *original* rather than *delegated* authority, an impression swiftly dispelled when the university's trustees, who are mostly successful businesspeople, intercede to overrule any particular decision that violates their own sense of how the institution should be run. "Authority comes from the top," remarked the erstwhile chairman of the regents of the University of Texas, the conservative businessman Frank C. Erwin, Jr., who with refreshing candor reminds us that faculty and students have nothing to do with governing the university, although he notes that during "peaceful times" faculties have been able to gain some measure of power "because there was no reason not to give it to them."[10]

As Erwin suggests, the relative infrequency of trustee intercession into everyday affairs is predicated on the assumption that these affairs will be run in ways compatible with the predilections of the trustees, the absence of supervisory intervention being indicative not of a low but a *high* degree of subordinate compliance. During such periods, decisions on personnel, budget, and other matters take on a routine quality. Controls tend to be delegated downward in the chain of command. Not wishing to be bothered with recruiting new personnel, for instance, the trustees leave this task to the president who in turn hands it over to the deans and department chairmen, the latter exercising de facto but *borrowed* power. However, should a particular hiring or tenure decision challenge the conservative interests of the directorate, then the delegated power is swiftly reclaimed. What has been delegated to administrative heads is the *task* of supervising performance but not the ultimate authority over performance. Superordinate interventions become increasingly frequent as dissenting elements gain visibility and challenge the predilections of the trustees. To repeat: in peaceful times, controls tend to shift *downward*, but they are delegated and not permanently surrendered. In times of conflict, as yesterday's routine becomes today's crisis, controls revert *upward*, being gathered back by those who occupy the seats of authority.

Intervention by superiors is not always explicitly coercive. Most superiors like to believe they are relying on persuasion to get things accomplished. Indeed, individuals at various levels within any organization may exchange conflicting views, but the efficacy of any persuasion rests on its ability to appeal to the interests of the other, and that ability is strengthened when one's argument is backed by the potential exercise of other resources. In a normal nondisruptive situation, the subordinate's words are usually his last and only reserve, while the superior's words are merely his first of many resources. This is why the superior's argument seems to "carry more weight" and commonly emerges as the more compelling—thus lending truth to La Fontaine's classic observation: "*La raison du plus fort est toujours la meilleure.*" ("The reason of the strongest is always the best.")

In modern American organizations, employers prefer to view themselves as sympathetic to, and understanding of, the needs and aspirations of their workers, but in practice, as Reinhard Bendix writes, "what workers say is called *information* which management can use to 'eliminate misunderstandings.' But what employers tell their employees are the *facts* (a free and steady flow of them at that), which 'will promote teamwork, cooperation and harmony.'" In these kinds of "two-way" communications, subordinates "are expected to listen so they may learn, while managers merely receive information which they can use." In business organizations there is "an unequivocal order of authority." Citing the General Motors Corporation as a case in point, Bendix observes that management alone decides what is the right job for each employee and what in general constitutes fair treatment. "Clearly, there is no suggestion . . . that orders will be executed only if employees give their tacit consent. The implication is rather that they will be executed because management has unquestioned authority." Whatever the emphasis on "human relations," the primary consideration of management remains "the stability and continued success of the company."[11]

It is the desire of all superiors at all levels of command to have subordinates so conditioned as to make direct supervisory intervention an infrequent necessity. Individuals in authority prefer to keep the whip on the wall, pointing to it occasionally but not having to use it. Given the volume of activity and the numbers of subordinates, control would be prohibitively costly and otherwise impossible were it to be constant and omnipresent. In order to be effective, control must be felt in the anticipation as well as the actuality. The *anticipation* of supervisory intervention is usually constant even if the *actual* intervention is not. Subordinates devote much time and psychic energy toward anticipating the reactions of superiors.

The necessity of having to consider the reactions of superiors while simultaneously trying to deal with the dissatisfactions of constituencies explains why many highly visible administrators, such as church leaders, public-agency heads, and college presidents and deans, take on disingenuous and cryptic appearances in the eyes of petitioners and protestors. The administrator is usually working in someone else's shadow. Criticisms from above cause him genuinely to fear for his career while challenges from below create only a passing discomfort—except when they lead to disruptions that invite criticisms from superiors who feel he is doing an insufficient job in keeping the natives (i.e., workers, slum dwellers, welfare recipients, students, etc.) properly in line. In such cases, the administrator's fear of lower-strata disruptions is but an expression, one step removed, of his fear of superiors.

THE LOYALTY OF
THE MIDDLE LEVELS

Those who hold a delegated power or who exercise "advisory power" will sometimes go to great lengths to maintain the illusion—for themselves if for no one else—that they are exercising an original authority. The faculty senates of most universities provide almost amusing illustrations of this. The typical faculty senate adheres to parliamentary procedures, appoints committees, issues reports, debates and votes; it is possessed of all the accoutrements of a legislature except the power to legislate. On occasions when confronted with decisions that might be overruled by the administration or the trustees, faculty senates have been known to withdraw their dissent so as not to diminish their prestige and "influence."

College professors are hardly the only ones who try to maintain the illusion of power in the face of their powerlessness by avoiding confrontations with power. In his extensive study of salaried white-collar workers, Carl Dreyfuss writes:

> Employees in various occupations and in different social positions, such as bank clerk, salesgirl, traveling salesman, stenographer, and manager, seem at first glance to have authority and responsibility in the artificial economic pyramid. All are swayed by a great many false conceptions as to their positions and functions in the process of distribution and by illusions as to the importance of their particular work, and their social status in general.[12]

The middle-level administrators, managers, and bureaucrats, the brokers of power whose initiatives and judgments are never wholly their own, see their interests as being compatible with those who hold positions of high authority. Participating in the exercise of delegated authority, they identify strongly with its source. This phenomenon has been noted by writers over the centuries. Rousseau referred to persons in the chain of command who allow "themselves to be oppressed so far as they are hurried on by blind ambition, and, looking rather below than above them, come to love authority more than independence, and submit to slavery, that they may in turn enslave others."[13] Adam Smith described a similar phenomenon:

> All the inferior shepherds and herdsmen feel the security of their own herds and flocks depends upon the security of those of the great shepherd or herdsman; that the maintenance of their lesser authority depends upon that of his greater authority, and that upon their subordination to him depends his power of keeping their inferiors in subordination to them.[14]

And more recently Dahrendorf notes:

For the bureaucrats the supreme social reality is their career that provides, at least in theory, a direct link between every one of them and the top positions which may be described as the ultimate seat of authority. It would be false to say that the bureaucrats are a ruling class, but in any case they are part of it, and one would therefore expect them to act accordingly in industrial, social and political conflicts.[15]

Along with the inflated sense of pride, power, and status which brings a vicarious identity with the ruling class, there is a more practical motive behind middle-level loyalty. As implied earlier, it is quite simply in the material interest of subordinates to serve their superiors, lest they suffer a loss of position. What they owe is a "hired-man's loyalty," to use Veblen's phrase, for often they have within themselves no original attachment to the institution. But if their dedication is not born of love, it has its roots in something more durable—self-interest.

The middle levels of modern organizations grow and grow. In business firms, universities, hospitals, government agencies, and charitable organizations, increasingly greater portions of the budget are devoted to the expansion of administrative and white-collar staffs. In American corporations, profits sometimes are so enormous as to allow for a substantial surplus even after providing for new capital outlays and paying handsome dividends to stockholders and fat bonuses and astronomical salaries to management. A portion of this surplus goes into hiring yet more white-collar employees. It is seldom clear that this growth in the work force is necessary, it being difficult to measure how such employees earn their salaries and difficult to relate their efforts to tangible outputs. Hacker mentions a corporation that retained full production and sales with no difficulty even after firing one-third of its white-collar staff.[16]

If not "functional" in the production sense, a large administrative and clerical staff serves other kinds of valuable purposes, above all acting as a visible manifestation of managerial importance and authority. In addition, the middle-executive and white-collar forces provide a ready supply of scab labor during strikes by blue-collar employees, as has been the case in recent years during work stoppages in telephone and utility companies, air terminals, schools and hospitals.

Organizational structures have a "natural" tendency to expand.[17] If advancement cannot come by moving up in the existing structure, it is sometimes achieved by broadening one's domain within it, creating new chores, new jurisdictions, winning a larger budget, and hiring more subordinates for one's office—"empire building," as it is called. This expansionism is not confined to top management but manifests itself within the lowest reaches of the administrative structure, where staffs of assistants and secretaries serve as insignia of managerial status and thereby help guarantee middle- and lower-middle level loyalty to the organization.

In time, the very growth of bureaucracy is a cause for its further expansion. Those who do not produce any really tangible product or service must justify their existence with a proliferation of meetings, discussions, correspondence, memoranda, questionnaires, records, forms, studies, reports, plans, proposals, and other products of white-collar work. As Hacker notes:

> There is emerging a vocabulary purporting to explain how the white-collar day is consumed: such individuals are paid to manage and plan and coordinate; they travel and confer and investigate possibilities; they sit at meetings and talk on the telephone; they write letters and draft memoranda; they check up to see how things are coming along; they accompany their superiors and provide additional opinions; they relate to suppliers and retailers, stockholders and unions, government agencies and the public. With all these tasks to be accomplished, their salaried time is easily filled, spreading over into prolonged lunch hours and often into dinner and the evening.[18]

Bureaucrats and their subalterns have a way of keeping each other busy. A growing staff consumes more and more staff time so that there is need for further staff increases. This is as true of the private bureaucracies of business as of the public ones of government, although only the latter have been subjected to popular criticism on this point.

EFFICIENCY OR CLASS DOMINATION?

It should be clear by now that authority is delegated downward within an institutional structure not that it be democratized, but that it be extended so as better to serve those at the elevated tiers. As the size of the organization increases, greater checks over work tasks, recruitment, and budget are instituted in order to ensure control by management. However, problems arise as the chain of command lengthens, increasing the subdivisions of discretion and pockets of inertia—at least in regard to certain operational matters.[19] The outcome is an organization that may sometimes prove unwieldy and congested.

Organizational inertia, however, has advantages for the people on top. The stalled elephant is less a hardship for its rider than for the people underfoot. A bureaucracy that takes things in its own slow stride poses fewer problems for persons whose interest is to maintain the status quo than for those who ache for a change. If "whirl is king" and power within the institution gives the appearance of being everywhere and nowhere, then attempts at confronting "the persons responsible" becomes an exhausting endless mission of most uncertain results. Nonaccountability in the face of protest is the first line of defense of any bureaucracy. Those who advise protestors to exhaust all available channels within an institution before resorting to other kinds of actions overlook the fact that such channels by their very nature are virtually inexhaustible.[20] Over time, a familiar pattern emerges: at the onset dissenters voice expectations about "making the channels work." After experiencing initial rebuffs, delays, and deceptions, they begin to voice disenchantment with the entrenched leadership. Finally they are seized by a sense of futility. Thus after working long and arduously for "student power" reforms, one campus protestor remarked, with an accuracy that transcends logic: "The channels are all never-ending dead-ends."[21]

There are two meanings to "inertia": (1) immobility and (2) the ability to move only in the direction one is already moving. Institutions suffer less from the first than from the second. Indeed, the second is sometimes described approvingly by institutional representatives as "continuity of policy." Perhaps all institutional affairs, like all human affairs, are to some degree encumbered by inertia, but this does not make inertia an innocent social condition, for it often reflects the established equilibrium of power and as such has a highly political content—be it in public or private institutions.

This is seen in governmental organizations. A maze of departments, agencies, bureaus, boards, committees, councils, and commissions, with their sometimes conflicting and ill-defined spheres of responsibility, intractable administrative procedures, and tendencies toward self-aggrandizement, self-protection, and secretiveness often make public bureaucracy the graveyard of public policy. But, again, the inertia of bureaucracy is more a problem for some interests than for others and is, in fact, something of an advantage for the established groups that are able to realize their own goals within the confines of that inertia. The truth is that the purported unwieldiness of bureaucracy does not prevent it from performing important tasks for dominant interests. Almost all major policy accomplishments, from the space program to the highway program, are bureaucratic achievements, that is, they entail the systematic mobilization and coordination of vast amounts of labor and material resources under centralized systems of command. With the right political support bureaucracies are capable of momentous undertakings. As I have noted elsewhere, the question is not "Why can't bureaucracies act?" but "Why are they able to act so forcefully and successfully in some ways and not at all in other ways?" The first question invites us to throw up our hands in befuddlement; the second requires that we investigate the realities of power and interest.[22]

Frequently the complaint is heard that one or another organization "lacks structure" when, in truth, there is no such thing as no structure; rather the choice is between informal, covert patterns of operation or more formalized, visible ones. The implicit, informal links are often developed by superiors themselves and are justified as being a way of keeping things "loose" and "open," when in fact they often have the very opposite effect and are valued for that very reason. While the covert linkages are no less structured than the formal ones, their advantage is that they are less visible and less accountable to troublesome outside critics.

The deliberate mystification of knowledge, a practice as old as the shaman, is still an everyday form of control exercised by administrators, technocrats, and other professionals. The monopolization of privileged positions and scarce resources by the hierarchical few is justified by the claim that only persons seasoned in command or trained as experts have the knowledgeability to participate in decision making. In truth, much of the allegedly technical expertise of top administrators is little more than window dressing. To a great degree, decisions are still made on the basis of political pressures, highly incomplete information, and imprecise assessments. An observation made about university administration may apply to other organizations, both private and governmental—that the institution

> is often forced to put on a dramatic show of scientific objectivity in its budgeting process in order to justify its requests for continued support, even though the dramatic props—elaborate formulas, statistical ratios, and so on—may have very little to do with the way in which decisions are actively made within the . . . establishment.[23]

The purpose of such "props" is not to manage the organization but "to manage the impression that outsiders have about it."[24]

More generally, modern hierarchical organization with its elaborate stratification of command and fragmentation of tasks may itself be less the outgrowth of technical necessity and more a means whereby the few control the many. The sociologist Norbert Wiley argues that bureaucratic structure "has two main functions: efficiency and class domination. The former is admitted, open and manifest; the latter covert, unrecognized (by many) and unadmitted."[25] Wiley notes that the credentials barriers imposed on personnel, the settings of educational and testing standards, and the constant upgrading of these standards, ostensibly to maximize the expertise of bureaucratic personnel, has the important consequence of creating artificial competitions and divisions among workers. The lack of educational credentials such as a college degree also keeps many talented workers from high positions, "a credential which is certainly an artificial one in many cases, and which has the effect of being a social class discrimination."[26] By requiring ever more elaborate and often unnecessary standards of performance, credentials barriers have the effect of keeping mature employees who aspire to advance, and young adults who aspire to be employed, in supplicant positions for protracted periods of time.

Dreyfuss's study of business organizations brings him to the conclusion that prestige differentials, elaborate division of labor, and impersonality in procedures are used as control devices for preventing white-collar employees from confronting their bosses as a homogeneous group and are largely unnecessary from a standpoint of technical efficiency.[27] Gouldner suggests that formal procedures and paperwork serve primarily not to advance work performance but to deflect, absorb, and discourage protest from wider constituencies.[28] Furthermore, the formal rules and procedures are not meant to be obeyed; they are meant as a threat against people who refuse to obey the "real" (i.e., informal) rules.[29]

Other investigations show that divisions between skilled and unskilled jobs and various minutely specialized work tasks in factories were developed for the purpose of dividing workers and better controlling them.[30] Studies of the factory system in Great Britain and the development of the steel industry in the United States demonstrate that the hierarchical, centralized ordering of work resulted not from technological necessity but from the desire of management to control the process of production.[31] To do so, management must deny the worker knowledge of the labor process and must concentrate this knowledge in its own hands. In this way directors are able to downgrade tasks and wages from skilled to unskilled categories and achieve a more complete monopoly over the labor process and its mode of execution.[32] As Braverman observes:

> A necessary consequence of the separation of conception and execution is that the labor process is now divided between separate sites and separate bodies of workers. In one location, the physical processes of production are executed. In another are concentrated the design, planning, calculation and record-keeping. . . .
>
> The concept of control adopted by modern management requires that every activity in production have its several parallel activities in the management center. . . . The result is that the process of production is replicated in paper form before, as, and after it takes place in physical form. Just as labor in human beings requires that the labor process take place in the brain of the worker as well as in the worker's physical activity, so now the image of the process, removed from production to a separate location and a separate group, controls the process itself. The novelty of this developmetn during the past century lies not in the separate existence of hand and brain, conception and execution, but the rigor with which they are divided from one another, and then increasingly subdivided, so that conception is concentrated, insofar as possible, in ever more limited groups within management or closely associated with it.[33]

Management can better control an organization composed of intermediate groupings, each with its own bit of specialized knowledge and delegated authority, each responsive to the level above. Without a division of labor, labor would be dangerously united, and management might find itself in confrontation with a hostile or indifferent mass. If all workers could perform all tasks, including budgeting and planning—as they do in some worker-controlled factories—it would not be long before they might try to assume control over the entire productive process and over the corporate property itself. Such autonomy would destroy the legitimacy of management's claim to being the necessary administrative, coordinating brain center of the organization, thereby threatening the class interests of those who own the companies but do not labor in them.[34] After reviewing numerous studies, Wiley concludes:

> Class conflict declines with the growth of bureaucracy, not because bureaucracy's efficiency and productivity satisfies potential dissenters but because *the very structural features of bureaucracy* stifle the power resources of potential dissenters. It would therefore be correct to say that bureaucratization is another form of class conflict, a form in which one side wins and the other loses and which might better be called class domination.[35]

Whether bureaucratic arrangements are part of a deliberate design to control dissenting elements may not be the most salient point. The question is not whether bureaucrats see themselves as instruments of class domination (most likely they do not), but whether their organizations have a class dominating effect. This distinction between class *intent* and class *effect* is often overlooked. Even if we were to accept the dubious contention that many social arrangements (from divorce and abortion laws to public programs in medicine, education, transportation, and housing) originate with no explicit class intent, they usually operate with class effects. The same distinction between intent and effect can be drawn when talking of "institutional racism." A particular organization in its real-estate dealings, growth policy or wage practices directly or indirectly may effect serious hardships on minority communities (and other lower-class communities) even as institutional leaders express their abhorrence for racism and point to their (selective and limited) recruitment of trained minority members. Since it is a common supposition that the ultimate commitments are to be found in the hearts and minds of individuals, then the conviction held by some institutional elites that they are dedicated to improving racial and class conditions, an expression of *intent*, is often taken as evidence of some kind of institutional *effect*. But professed intentions are one thing and the social actualities of institutional structure are something else.

NOTES

1. Ralf Dahrendorf, *Class and Class Conflict in Industrial Society* (Palo Alto, Calif.: Stanford University Press, 1959), p. 137

2. See James Boyd, "Men of Distinction," in Robert Heilbroner et al., *In the Name of Profit* (Garden City, N.Y.: Doubleday, 1972), pp. 154–219; also Thomas McCann, *An American Company: The Tragedy of United Fruit* (New York: Crown, 1976).

3. G. William Domhoff, *Who Rules America?* (Englewood Cliffs, N.J.: Prentice-Hall, 1967), p. 39; also Paul M. Sweezy, *The Present as History* (New York: Monthly Review Press, 1953), pp. 120–138.

4. Michael Walzer, "Civil Disobedience and Corporate Authority," in Philip Green and Sanford Levinson (eds.), *Power and Community, Dissenting Essays in Political Science* (New York: Pantheon, 1969), p. 226.

5. Bruce J. Berman, "Richard Nixon and the New Corporate State," *Queens Quarterly*, 80 (Autumn 1973), 426.

6. Eugene V. Rostow, "To Whom and for What Ends Is Corporate Management Responsible?" in Edward S. Mason (ed.), *The Corporation in Modern Society* (Cambridge, Mass.: Harvard University Press, 1960), p. 51

7. Edward S. Herman, "Do Bankers Control Corporations?" *Monthly Review*, June 1973, pp. 15–16.

8. Matthew Josephson, *The Robber Barons* (New York: Harcourt, Brace and World, 1962), p. 317; also Domhoff, *Who Rules America?*, p. 21, and the studies cited therein.

9. Hans Gerth and C. Wright Mills, *Character and Social Structure* (New York: Harcourt, Brace and World, 1953), p. 328.

10. Quoted in *The Daily Texan* (Student newspaper, University of Texas at Austin), January 24, 1971.

11. Reinhard Bendix, *Work and Authority in Industry* (New York: Harper & Row, 1963), pp. 326–328.

12. Carl Dreyfuss, *Occupation and Ideology of the Salaried Employee* (New York: Works Projects Administration, 1938), II, 133.

13. Jean Jacques Rousseau, "A Discourse on the Origins of Inequality," in *The Social Contract and Discourses* (New York: Dutton, 1950), p. 264.

14. Adam Smith, *The Wealth of Nations* (Chicago: Encyclopedia Britannica, 1952), p. 311.

15. Dahrendorf, *Class and Class Conflict*, p. 56.

16. Andrew Hacker, *The End of the American Era* (New York: Atheneum, 1970), p. 50; also pp. 16–17.

17. See C. Northcote Parkinson, *Parkinson's Law and Other Studies in Administration* (Boston: Houghton Mifflin, 1957).

18. Hacker, *The End of the American Era,* pp. 18–19.

19. Bendix, *Work and Authority in Industry*, p. 336.

20. See my account of attempts by Black protestors in Newark to confront, and in fact to locate, the public officials responsible for certain conditions, "Power and Pluralism: A View from the Bottom," *The Journal of Politics*, 3 (August 1970), 501–530; reprinted in a slightly expanded version in Marvin Sarkin and Alan Wolf (eds.), *An End to Political Science, The Caucus Papers* (New York: Basic Books, 1970), pp. 111–143.

21. Quoted in Michael Parenti, "Campus Disorders: A Case of Successful Communication," *New Politics*, 9 (Spring 1970), 27.

22. Michael Parenti, *Democracy for the Few*, 2nd ed. (New York: St. Martin's, 1977), p. 280

23. Francis E. Rourke and Glenn E. Brooks, *The Managerial Revolution in Higher Education* (Baltimore: Johns Hopkins University Press, 1966), p. 103.

24. Ibid.

25. Norbert Wiley, "Surplus Power and Modern Bureaucracy" (unpublished monograph, 1970), p. 2.

26. Ibid., p. 8.

27. Dreyfuss, *Occupation and Ideology of the Salaried Employee*, I, 1–18.

28. Alvin Gouldner, "Red Tape as a Social Problem," in Robert Merton et al. (eds.), *Reader in Bureaucracy* (Glencoe, Ill.: Free Press, 1952), pp. 410–418.

29. Alvin Gouldner, *Patterns of Industrial Bureaucracy* (Glencoe, Ill.: Free Press, 1954), pp. 157–180.

30. Peter F. Drucker, *Concept of the Corporation* (New York: John Day, 1946), p. 176 ff.

31. Stephen A. Marglin, "What Do Bosses Do? The Origins and Functions of Hierarchy in Capitalist Production," *Review of Radical Political Economics*, 6 (Summer 1974), 60–112; and Katherine Stone, "The Origins of Job Structures in the Steel Industry," *Review of Radical Political Economics*, 6 (Summer 1974), 113–173.

32. See Harry Braverman, *Labor and Monopoly Capital* (New York: Monthly Review Press, 1974), pp. 119, 212.

33. Ibid., pp. 124–125.

34. Marglin, "What Do Bosses Do?"; also Samuel Bowles and Herbert Gintis, "Class Power and Alienated Labor," *Monthly Review*, March 1975, pp. 9–25.

35. Wiley, "Surplus Power and Modern Bureaucracy," p. 2.

11

The Class Interest
Of Institutions

While ostensibly unrelated to each other because of differences in constituencies, most institutions are linked by a commonality of class interest. Their wide range of activities is enough to obscure this fact, leading us mistakenly to treat the diversity of organizations as a manifestation of the diffusion of power. But as Robert Lynd pointed out years ago: "Sheer multiplicity of organizations in a society may not be assumed to indicate their discreteness and autonomy. . . ." More often, the interplay of power between institutions is neither voluntary nor equal, since some institutions "occupy positions of established dependence upon other institutions. One may illustrate this by the cases of education and of the Protestant churches which trade their respective prestige and something of their integrity for financial support from business."[1] Instead of being led astray by the seemingly varied institutional powers in our society, Lynd suggests, we need to concentrate on the organization of these powers. Let us consider some specific cases.

148

PRESS AND PULPIT

Many institutions that give an appearance of autonomy on closer examination show themselves to be operating either as profit-making components of big business or as ideological propagators of capitalist values—or both. Consider the mass media. It is commonly presumed that we are blessed with a free and independent press. Actually the media are so thoroughly tied to the business class as to make their claims to being the guardians of the public trust a subject of some mockery. The major newspaper chains, magazines, wire services, radio and television networks, and their many subsidiaries are controlled by a few powerful financial interests centering on the Morgan and Rockefeller empires.[2] The smaller "independent" media outlets also are owned by wealthy persons whose political orientations rarely stray beyond conservative boundaries. Among the better known media tycoons are or were Henry Luce, William Randolph Hearst, John Knight, and Walter Annenberg. Consider the last mentioned: Annenberg once owned the *Philadelphia Inquirer* and *Daily News*. As of 1976 he still owned *TV Guide* (the weekly with the largest circulation in the world), *Seventeen*, the *New York Morning Telegraph*, a dozen radio and television stations, and seven cable television companies. He was the largest stockholder in Penn Central and an important investor in the Gerard Trust Bank and the Campbell Soup Company and an active director of these enterprises. Annenberg has been the key contributor to the Annenberg School of Communications, with branches at two major universities.[3] In return for his generous donations to the Republican party, he was selected by President Nixon to serve as ambassador to Great Britain, a position he held for over five years. As a rich, politically influential, conservative businessman, he is representative of the kind of people who own the media.

"The schools and the mass media," Lenski writes, "are dominated by the propertied, entreprencurial and managerial classes, and while they permit a certain amount of criticism to be reported there, in the main, these institutions are supportive of the system."[4] Reviewing the many county weeklies published in America, Calvin Trillin concludes that very few "ever print anything that might cause discomfort to anyone with any economic power."[5] Foreign journalists have noted the ideological orthodoxy encountered in the American press. To quote one who made an extended firsthand study of American newspapers: "A newspaper editor will censor himself . . . because he knows he has to say more or less what the owner of the paper wants him to say. . . . Almost all the publishers in the United States have [one] way of thinking, and so the editors and reporters have to write in this direction."[6] After losing the support of a liberal donor for espousing views beyond those the donor could tolerate, the editors of *Ramparts* observed: "Ideas that money supports are generally heard; those that money finds offensive or irresponsible languish for want of a powerful and costly public voice."[7]

When treating political events at home and abroad, the media rather consistently share the counter-revolutionary anti-Communist perspective and assumptions of the Pentagon, the State Department, and the multinational corporations, staying within the limits of a fairly narrow political orthodoxy. Despite an occasional exposé, and for all the talk about "investigative journalism," the media, both in their entertainment and feature sections and their news coverage and analysis, propagate conventional values, cooperate with government officials in withholding information from the public, have almost nothing to say about the more damaging aspects of the corporate politico-economy, refrain from any examination of fundamental precepts upon which policy is based, and regularly and uncritically disseminate distorted and fabricated information about countries with leftist governments.[8] By omission and commission, complicity and docility, the media seldom stray from the ideological fold. Far from being the independent "watchdogs of democracy," they are among the most representative products of the existing politico-economic system.

Along with the ability to censor ideas and information is the media's capacity to confine the social imagination of the populace, defining people's needs and life-styles in accordance with the dictates of the commodity market, selling not only products but a social consciousness, a manner of life, and a definition of reality, instilling the kinds of fears, fantasies, titillations, and discontents that express themselves through the fabricated necessities of compulsive production, joyless consumption, and economic and psychological scarcity.[9]

Of the other social institutions none makes greater claim to placing spiritual concerns above material ones than do the churches. Indeed there is some ironic truth to this insofar as prelates have concentrated on otherworldly matters rather than worldly injustices and have taken care that their moral injunctions be inoffensive to their wealthier patrons. In an earlier epoch religious ideology exercised a greater control over business ideology than vice versa, but this was due as much to the church's powerful economic and political position as to any desire on the part of merchants to submit their interests to ecclesiastical dictates. Over the centuries, as entrepreneurs gathered power so did they free themselves from the constraints of the church until those who were once their masters became their servants.

As early as the mid-seventeenth century in England a typical Puritan moral code would enumerate the sabbath pieties to be upheld and the sins of lust and profanity to be avoided. But as Hobbes tells us: "Nothing else was sin," not even "malice or greed." The ministers "did not inveigh against the lucrative vices of men of trade or handicraft." Reviewing such codes, the historian H. N. Brailsford reports there is no mention of the sin of exploiting one's workers. "Misconduct in business is expressly excluded from review."[10] From the seventeenth century onward, evangelical preachings defined "sin" in strictly personal terms, as indulgence in worldly pleasures and sensual impulses. Sin was the peculiar infection of the soul arising from flawed spiritual development rather than from oppressive and exploitative social conditions. Poverty itself was treated as a manifestation of personal venality. For Henry Ward Beecher, it was a "general truth" that "no man in this land suffers from poverty unless it be more than his fault—unless it be his *sin*."[11]

As industrial capitalism reached its apotheosis in the early twentieth century the majority of the Protestant and Catholic clergy gave religious sanction to the businessman's views of property, labor, and economic inequality. Labor unions, strikes, minimum wage laws, the eight-hour day, and other social reforms were denounced as interferences with "natural law." Forms of collective action along class lines were met with overt opposition from the clergy. The poor were urged to work hard, obey their superiors, and be content with the station to which God had called them.[12] Imperialistic aggrandizement against Third World peoples won the support of churchmen, who saw in such ventures an opportunity to spread the Gospel, it being maintained, in the words of a well-known Protestant hymn, that darker peoples "from many a balmy plain . . . call us to deliver their land from error's chain."

This is not to deny that a minority within the various denominations became champions of social reform, but most of these "Social Gospel" advocates directed their efforts at certain of the abuses of the corporate system without attacking or seeking to eliminate the system itself. They were clerical muckrakers, genuinely appalled by capitalism's "excesses," yet eschewing advocacy of any alternative economic system, and offering Christianity as the solution.[13] Today, compassion for the poor and concern for the Golden Rule are expressed by the more socially conscious religious leaders, but the exploitative practices of capitalism are seldom accorded the attention they might deserve and the conceptions of sin and virtue remain couched in essentially privatized and inspirational terms. With a few notable exceptions, the pulpit is guardian of the values of its trustees and patrons. The rare priest, minister, or rabbi who voices an explicit opposition to capitalism would find himself an object of heated controversy and would run the risk of being deprived of a congregation. In regard to the world of politics, as it is normally and narrowly defined, the churches of all capitalist nations have evidenced, with varying degrees of intensity, hostility toward leftist political parties and movements, and amity and support for conservative political forces.[14]

Religious institutions are financially linked to corporate America. Successful business people dominate the church boards of most denominations and the churches themselves are deeply involved in secular, pecuniary affairs. With their lawyers, accountants, brokers, and managers, the churches preside over commercial empires that are indistinguishable from those of more profane organizations. The Catholic church and the leading Protestant denominations hold corporate investments valued at several billion dollars in defense and armaments, banking, housing, insurance, agriculture, utilities, pharmaceuticals, television, radio, publishing, liquor, and other enterprises.[15] If religious organizations are conservative, it is not only because they are dependent on wealthy contributors but because they themselves are wealthy.

UNIONS AND UNIVERSITIES

Another institution thought to be fulfilling an autonomous function, indeed an explicitly antagonistic or competitive role vis-à-vis the business class, is the trade union. To be sure, unions have brought a measure of material betterment to workers of a kind only dreamed of in the earlier days of industrialization. Gains in benefits and wages have been wrested from management after prolonged and bitter struggles, and the conditions of labor exploitation are such that sometimes even a weak and conservative union is better than none at all. Yet four out of five workers in North America still toil without benefit of a union and most unions after an initial period of militancy become flaccid and accommodationist in their relations to management.

Having accepted the capitalist mode of ownership as the only legitimate one and denying themselves any direct claim over production, organized labor, in effect, has agreed to play a subservient role in relation to management. The unions are caught in the contradiction of having to make demands against the very industry whose good fortunes they depend upon. Rather than struggle for hegemony, they settle for a "trickle-down" system of recompense.

While supposedly maintaining an independent material base by directly taxing their own membership, trade unions perforce limit their demands so as to accommodate the market interests of the "parent" industry, it being felt that the union's survival ultimately depends on the prosperity of the industry which employs its rank and file. Unions enter into what was described earlier as a "forced collusive interest," accepting layoffs, cutbacks, and contracts that bring a net loss in real wages and a diminished control over work conditions. For decades the United Mine Workers was so concerned with preserving the coal industry's competitive positions and collecting the royalties that come from production (allocated by management as a bonus for union cooperation) that it abandoned all interest in the safety and health of its members.[16] The union's former president, W. A. Boyle, was unequivocal in his dedications of loyalty to the coal owners when he told a Senate subcommittee: "The UMWA will not abridge the rights of mine operators in running the mines. We follow the judgment of the coal operators, right or wrong."[17]

Unions provide some of the best examples of how *competitive vertical* identities (particular industry interests) mold consciousness in a more immediate way than do *cooperative lateral* identities (common working-class interests). When labor leaders do think beyond the confines of a particular industry to include all of labor, they see unions today, as did Samuel Gompers almost a century ago, as "Industry's most able helpmate." "Trade unionism," said David Dubinsky, former leader of the ILGWU, "needs capitalism like a fish needs water."[18] The collusion between labor and management in America was expressed with unreserved candor by George Meany, AFL-CIO president, in a speech before the National Association of Manufacturers in 1956: "I never went on strike in my life, never ran a strike in my life, never ordered anyone else to run a strike in my life, never had anything to do with a picket line. . . . In the final analysis, there is not a great difference between the things I stand for and the things that NAM leaders stand for."[19] Quite so. Tracing the development of the American Federation of Labor, Michael Rogin writes:

> The more established their organizations and the longer they remained in office, the friendlier the AFL officials became toward business leaders and others powerful in the outer world. They developed continuing relations with these men, which often turned to admiration. They often used their organizational positions to obtain wealth and status outside the labor movement. Many writers now praise this process of embourgeoisement, arguing that it creates moderate leaders more willing to compromise. Yet the embourgeoised AFL leadership of the 1920's was more extreme in its antipathy to politics, its suppression of internal disagreement, and its superpatriotic rhetoric, than at any other time in its history. Surely much depends on what leaders become embourgeoised into. AFL leaders in the 1920's resembled the nationalistic, Social Darwinist businessmen against whom their unions had originally been organized.[20]

Historically union leaders have been less militant than rank and file and more concerned about appearing "responsible" vis-à-vis management and the public. They have been less committed to strike actions and when a strike has occurred more inclined to end it quickly.

They have frequently and sometimes violently discouraged rank-and-file involvement in labor parties and other "militant" political organizations.[21] Leaders like Samuel Gompers showed unmitigated hostility toward leftist movements. He and his associates in the AFL were not even enthusiastic about the agitation for an eight-hour day. Only pressure from the ranks induced the AFL leadership to lend lukewarm support for a shorter work day in 1888. In the words of one historian, Gompers "had been compelled to endorse the eight-hour agitation of the rank-and-file of the union, but in his heart and mind he opposed it. The idea was too radical; it endangered his conservative policies, to say nothing of his position as president of the A.F. of L."[22]

Almost a century after Gompers, the AFL-CIO leadership still adheres to an anticommunism that is to the right of most mainstream politicians. Under the guidance and with the financial aid of corporate leaders and the United States government, labor leaders have played an active role in advancing the interests of American capitalism against the challenges of domestic and overseas socialist movements. In places like Western Europe and Latin America, United States union leaders have helped build conservative procapitalist labor organizations to compete against leftist-oriented ones.[23] As a faithful and unequal member of the corporate-military establishment, labor offers no divisive class aims of its own. Miliband concludes:

> Labor has nothing of the power of capital in the day-to-day economic decision-making of capitalist enterprise. What a firm produces; whether it exports or does not export; whether it invests, in what, and for what purpose; whether it absorbs or is absorbed by other firms—these and many other such decisions are matters over which labor has at best an indirect degree of influence and more generally no influence at all. In this sense labor lacks a firm basis of economic power, and has consequently that much less pressure potential vis-à-vis the state. This is also one reason why governments are so much less concerned to obtain the "confidence" of labor than of business.[24]

Although unions are relatively weak compared to government and business, they exercise a tight control over their own rank and file. The function of the labor bureaucracy is to guarantee the stability of the nation's labor force. In return the labor bureaucrats are afforded by government and management a more or less free hand in running their unions as they choose. Union officials stress "productivity" and "cooperation" with the companies and sometimes enter into sweetheart contracts with management. Workers who display wildcat tendencies and class consciousness are often coopted or intimidated into silence. The close ties many unions have with gangsters is not just a matter of personal corruption but is a functional relationship: in return for part of the take, the racketeers terrorize potential rank-and-file opposition. The structure of most unions is totally hierarchical. Rank-and-file committees, when they do exist, are usually limited to minor advisory roles and remain tightly controlled by the union's staff. Regarding a teamster local, one writer concludes:

> The union . . . is generally seen as simply one more repressive institution in the workers' lives. It's not that the union is necessarily worse than the companies; it's just that the companies are supposed to act that way and the union is supposed to be on your side. . . . Rather than building self-affirming actions and programs, the union contributes to the alienation and powerlessness felt by the average worker. "Apathy" is used as an ideological weapon to show workers that their self-hatred is justified, that workers are powerless because they are unworthy of power, and consequently that the union has power because it is worthy.[25]

Among the institutions enjoying an undeserved reputation for autonomy while being closely bound to the interests of the business class are the schools and colleges. In chapter 9 it was noted how public schools served as propagators of business ideology and as agents of conservative socialization. Here I might add that this function was not accidentally arrived at. The expansion of public education in the nineteenth century was an offshoot of industry's growing need for a more literate work force. It was anticipated in many locales that a better-educated populace would offer inducements to commercial growth and attract capital investment.[26] But more importantly, local school committees, dominated by the more affluent elements, saw schools as a place for teaching punctuality, regular attendance, and other attitudes useful for future employment. In the words of one nineteenth-century teachers' magazine: "That the habit of prompt action in the performance of duty required of the boy, by the teacher at school, becomes in the man of business confirmed; thus system and order characterize the employment of the day laborer."[27]

Persons of property saw the "ignorant and uneducated" as "the most turbulent and troublesome" element. Education imposed from above was a cure, a way of teaching orderly living and obedience to authority. The schools also were expected to promote harmony and unity among the social classes. Business and educational leaders hoped that better-schooled laborers would be less militant workers. With the benefit of a high-school education, the more intelligent sons of workers were expected to find profitable positions within the existing industrial system rather than becoming agitators for the discontented masses.[18] They would learn respect for social order, that is, respect for the existing social order. (In fact, high-school education seldom reached the children of the laboring poor.) Something of the same anticipation could be observed a century later regarding Blacks. College scholarships were made available to select numbers of Black youth in the 1960s in the hope they might be better integrated into the affluence of White America and refrain from creating disturbances in the streets.

Of all educational organizations none has become more closely linked to capitalism than the university. With the advance of industrialization the university evolved from a clergy-dominated institution concentrating on classical education and theology to one that served industry's growing need for managers, technicians, and bureaucratic workers. Through the early decades of the twentieth century, the business class tightened and systematized its hold over the colleges, using tax-free foundations and state and federal money to build select liberal arts, science, agricultural, law, engineering, and business schools. Far from being independent of the business world, the universities now provide the corporations with a wide range of services, are financially dependent on corporate endowments and private foundations, and have substantial investments in big business.

The university no longer governs itself, but is directly managed by business elites. Describing conditions at the turn of the century, one scholar writes:

> On the whole, the sound conservative men of wealth who came to dominate the college governing boards were pillars of the better classes, and while their duties permitted them to perform a social responsibility, their authority also enabled them to keep the colleges true to the interests and prejudices of the classes from which they were drawn.[19]

In 1969 the twenty-three trustees of Columbia University, to cite a typical example, were mostly real-estate magnates, bankers, and directors of such corporations as Lockheed Aircraft, Consolidated Edison, IBM, and CBS. The average age of those who sat on the self-appointed, self-perpetuating Columbia board was over sixty.[30] As Peter Schrag notes: "Insofar as American colleges and universities still retain any independence, they tend to be rather like individual suppliers in a market dominated by corporate giants."[31] "The University and segments of industry," Clark Kerr concludes, "are becoming more and more alike. As the University becomes tied to the world of work, the professor—at least in the natural and some of the social sciences—takes on the characteristics of an entrepreneur . . . the two worlds are merging physically."[32]

After World War II, the major universities moved increasingly toward research for monetary gain or—as it is called—"project-oriented research." These endeavors have been massively financed by the federal government and are of special use to the military and private industry. Numerous faculty and administrators are employed as advisors and consultants for the Department of Defense, the CIA, and numerous other security agencies. For handsome fees and contracts, faculty members provide a variety of brainpower services to business, law, industry, engineering, and agribusiness, whose firms in turn frequently service that biggest and most energetic part of the federal government, the Pentagon.

Not only do many professors do consulting work for companies like Exxon, IBM, and General Motors, but the boards of directors of the giant firms harbor a surprisingly high number of well-paid academics with close links to the scientific-governmental-industrial establishment.[33]

How . . . did these academic scientists achieve these positions of great importance? Certainly, the professional prestige of these individuals in scientific and academic circles was essential; but it is not the only criterion. In order to be invited inside sensitive governmental activities one must be considered safe—a team player, not a boat rocker. . . . However, the requirements for elevation to the board of directors of a major corporation must be even more selective. Here, it must be assumed that one is dedicated to serving the self-interest of that particular corporation and, by implication, to supporting generally the values and the goals of the capitalist class. This is where political concerns become more acute, since corporate interests are so often opposite to the general public interest. Such an interpretation destroys the basis for considering these corporate-connected academic scientists as being independent advisors on public policy matters.[34]

As technical knowledge increases in importance so does the social and political power of the institutions that hold a near monopoly over its practical use. This concentration of knowledge further reduces the capacity of ordinary persons to control their society.[35] However, technical knowledge is not controlled by service institutions like the university but by the organized centers of politico-economic power.

Lowi reminds us of "the impossibility of establishing a university that does not have a systematic bias toward one set of social interests and against some other."[36] Yet within most institutions of higher learning can be found faculty and administrators, including many engaged in the corporate and governmental activities mentioned above, who argue with all apparent seriousness that a university is a place apart from the immediate partisan interests of this world. As Yale's president, Kingman Brewster, claimed, the university serves no social end "other than the advancement of learning."[37] Other people such as Ronald Reagan, former governor of California, spoke with greater accuracy: "Higher education should be looked upon as a capital investment . . . the university is not a sanctuary for someone who wants to pursue knowledge for knowledge's sake."[38]

With greater business controls came tighter business ideological controls. For the last one hundred years persons of Marxist or other left persuasions have been purged from academia or prevented from entering its ranks. The first president of Cornell, Andrew White, observed that while he believed "in freedom from authoritarianism of every kind, this freedom did not, however, extend to Marxists, anarchists, and other radical disturbers of the social order."[39] And in 1908 Charles William Eliot of Harvard expressed relief that the private colleges of his day were free of the dangerous "class influences such as that exerted by farmers as a class, or trade unionists as a class." Higher education, he added, rested safely in the hands of the "public-spirited, business or professional man,"[40] whose biases, being of the kind that Eliot shared, were not perceived as class influences.

University courses usually are devoid of radical political content or are taught by men whose ideological perspectives rarely stray beyond respectable, albeit sometimes critical, persuasions. Noncontroversial subject matter is defined as "scholarly" and "professional," while heterodox constructions are frequently dismissed as beyond the pale of proper scientific inquiry. Thus for an aspiring young economist, career advancement is contingent upon publication in professional journals which define scholarly work as that which concerns itself with the operational problems and theories of a capitalist system, while those analyses developed from an anticapitalist perspective are treated as inherently lacking in professional standards. In most of the other social-science disciplines the situation is the same. Students who wish to explore heterodox perspectives are not encouraged to do so by those armed with the power of certification. While making claim to intellectual and ideological independence, most departments produce Ph.D's who are remarkably standardized in their views about what constitutes acceptable research, and how ideas (and careers) are to be advanced.[41]

The call for "professionalism" in higher education frequently is an invitation to avoid controversial ideas and to concentrate on fortifying prevailing power relations. The concern of graduate and professional schools rarely extends beyond the training of people for service roles within the existing institutional order. Usually the school itself is staffed by persons who, drawn from established professions and industries, define the problems of their discipline from the perspective of the corporate world and see it as their tasks to socialize students to the devotions of future employers. Commerce students, of course, learn that their business is business, but similarly students in the various sciences and technologies devote their best efforts to the interests that control research funds and jobs—in most instances this means the corporations and the Pentagon.[42] The student of journalism is taught to write a lead paragraph but receives little encouragement in developing an awareness of the socio-economic forces and institutions that shape the world he or she is supposed to be discerning. The "news" is composed of a series of immediate controversies, events, and personalities. Newspeople, like so many gossips, develop an instinct for the simplified and superficial at the expense of the more penetrating questions which go unanswered because they go unasked.

Similarly, the law schools of America, as Ralph Nader points out, take "the very bright young minds of a nation, envelop them in conceptual cocoons and condition their expectations of practice to the demands of the corporate law firm."[43] The law curriculum is in large part a reflection of the commercial interests which command the talents of lawyers: tax, corporate, securities, and property law are the prestige areas. Realty law is studied from the viewpoint of the landlord rather than from the needs of the tenant. The rights of creditors and producers are afforded careful attention while the legal problems of the indebted are generally ignored. But such training is an accurate reflection of the occupational roles performed by lawyers; as Nader concludes:

> Lawyers labored for polluters, not anti-polluters, for sellers, not consumers, for corporations, not citizens, for labor leaders, not rank and file, for, not against, rate increases or weak standards before government agencies, for highway builders not displaced residents, . . . for preferential business access to government and against equal citizen access to the same government, for agricultural subsidies to the rich but not food stamps for the poor, for tax and quota privileges, not for equity and free trade. None of this . . . seemed to trouble the law schools.[44]

Watergate revealed to the public that venality and knavery exist at every level of the legal profession. For every Clarence Darrow produced by the profession there are a score of lying, hustling, reactionary Kleindiensts, Kalmbachs, Mitchells, Ehrlichmans, and Haldemans who win fame and fortune by serving the interests of the powerful.[45]

In sum, what is normally designated as "higher" education or "professional" education gives little encouragement to the socially heretical elements within various disciplines—which may explain why great intellectual upheavals usually come from *without* rather than within the academy and with the opposition rather than the support of the established academics. The people who are graduated from such institutions run the risk of becoming, to use Kenneth Dolbeare's words, "mere technocratic instruments of the status quo," their perceptions of social policy alternatives being so institutionally predefined as to fortify the very values and social relations which sustain existing problems.[46]

Some people would take issue with the view that the universities have been schools for conformity. Pointing to the confrontations of the late 1960s, they argue that the campus has been a place of ferment and dissent. But a moment's reflection should tell us that the university was not the *source* but the *target* of protest. The university was under attack because of its ROTC programs, military research, complicity with the Vietnam War, irrelevant and conformist courses, institutional racism, and absence of student participation in decision making. When workers strike against their bosses for better work conditions, we usually do not credit management with having fostered a spirit of activism and dissension in their employees, although their policies may well have inadvertently instigated such sentiments. So should we not credit the university with propagating heterodoxy when students rebel against its orthodoxy. To the extent that students participated in the protest movement, it was not due to but *despite* their education. In any case, only a relatively small portion of students and faculty actually engaged in the confrontation politics of the 1960s, the remainder having given themselves to the uninterrupted pursuit of their careers and to the defense of their vested interests, a testimony to the successful effects of their conservative socialization.

As a means of preserving its establishmentarian ideology, the university mirrors the larger corporate society in its hierarchical structure: an all-powerful decision-making board of trustees at the top, followed by an obedient level of senior administrators, influential alumni, and some senior faculty. At the very bottom are the students and working staff.

The academic profession itself is divided by prestige, money, and employment conditions. Most academicians who work their hours in anonymous classrooms continue to make do without benefit of fat consultation fees, foundation grants, or corporate and government appointments. These hewers of wood and drawers of water, comprising the great majority of the disciplines, defer to the luminaries of their profession, those of the big time and big money. Though small in number, the luminaries, through their research, publications, elite university positions, governmental and corporate funding, foundation support, advisory council positions, and control over graduate training and professional associations and publications, define the direction of the profession, its subject matter, intellectual biases, implicitly centrist ideological limits, and standards of professional success.[47]

SCIENCE, ARTS, AND SPORTS

In modern times science has become something more than the work of scientists. Today it is an industry. The spontaneous invention has been replaced by the planned investment.

> This was accomplished by means of the transformation of science itself into a commodity bought and sold like the other implements and labors of production. . . .The scientific-technical revolution, for this reason, cannot be understood in terms of specific innovations—as in the case of the Industrial Revolution, which may be adequately characterized by a handful of key inventions—but must be understood rather in its totality as a mode of production into which science and exhaustive engineering investigations have been integrated as part of ordinary functioning. The key innovation is not to be found in chemistry, electronics, automatic machinery, aeronautics, atomic physics, or any of the products of these science-technologies, but rather in the transformartion of science itself into capital.[48]

The way the scientific disciplines are financed determines in large degree the development of their subject matter. Over forty-five years ago, Wilhelm Reich wrote:

> We need to take a close look at the . . . structure of bourgeois science in general. It is broken up into a hundred thousand individualistic fragments. . . . Bourgeois science is academic not only in its language but also in its choice of subjects (compare the number of papers on the fine structure of brain tissue in chronic alcoholics with that of papers on the social conditions which cause alcoholism). And the closer the subject studied is to real life, the more remote from life is bourgeois science, the more grotesque the theories it produces, the more abstract the discussions around these theories. For this reason a science like, say, mathematics is the most free from the influences of bourgeois thinking, while, say, research into tuberculosis has not yet got to the point of thoroughly studying the effect of poor food and housing on the human lungs.[49]

Certainly medical science offers enough examples of Reich's complaint, most notably in its tendency to define diseases by the chemistry of their symptoms while ignoring the organism as a functioning entity and disregarding the related social causes of illness. Today the multibillion-dollar search continues for a "cure" for cancer while the causes are known to be human-made, linked to industrial pollutants and chemical additives and emissions in the air, water, and food. Scientifically it would be easier to *prevent* cancer by removing the human-made causes than to try to cure what may often be incurable. But medical problems have an important class-political dimension. Given the wider realities of power, it is easier to spend billions looking for a cure than to challenge the big economic interests that are part of the cause. The tendency to define medical problems as separate from politico-economic power is itself a profound concession to politico-economic power.

The way the medical profession itself has evolved reflects the profound influence of the capitalist system and the capitalist mentality. Rather than being organized as a public service for the entire community, medical doctors operate as do any self-enriching entrepreneurs, setting up their private businesses ("practices") on a market basis, selling medical treatment to customers ("patients") who can pay, while denying it to persons who cannot. Prices ("fees") are fixed by the regional chapters of the American Medical Association (AMA). Those few doctors who try to charge below the inflated monopoly rates often run into trouble with the AMA and find their referrals and their access to hospitals cut off. The medical profession keeps prices exorbitantly high and is the richest of professions, with incomes equaled or excelled only by those of the top managerial elites of business. High profits are achieved by limiting the number of medical schools and the supply of doctors, and by getting the Food and Drug Administration and the state legislatures to outlaw competing practices such as naturopathy, homeopathy, and other nutritional, herbal, and nonchemical treatments. The effect of these practices is to deny people the right to alternative forms of medicine. The M.D.s also monopolize access to health insurance benefits, amounting to a $30 billion yearly gross. This amount represented nearly half of the total United States insurance industry in 1976.[50]

M.D.s are arrogantly ignorant of nutritional and other non-chemical cures, being required to take no courses in nutrition while in medical school. Rather, they rely on expensive chemical drugs marketed by the drug industry, which has annual sales of $10 billion and which has enjoyed the first or second highest profit rate in manufacturing over the past decade. These drugs are elaborately packaged in eye-catching displays and are advertised in fancy, elaborately colored brochures designed by Madison Avenue advertising companies and peddled by drug company salespersons who have no medical training but whose opinions doctors tend to rely on. Such drugs are often untested and unsafe, are designed to ignore causes and attack symptoms, and often worsen the illness by causing serious side effects.[51]

The existing system's distorting effects can be seen in other areas of science. More than two-thirds of the technical research done in the United States is financed and consumed by the military and is used for new weapons systems, chemical and bacteriological warfare, counter-insurgency technology, communications systems, and similar endeavors. There is not a natural science that has not felt the effects of corporate-military financing in one way or another. The social sciences have experienced a similar impact. By the early 1960s the Pentagon was spending millions each year on social-science research. Spurred on by this kind of largesse, there arose a vast array of "institutes," "projects," and "councils," populated by teams of behavioralist researchers who produced elaborate studies on such subjects as the American soldier, consumer buying habits, work motivation in the factory, urban riots, student protests, savings-bond sales campaigns, military recruitment campaigns, effective lobbying techniques, budget and management control problems, "instability" in Third World nations, police control methods at home and abroad, insurgency and counter-insurgency, and the like.

Whether it was a question of developing new techniques for making the tax burden less visible, or weeding out potentially dissident college applicants, or making consumers more responsive, or assembly-line workers, ghetto residents, and Latin American and Asian villagers more compliant, the social-science "teams" were there with bright and often ruthless ideas, never defining new goals nor challenging the interests and ideological premises of their corporate-governmental patrons, but always trying to find ways of reaching— and justifying— the objectives desired by the interests that employed their talents. Their task has been not to change the world but to help those in power to control it. As the Advisory Committee on Government Programs in the Behavioral Sciences proudly put it: "The behavioral sciences are . . . an important source of information, analysis and explanation about group and individual behavior, and thus an essential and increasingly relevant instrument of modern government."[52]

The image of the scientist engaged in a dispassionate, sacred search for truth free from the influences of vested interests is nothing more than an image. Without needing to repeat what was noted about the universities, suffice it to say that the "scientific establishment" is a highly controlled service adjunct to the powers that be. It was Gramsci who noted that intellectuals are allowed the trappings of independence: professional certification, scholarly overproduction on specialized subjects, academic posts that suffer only indirect supervision on many matters, a social status that developed historically apart from the clerics who themselves were closely tied to the landowning class. "Just as . . . intellectuals have a sense of their own uninterrupted historical continuity, of their 'qualifications' and of *esprit de corps*, so they see themselves as autonomous and independent of the ruling social group."[53] That they see themselves as independent does not mean they are since they are tied by economic necessity to the corporations, government agencies, and academic institutes that pay their salaries and set the conditions of their labor.

Areas of social activity once belonging to the people, and meriting the name of "folk culture," have been expropriated by the corporate economy. In their constant search for investment opportunities and profit, capitalists move into all areas of human experience. This process can be seen not only in the way people work but in the way they create, play, and consume. The storytelling arts have given way to the canned dramas of Hollywood and television. Much of folk music has become professionalized, with a relatively few high-priced performers playing before audiences who pay to listen or who purchase the tapes and recordings. As with most of what now passes for "entertainment," music and cinema belong to a handful of corporate promoters, distributors, agents, public relations experts, and "stars."

The image we have of the artist as the independent explorer, challenger, and even creator of culture may be as misleading as the one we have of the scientist. What is referred to as the "art world" is not a thing apart from the art market, the latter heavily influenced by a small number of moneyed persons like the Huntington Hartfords, J. Paul Gettys, and Nelson Rockefellers, who treat art works not as part of the communal treasure but as objects of pecuniary investment, personal acquisition, and conspicuous consumption.[54] They own and finance the museums and major galleries, the publishing houses that print art books, the expensive art magazines, and the university endowments and art centers. If they do not exercise daily decision-making power over every twist and fad of art, as trustees, publishers, patrons, and speculators they exercise an influence over the means of artistic production and distribution, setting the political limits of artistic expression. The artist who moves beyond these political limits

> produces for himself and for those whom his message cannot reach because his means of access are closed when he refuses to produce in accordance with an external need, that is, for the market; his work, moreover, comes into contradiction with the tastes and ideals which govern the production of commodities, and therefore he cannot find a buyer.[55]

Many politically conscious artists have learned either to avoid controversial themes or touch upon them only in oblique fashion. If they become too explicit they run the risk of not being shown. Thus in 1971 the Guggenheim Museum canceled a show by the European artist Hans Haacke because he portrayed certain noted art-world patrons as the slumlords they were.[56] Art with a radical political content is labeled "propaganda" or "ideology" by those who preside over the art market. While professing thereby to keep art free of politics, these influential persons impose their own politically motivated definition of what is and is not art. Whether consciously or not, this definition has come to be accepted by most gallery operators, critics, art professors, aspiring artists and by the public itself.

Volumes have been written on the purpose and meaning of artistic creation. There is art as "an instrument of war" (Picasso's words) to be used in the struggle for social justice; art as an expression of realities yet to come, with the artist acting as prophet; and art as the highest aesthetic experience, something above society ("for art's sake"); art as a manifestation of emotive, spiritual longings. Giving us a glimpse of the world beyond, art may assume disembodied forms in attempting to describe that which is ultimately ineffable, going beyond nature and beyond the senses.[57]

While not every artist can successfully explore the farthest edges of religious, spiritual, aesthetic, or emotional experience, enough of them will embrace the individualist, elitist attitudes that are taken to be symptomatic of such experience. Whether or not these attitudes are a necessary adjunct of genuine artistic creation, they certainly are congruent with the socio-political values of a capitalist society. Artists move beyond their public, scorning the populace for being aesthetically untutored. While moving away from their society, indeed, while supposedly rebelling against it, most artists unbeknownst to themselves are faithful products of it. They may be opposed to "bourgeois values" as emodied in the stuffy, complacent, conventional life, but most of them are not opposed to the bourgeoisie. If they feel superior to the life-styles of society's more affluent consumers, they are also dependent on these same consumers for their market and have next to nothing to say about the privileges, oppressions, and deforming effects of class power.

In keeping with the notion that art was something that transcended ordinary perceptions and belonged to the interior experience of the artist, Western art in the modern period became dominated by a formalistic perspective. Effort was directed at creating visual, spatial experiences to the exclusion of the substantive connections art might have to the objective world. Such art was called "nonobjective," and "nonrepresentational." When art did consist of representational images and themes from the real world, these were notably devoid of any socio-political content. And what has been true of painting and sculpture has held more or less for much of poetry, photography, film, dance, drama, and literature.

As art became further removed from important aspects of social reality, it became ever more open to the gimmicks of charlatans and opportunists. In recent years a painter in New York exhibited works done in human excrement; another cut off pieces of his own flesh and photographed them; another had himself shot in peripheral areas of the body and exhibited photographs of his wounds; another exhibited plastic genitalia around a coffin in which he himself lay naked. One artist filled an exhibition room with old rubber tires, another with dirt, and these were presented to the public as shows. A painter turned film maker made an eight-hour movie consisting of a man sleeping. A noted modern composer performed concerts of static from radio sets and women danced past photoelectric cells to start recorders going. Another's composition consisted of two performers hitting a piano case irregularly with wooden mallets for eleven minutes.[58] To retain "freshness" some artists have had to supersede previous efforts with new contrivances, each making a claim to being the avant-garde. "New and better" commodities have to be produced for a fickle, competitive market.[59]

It is not my intent to argue that all art must be expressly political in its content but to point out how the kind of yearnings, images, and experiences that are politically unacceptable to the moneyed elites find almost no outlet and distribution in the mainstream art market. Protest art of social content, art moved by the struggle for justice, has seldom been encouraged or tolerated in the capitalist art world. Proponents of such art seek not to replace the existing abstract productions, of which some are silly and some sublime, but to supplement them with kinds that can explore other dimensions of the human experience besides the privatized, the formalistic, or the grotesquely contrived.

If much of art seems to have turned into mindless play for the commodity market, play has been turned into something of a sinister art. Sports have become organized, institutionalized, and "professionalized," with the playing done by salaried persons of specialized skill who perform before masses of paying spectators for the profit of a few owners. The first baseball teams were cooperative ventures owned by the players. But in the 1870s, as the game attracted a popular following, capital moved in and there began what the early baseball entrepreneur, A. G. Spaulding, called

> the irrepressible conflict between labor and capital. . . . Like every other form of business enterprise, baseball depends for results on two interdependent divisions, the one to have absolute control and direction of the system, and the other to engage—always under the executive branch—in actual work of production.[60]

By the end of the 1880s the players revolted against the owner-monopolized game and formed a Players League which promptly attracted more fans than the owners' leagues. But the moneyed class closed ranks against the worker-controlled enterprise. The Players League found it impossible to get bank loans and its games received almost no coverage and much bad publicity from the business-owned newspapers. Within a year it folded.[61]

In contrast, basketball remained dominated by player-controlled teams until after World War II, when owners of sports arenas decided there was money to be made from professional basketball. As Paul Hoch notes, through their control of the sports arenas (i.e., the means of sports production), the owners were able to exclude player-controlled teams:

> So throughout the sports industry, as in every other industry under capitalism, control is exercised, not by the consumers (fans), nor by the producers (players), but by the owners of capital. It is they who decide whether or not to stage their spectacles and when, where and how to do so. Ownership gives them the power to dictate the complete development or nondevelopment of the industry, the very life and working conditions of those (players) whose labor they buy and the nature of the product they produce. And the basis of their decisions is, first and foremost, personal profit.[62]

"Spectator sports" is anything but play and is more correctly identified as a business, technically organized, ruthlessly competitive, profit-oriented, and deficient in artlessness, frivolity, and spontaneity. As the sport becomes less of a game and more of an enterprise it develops newly rationalized forms. The players are encouraged to take drug stimulants, give unquestioning obedience to coaches and owners, and devote themselves totally to performance, sometimes at great risk to their health and safety, often sustaining repeated injuries.[63] The game is controlled by a "game plan," with patterns of movement and strategies brought increasingly under the control of nonplaying managerial technocrats who dictate decisions and plays. Play, like work, is becoming Taylorized.

Competitive sports is closely associated with nationalistic, militaristic, and male-dominated values. Indeed, sports are quite explicitly treated by owners, promoters, coaches, sportswriters, educators, military men, and politicians as not only a national institution but a nationalistic one, building fitness of mind and body and a spirit of sacrifice, discipline, and toughness of the kind needed for a strong America. During the Vietnam era, Hoch observed:

every U.S. sports event seems to be turning into a pro-war rally, complete with speeches from the Secretary of Defense at the baseball opener, Air Force jets flying overhead at football bowl games, moments of silence for "our boys in Vietnam," and everywhere the flag and the National Anthem.[64]

The first principle of professional sports and, increasingly so, college sports, is not sportsmanship but winning. Rather than being seen as a group of people engaged in a commonly enjoyable activity, the other team is treated as the opponent and the enemy. Ruthless competition, spectator fanaticism, the need to "beat" others totally and decisively, exclusive possession of the ball, dominance of the field or court, legalized violence and aggression, craft and guile—with such values, organized sports support and reflect the society that produces them.

To summarize some of the observations in this chapter: the major institutions of society, far from being autonomous bastions of pluralistic power, are tied by purchase and persuasion to the corporate system. The linkages are several: first, the financial resources essential for the maintenance of the nonbusiness institutions are in the hands of the corporate class. In fact, on closer examination some of the "nonbusiness" institutions turn out themselves to be corporate profit-making enterprises. Second, the business elites usually exercise direct decision-making power through directorships, giving them control over the property of the institution, a control enforced by the police powers of the state.[65]

Third, the influence of capitalist values can be felt within the very content of various institutional practices, as when the churches preach obedience to authority and the unions call for loyalty to the existing economic order. With few exceptions institutions also filter out heterodox ideas and censor ideological dissenters. Fourth, an area barely touched upon here and needing further development: the above conditions of capitalist control operate with distorting effects on ordinary interpersonal institutional experiences, for instance, the way medical personnel treat patients in understaffed hospitals run for the profit of private suppliers and doctors, or the way teachers treat students—and vice versa—in crowded, demoralized slum schools. Also needing greater investigation is how the values, imperatives, and anxieties propagated by the existing socio-cultural system permeate the very intrapsychic experiences of the individual in what might be referred to as "the presentation of the *capitalist* self in everyday life."[66]

The corporate elites do not attempt to control every level of decision making nor every resource allocation within every social organization at every moment. No elite has the interest or ability to function in that way. What they have is the ability to prefigure the overall activities of other institutions. The business class exercises a reach over social institutions which the institutions do not exercise over the business class. As former FCC commissioner Nicholas Johnson complained:

> The difficulty in America today is that we have turned it over to the big corporations. . . . Our colleges, churches, foundations and public broadcasting stations tend to be presided over by the same guys who decide what automobiles we'll buy and what cereal we'll eat. They publish our children's schoolbooks; they own most of the nation's artistic talent—and they have little hesitation in censoring the copy of both.[67]

Americans have been taught to see the material prosperity of their nation as inextricably bound up with the interests of the corporate economy—and, in a sense, correctly so. The error was in assuming that the linkage was necessarily a benign and providential one and that society could achieve growth and fulfillment only by giving free rein to its "private sector." "Capitalist society," Tillich reminds us, "took its rise with the emancipation of economic activity from control by a superior social power and the development of an autonomous economic system subject only to its own laws."[68] The idea of society as an entity dedicated to the propagation of a communal life makes no noticeable appearance in capitalist ideology. Instead, society is seen as an agglomeration of individuals and groups engaged in the competitive pursuits of the marketplace. Defined in terms of its market activities, society was "submerged in its economic institutions."[69]

If the social structure itself is organized first and foremost around the interests of one institution, then "that institution tends to become dominant over other institutions in the society."[70] If the supportive functions of other social institutions are properly performed, then the conditional powers of these institutions, as related to activities not challenging owning class interests, are allowed to continue. "But with the onset of insecurity in the dominant power, these . . . secondary powers tend to lose those parts of their freedom that conflict with the interests of the dominant power."[1] The "freedom" of the powerless is conditional upon their remaining in their place.

The reason the never-ending discussions on "What is wrong with American society?" as conducted within our educational, political, labor, religious, and communicational organizations are usually devoid of any attack on capitalism is that these institutions are materially beholden to that system, defensive of its interests, and purveyors of its culture. But if the power of "private" institutions is so preempted by those who control the material resources of society, what of the public sector, that portion of authoritative decision making supposedly organized for the purpose of giving the populace a say in their own destiny. To pursue that question, we must turn to the political system.

NOTES

1. Robert S. Lynd, "Power in American Society as Resource and Problem," in Arthur Kornhauser (ed.), *Problems of Power in American Democracy* (Detroit: Wayne State University Press, 1957), p. 30.

2. For a more detailed account of the ownership of the media see Herbert I. Schiller, *The Mind Managers* (Boston: Beacon Press, 1973); also Michael Parenti, *Democracy for the Few*, 2nd ed. (New York: St. Martin's, 1977), p. 188 ff.

3. Gaeton Fonzi, *Annenberg: A Biography of Power* (New York: Weybright and Talley, 1970); also *New York Times*, March 15, 1977.

4. Gerhard Lenski, *Power and Privilege* (New York: McGraw-Hill, 1966), p. 421. See also Tom Bethell, "The Myth of an Adversary Press," *Harper's*, January 1977, pp. 33–40.

5. Calvin Trillin, "U.S. Journal: Kentucky," *The New Yorker*, December 27, 1969, p. 33.

6. "A Foreign Look at the American Press," *Mass Communication* (Santa Barbara, Calif.: Center for the Study of Democratic Institutions, 1966); see pp. 3–5 for this and similar observations by visiting journalists.

7. The Editors, *Ramparts*, October 1970, p. 52. In 1975 *Ramparts* ceased publication because of lack of funds.

8. For documentation of these observations see Robert Cirino, *Don't Blame the People* (Los Angeles: Diversity Press, 1971); James Aronson, *The Press and the Cold War* (New York: Bobbs-Merrill, 1970); Parenti, *Democracy for the Few*, pp. 180–188.

9. Stuart Ewen, *Captains of Consciousness* (New York: McGraw-Hill, 1976). See also the discussion on "Consumers and Spectators" in chapter 8.

10. H. N. Brailsford, *The Levellers and the English Revolution* (Stanford, Calif.: Stanford University Press, 1961), p. 29. Hobbes's observation is from *Behemoth* and is quoted in Brailsford, p. 28.

11. Quoted in Sidney Fine. *Laissez Faire and the General-Welfare State* (Ann Arbor: University of Michigan Press, 1956), p. 119.

12. Reinhard Bendix, *Work and Authority in Industry* (New York: Harper & Row, 1963), p. 68; and Fine, *Laissez Faire*, pp. 117–125.

13. Fine, *Laissez Faire*, p. 179.

14. For a discussion of the conservative political role of the church see Ralph Miliband, *The State in Capitalist Society* (New York: Basic Books, 1969), pp. 198–205. The conservative role of the church in a labor dispute is discussed in Liston Pope, *Millhands and Preachers* (New Haven: Yale University Press, 1942).

15. Martin A. Larson and C. Stanley Lowell, *The Religious Empire* (Silver Spring, Md.: Americans United Research Foundation, 1976). The ten major Protestant denominations held securities valued at over $200 million with some thirty corporate military contractors. See *The Progressive*, March 1972, p. 7. Also Nino Lo Bello, *The Vatican Empire* (New York: Trident Press, 1968) and Nino Lo Bello, *Vatican, U.S.A.* (New York: Trident Press, 1973).

16. See Ben A. Franklin. "The Scandal of Death and Injury in the Mines," *New York Times Magazine*, March 30, 1969, p. 127 ff.

17. As quoted in "Showdown in the Mines," *Guardian*, 23 (January 16, 1971), 8.

18. Quoted in Michael Myerson, "ILGWU: Fighting for Lower Wages," *Ramparts*, 8 (October 1969), 55.

19. Meany's speech is quoted in *Wildcat* (Chicago), July 1969, p. 2.

20. Michael Rogin, "Nonpartisanship and the Group Interest," in Philip Green and Sanford Levinson (eds.), *Power and Community* (New York: Vintage, 1970), p. 133. For a specific case, see Paul Schrade, "Growing Bureaucratization of the UAW," *New Politics*, 10 (Winter 1973), 13–21.

21. See the observations by V. L. Allen, *Militant Trade Unionism* quoted and discussed by Miliband, *State in Capitalist Society*, p. 159; also Rogin, "Nonpartisanship and the Group Interest," p. 128.

22. Louis Adamic, "Dynamite: The Story of Class Violence in America," in Thomas Rose (ed.), *Violence in America* (New York: Vintage, 1969), p. 142.

23. Ronald Radosh, *American Labor and United States Foreign Policy* (New York: Random House, 1969); also Sidney Lens, *The Military-Industrial Complex* (Philadelphia: United Church Press, 1970), pp. 99–122.

24. Miliband, *State in Capitalist Society*, p. 155.

25. George Lipsitz, "Beyond the Fringe Benefits: Rank and File Teamsters in St. Louis," *Liberation*, July-August 1973, pp. 31–45.

26. Michael B. Katz, *The Irony of Early School Reform* (Boston: Beacon Press, 1968), p. 37.

27. *The Massachusetts Teacher*, September 1861, quoted in Katz, *The Irony of Early School Reform*, p. 87.

28. David N. Smith, *Who Rules the Universities?* (New York: Monthly Review Press, 1974), p. 84; and Katz, *The Irony of Early School Reform, passim*. For an excellent account of how the public school performs a class control function among the present-day poor, see Gerald E. Levy, *Ghetto School: Class Warfare in an Elementary School* (New York: Bobbs-Merrill, 1970); also Norman Diamond, "Against Cynicism," *Monthly Review*, June 1976; and Anonymous, "More Against Cynicism," *Monthly Review*, January 1977, pp. 61–64.

29. Frederick Rudolph, *The American College and University: A History,* quoted in Smith, *Who Rules the Universities?,* pp. 86–87.

30. Jerry L. Avorn et al., *Up Against the Ivy Wall* (New York: Atheneum, 1969), p. 8.

31. Peter Schrag, "The University: Power and Innocence," *Saturday Review,* October 21, 1967, p. 69.

32. Quoted in Robert Lichtman, "The University: Mask for Privilege?" *The Center Magazine* (Publication of the Center for the Study of Democratic Institutions), January 1968, p. 3; see also Robert Rainhold, "In Academic Jet Set, Schedule is Hectic, Rewards High," *New York Times,* June 18, 1969.

33. Charles Schwartz, "The Corporate Connection," *Bulletin of the Atomic Scientists,* October 1975, pp. 15–19.

34. Ibid., p. 18. For a good account of how scientists are acculturated into powerful corporate and governmental organizations, see Philip Green, "Science, Government and the Case of RAND: A Singular Pluralism," *World Politics,* 22 (January, 1968); also Loren Baritz, *The Servants of Power: A History of the Use of Social Science in American Industry* (New York: Science Editions, 1960).

35. John McDermott, "Knowledge Is Power," *The Nation,* April 14, 1969, p. 458.

36. Theodore Lowi, *The Politics of Disorder* (New York: Basic Books, 1971), p. 128.

37. Kingman Brewster as quoted in the *New York Times,* December 14, 1969.

38. Quoted by Marjorie Heins, "Los Siete de la Raza," *Hard Times,* no. 59 (January 5–12, 1970), 4.

39. Smith, *Who Rules the Universities?,* p. 88.

40. Ibid., pp. 85–86.

41. For firsthand observations on the persistent anti-Marxist biases at one leading university, see Marsha Forest, "Why I'm Becoming a Marxist," *Monthly Review,* December 1974, pp. 31–35; see also Michael Parenti, "Orthodoxy and Challenge in the Social Sciences," *Book Forum,* 1 (Summer 1974), 81–91.

42. Some 80 percent of all basic research is financed by the Department of Defense. For detailed discussions on the ways the universities service the corporations and the military, see Sidney Lens, *The Military-Industrial Complex* (Philadelphia: United Church Press, 1970), pp. 123–138; also James Ridgeway, *The Closed Corporation, America's Universities in Crisis* (New York: Ballantine Books, 1969).

43. Ralph Nader, "Law Schools and Law Firms," *New Republic,* 161 (October 11, 1969), 20.

44. Ibid., p. 21; see also Scott Turow, *One L* (New York: Putnam's, 1977).

45. Jerold S. Auerbach, *Unequal Justice: Lawyers and Social Change in Modern America* (New York: Oxford University Press, 1975).

46. Kenneth M. Dolbeare, "Public Policy Analysis and the Coming Struggle for the Soul of the Postbehavioral Revolution," in Philip Green and Sanford Levinson (eds.), *Power and Community, Dissenting Essays in Political Science* (New York: Pantheon, 1969), p. 86.

47. See Martin Nicolaus, "The Professional Organization of Sociology: A View from Below," in Robin Blackburn (ed.), *Ideology in Social Science* (New York: Vintage, 1972), pp. 45–60.

48. Harry Braverman, *Labor and Monopoly Capital* (New York: Monthly Review Press, 1974), p. 166–167; an excellent treatment of this subject is David F. Noble, *America by Design: Science, Technology, and the Rise of Corporate Capitalism* (New York: Knopf, 1977).

49. Wilhelm Reich, "What is Class Consciousness?", *Liberation*, October 1971, p. 43 (originally published in 1934).

50. Vincente Navarro, *Medicine Under Capitalism* (New York: Prodit, 1976).

51. Ibid.; also Omar V. Garrison, *The Dictocrats' Attack on Health Foods and Vitamins* (New York: Arco, 1971).

52. "Summary and Recommendations of the Report of the Advisory Committee on Govermnent Programs in the Behavioral Sciences, National Research Council," *P.S.*, Fall 1968, p. 5.

53. Antonio Gramsci, "The Formation of Intellectuals," *The Modern Prince and Other Writings* (New York: International Publishers, 1976), p. 120.

54. See Matthew Josephson, *The Robber Barons* (New York: Harcourt, Brace and World, 1934), pp. 340-346, for an interesting and revealing picture of how the early tycoons of business treated art.

55. Adolfo Sanchez Vazquez, *Art and Society: Essays in Marxist Aesthetics* (New York: Monthly Review Press, 1970), pp. 212-213. Also see the forthcoming work by William Roth, tentatively entitled *Art, the Market and Public Policy*.

56. Kay Larson, "Art Critics of the World, Unite," *Boston After Dark*, October 5, 1976, p. 18.

57. See Jacques Barzun, *The Use and Abuse of Art* (Princeton, N.J.: Princeton University Press, 1974), p. 30.

58. Barzun, *The Use and Abuse of Art*, pp. 14-15, and passim.

59. Larson, "Art Critics of the World, Unite," p. 19.

60. "Depreciating the National Pastime," *Dollars and Sense*, May-June 1977, p. 4.

61. Paul Hoch, *Rip Off the Big Game: The Exploitation of Sports by the Power Elite* (Garden City, N.Y.: Doubleday, 1972), pp. 41-42.

62. Ibid. p. 46.

63. See Dave Meggyesy, *Out of Their League* (Berkeley, Calif.: Ramparts Press, 1970); Bernie Parrish, *They Call It a Game* (New York: Dial, 1971); Jack Scott, *The Athletic Revolution* (New York: Free Press, 1971).

64. Hoch, *Rip Off*, p. 1.

65. The question of corporate directorships was treated more fully in the previous chapter. See also chapter 12 for a discussion of property.

66. The phrase might serve as the title of a much-needed sequel to Erving Goffman's *The Presentation of Self in Everyday Life* (New York: Overlook Press, 1974).

67. Quoted in Frank Browning, "Cable TV: Turn On, Tune In, Rip Off," *Ramparts*, 9 (April 1971), 38.

68. Paul Tillich, *The Religious Situation* (New York: Meridian Books, 1956), pp. 105-106.

69. Lynd, "Power in American Society," p. 24.

70. Ibid., p. 25.

71. Ibid.

Part Three

On Politics

12

Public Service, Private Interest

While the political system is usually treated as a lesser component of the social system, its distinctive characteristic is that its decisions, the decisions of civil authority, are made in the name of that most inclusive of social units, the society itself, and, unlike those of a private group, apply authoritatively to all members of the polity. This is not to say that governmental decisions always have a greater effect on people's lives than those of private institutions, but that they play a unique role in securing private interests, doing for these interests what they cannot do for themselves. Private interests are greatly affected by public authority and public authority is heavily penetrated by private interests. It is one thing to postulate analytic distinctions between "public" and "private," and another to make empirical delineations, the difference between them being even more blurred in practice than in theory.

PRIVATE POWER AND PUBLIC RESPONSIBILITY

By controlling society's capital and labor, corporate conglomerates are able to build and demolish whole communities, preempt vast acreages of land, plunder and pollute the natural environment, manipulate entire technologies, shape the development of whole regions, obliterate fragile ancient cultures, map the lines of national and international trade and transportation, control media content, create new wants and markets, destroy old skills, values, and tastes, and control the destinies of peoples throughout the world. The multinationals exercise a coercive power of a magnitude difficult to comprehend, impinging upon our lives in a multitude of ways, often without our knowing it. How then can anyone speak of the corporation as a "private" organization, as if its decisions and actions had no effect on our collective destiny?

> The meaning of "private" as applied to the leading American corporations means merely that their policy makers are not publicly accountable for the decisions—so long as they "stay within the law" which is often loosely defined and perhaps necessarily vague about the latest business practices.[1]

No matter what one thinks of the giant corporation, Dahl notes, "surely it is a delusion to consider it a private enterprise."[2] Yet the modern capitalist state is organized around that delusion. The harmful effects of corporate activities on the nonmarketable needs and values of the populace are usually accorded neither lawful nor unlawful determination, but are left outside the scope of the law, treated as the private doings of private industry.

Enterprises have expanded beyond their economic scale, creating costs that are transferred to the consumer and the community at large. The costs of wasteful productive systems, unused surplus capital and misused and underemployed labor, excessively high prices and oppressive taxation levels, damages to health and environment, the glut of frivolous commodities, and the neglect of essential social services—these are some of the "external diseconomies unrecovered by society from the industries whose activities generated them."[3] Ironically enough, when account *is* taken of these costs, or certain of their more obvious manifestations, it is as part of a gross national product which presumedly measures our wealth and well-being. Higher commodity sales, including riot equipment for police and shoddy, overpriced goods for wage earners, become an indicator of consumer affluence. More automobiles and highways, with all their noise, pollution, and carnage, are represented as advances in transportation. Bigger profits for construction firms and realty developers are thought to bring improved housing. Greater military expenditures supposedly buy us national security. Such measurements of prosperity offer, at best, a most haphazard accounting of the many qualities of social life extending beyond the GNP.

The policies of government are made in the name of society itself but policy outputs commonly serve partial or special interests rather than universal ones, their costs and benefits rarely reaching everyone with equal effect. The highly uneven distribution of resources in the private sector leads to a like concentration in the public sector. Instead of acting as an equalizer of social outputs, the political system reflects and even augments existing socio-economic inequities. There is a saying that economic power is to political power as fuel is to fire. But the metaphor is misleading, for the "fire" actually feeds back onto the fuel and increases rather than depletes it. When properly harnessed, public authority becomes a most valuable source for expanding the prerogatives of economic power.

For all its activities on behalf of business, government has remained remarkably laissez-faire when holding industry accountable for the social costs of its enterprises. The concept of "limited government," so often violated in the area of civil and personal liberties, holds firmest when applied to business. The coercions of the corporate system are protected by notions of free labor, free market, and free contract which have long become obsolete—not in law but in practice. These coercions, as Veblen noted, are given no formal recognition; they are seldom taken into account by the legal mind. The social power of the industrial corporations compose a new historical reality

> which fits into the framework neither of the ancient system of prescriptive usage nor the later system of free personal initiative. It does not exist *de jure* but only *de facto*. . . . It is, as within the cognizance of the law, non-existent. . . . Such coercion as it may exert, or as may be exercised through its means, therefore, is in point of legal reality, no coercion.[4]

Despite more recent efforts by environmentalists and other reform-minded groups to hold corporations accountable for their actions, Veblen's observation still holds. Neither the public nor its elected representatives govern the economic development of the country nor regulate to any appreciable degree the coercive effects of the corporate economy. There is no involvement of the people, no citizens' advocacy procedure to challenge what the giant firms are doing to the natural and social environment. There exist few legal provisions that oblige business to take account of the nonmarketable needs of the public.

> The power to make investment decisions is concentrated in a few hands, and it is this power which will decide what kind of a nation America will be. Instead of government planning there is boardroom planning that is accountable to no outside agency: and these plans set the order of priorities on national growth, technological innovation, and ultimately, the values and behavior of human beings. Investment decisions are sweeping in their ramifications—no one is unaffected by their consequences. Yet this is an area where neither the public nor its government is able to participate.[5]

It is not exactly true that existing conditions result from no planning, for the large companies "have a keen sense of plan and purpose. It is rather that the plans which do exist are created and executed without public scrutiny or control."[6]

On most issues business, in effect, claims itself to be unaccountable before the law. Bachrach observes how U. S. Steel declared its neutrality during a 1963 civil rights struggle in Birmingham, announcing that it would refrain from injecting into the issue what it candidly described as the "considerable amount of power and authority" it wielded in Birmingham. In deciding not to support the integration cause, the corporation made a decision favoring the status quo, unilaterally declaring that it had no obligation to abide by the Fourteenth Amendment of the U.S. Constitution, thereby removing itself from the rules that supposedly govern the rest of the nation.[7]

The public is quicker to discern the coercive aspects of government than of the corporate economy. The constraints of the economic system are seldom defined as coercive, being seen more as inducements, agreements, contractual accords, or just as conditions of life. Workers who are laid off from their jobs by management are more likely to be considered subjects of ill fortune than objects of coercion.

Business has a variety of resources to induce citizen compliance, not the least being control of services and production itself. Thus, when "agreements" are violated, as when one has failed to pay one's utility bill, services are withheld and one's electricity is cut off. If more overt forms of coercion are required to enforce economic agreements, as when court orders are issued against debtors, tenants, or striking workers, such functions are carried out by agents of the *political* system. The political system performs many of the cruder coercive tasks of the private economy, enabling the economic system to be seen as one of choice, negotiation, voluntary exchange, opportunity, and reward, and seldom as the world of severely prestructured, one-sided constraints which it is for most employees, consumers, tenants, small businesspeople, and homeowners.[8]

If industry brings unemployment, inflation, low wages, and pollution, then community leaders, media commentators, and ordinary citizens look to the *government* to do something. Timber and mining companies may plunder the natural wealth of Appalachia, but the wreckage they leave in their wake—recalling the official rhetoric of the early 1960s—is called "the shame of the nation" and not "the shame of the corporations," and is defined as a "poverty" problem for which the entire American people and their government are responsible. During 1977, when strip mining so devastated the land as to cause floods and avalanches in Kentucky, taking a score of lives and destroying many homes, Appalachian community activists demanded disaster relief from the federal and state governments. The coal companies, of course, were denounced for their practices and for evading the land-reclamation laws, but it was assumed that compensation for the devastation they caused should be drawn from the public treasury. At no time were the companies held materially accountable for the social costs of their plunder. Far from directing actions against large firms, government officials enlist business "cooperation" in planning public spending programs, such as the billions allocated for the "war on poverty," at a generous profit to the enlistees and with no measurable benefit to the needy.

The same public that protests the loss of jobs when a government navy yard is phased out is likely to accept the decision of a private firm to shut down its factory as being within management's right. If one person is free to sell his home, then another should be free to sell his factory. The tendency to subsume both *personal-use commodities* and the *means of production* under the same rubric of "property" has served the corporate system well. The giant conglomerates represent themselves as being nothing more, and nothing less, than "private property," to be accorded all the same rights—and then some—that people might wish for their personal-use property.

Recent years have seen a shift in attitude on the question of corporate accountability. Despite the corporation's unchanged private status in the eyes of the law, beginning in the late 1960s, protestors have attempted to hold business firms directly accountable for their activities. Legal suits, pickets, boycotts, confrontations at stockholders' meetings, and sit-ins have been directed at many large companies deemed guilty of such things as racist hiring practices, manufacturing napalm, supporting overseas fascist coups, polluting the environment, and investing in South Africa. The citizen-consumer actions against big business challenge the presumed value neutrality of business decisions by suggesting that nothing one does in the marketplace is value-free and irrelevant to the public interest.[9] While growing numbers of people are embracing this view, many, perhaps most, still hold to the older notion of the unaccountability of "private" undertakings and have yet to draw the links between the hardships and impoverishments of society and the power and wealth of business.

PROPERTY AND THE STATE

Property, that seemingly most material thing, is really of a nonmaterial nature. In a strict sense, goods and land are not property as such but tangible representations of it, for property is a concept, a convention, a social fiction. The material representations of property cannot really *belong* to anyone as might the natural attachments of one's body. (Not even one's body belongs to oneself, some would argue on theological grounds, but is God's possession and must be cared for as such.) In Rousseau's memorable words:

> The first man who, having enclosed a piece of ground, bethought himself of saying "This is mine," and found people simple enough to believe him, was the real founder of civil society. From how many

crimes, wars, and murders, from how many horrors and misfortunes might not any one have saved mankind, by pulling up the stakes, or filling up the ditch, and crying to his fellows: "Beware of listening to this imposter; you are undone if you once forget that the fruits of the earth belong to us all, and the earth itself to nobody."[10]

To say this land or artifact is "mine" is to claim an exclusivity of use and abuse that must be recognized by others and supported by the powers of the state. The irony, then, is that a relationship which is treated as quintessentially private and individualistic ("No one can tell *me* what *I* should do with *my* property") actually gets its meaning from its public dimension, from the willingness of others to agree to it and accept the collective rule that enforces it. The social fiction of private property is secured through the public agency. In this respect, it does not differ much from other "individual" rights.

However, there is an exceptional quality about the right of property. Most social roles are defined in terms of reciprocal, albeit asymmetrical, relations between persons. The saying that there are "no rights without responsibilities" is a way of recognizing the mutuality of role obligations. But unlike other roles, the property owner is defined by law as having entered a relationship with a thing or object rather than with another person, a relationship burdened by no reciprocity of obligation and of no concern to other persons except as they are expected to accord it full respect. The owner's claim over his possession tends to be treated as an absolute right by the state, so that the rule of "no rights without responsibilities" is inverted to become "all rights with no responsibilities."

The effects on other *persons* perpetrated by the owner when using his property are treated as secondary to the bond between him and his possession. The owner is slow to recognize his obligations to others when exercising his proprietary role, but quick to call in the state when others violate what he takes to be his rights. "The basic effect of defining an object as someone's 'property' is to *exclude* all others except the state; it establishes by definition that others have no rights in this object except insofar as the proprietor expressly permits them such rights."[11]

The adage "no rights without responsibilities" takes the form of an admonition when applied to the more deprived elements of society.

The conservative argument is that have-nots should first demonstrate their capacity and worthiness to assume the responsibilities that go with certain rights. The supposedly inherent right is thus reduced to a conditional privilege. At the same time, certain privileges are elevated to rights. The need to demonstrate one's worthiness to enjoy access to riches is never made of the propertied class, it being assumed that the possession of wealth is itself evidence of capability. No one ever asked David Rockefeller to explain, let alone demonstrate, why he should have the powers and privileges he enjoys.

The absence of social obligations within property rights is a condition sustained by laws which themselves have been written by persons of property. And if these persons are often above the law, they are not for a moment without it, for no element in society places such a close reliance on civil authority as do they. Gouldner writes:

> The inviolability of property rights is more closely monitored and protected by the legal and state apparatus, in the normal course of events, than any other "right" except that of protection from bodily harm. The use of the state's force to protect property is not at all an instrument of "last resort," but a *routine* method of enforcement. Normally, one does not bargain, negotiate, remonstrate, or appeal to a thief; one calls the police. This implies something about the priorities that the state assigns to the protection of property rights; but more than that it implies something about the nature of the state itself.[12]

It implies that in any dispute between two private groups, the capitalist state almost always intervenes on the side of the propertied interests, treating them as tantamount to the public interest. This is not just one of those peculiar biases of the state; it is its essential function. Besides protecting property, the state *creates* it. The private corporation must be publicly incorporated by law. Private wealth is defined by its stocks, mortgages, deeds, accounts, legal currencies, all of which exist by public investiture, that is, by authority of the state. In this sense, private property is a "derivative" of public sovereignty, even as it exercises a dominant influence over the state.

Property rights are dressed in universalist rather than class terms and deemed to be the necessary and proper condition of a civic order serving the interests of all citizens, even the propertyless. In contrast, those who make claims *against* property are said to be moving in self-interested, even antisocial, directions of a kind frequently treated with suspicion and hostility by civil authorities. Property owners, trustees, and landlords have "rights" that are written into law, and protected by courts and police. But propertyless workers, students, and tenants have "demands" that have no legal status. Attempts to organize concerted actions in support of these demands, as with strikes, sit-ins, and boycotts, are often in violation of the law.

As said, the stability of one's property rests upon the willingness of the populace to accept the property convention, an acceptance shaped by long standing forces of socialization, legitimation and hierarchical coercion, of the kind discussed in earlier chapters. But in a changing, tumultuous world, the efficacy of such socializing forces is not always certain. One's claim to property may pretend to be absolute but one's property is never absolutely secure, given the chronic instability of prices, currencies, market conditions, and political regimes. Be it in the form of personalty or realty, be it money in the bank or vast industrial enterprises, there is always the problem of finding ways of holding onto wealth. As one's wealth increases so does the scope of one's financial concerns. The very rich worry about the security of their vast holdings as does the small owner, albeit within a markedly different frame of reference.

Behind all wealth and privilege there lurks the specter of revolution, the apprehension that the mass of have-nots will no longer accept the social fiction nor give obeisance to the sacred symbols of authority and property. The first stirrings of rebellion thus become the cause of great alarm and drastic repression. While governor of New York, Nelson Rockefeller saw the riot against inhumane prison conditions at Attica in 1971 as the work of "revolutionaries" seeking to overthrow the system, an analysis that had escaped less alert observers. To defend against this impending revolutionary upheaval, he ordered an armed assault by state troopers which resulted in the death and injury of many prisoners and guards. Revolutionary actions, persons, and ideas—or what might be taken for such—must be hunted down and eradicated. One cannot be too careful when one's fortune and way of life are at stake.

Given this eternal vigilance on behalf of wealth, the rights of property are often *more* thoroughly protected than the right to life, contrary to Gouldner's observation quoted earlier. The state's protection of corporate interests often comes at a great cost to life. When contradictions arise between the liberal principles and class interests of the dominant class, the guardians of the law are just as likely to become its violators. Individual rights and due process become something of a hindrance for police, military, and judiciary, whose first task is to protect the existing social order. Unauthorized surveillance, harrassment, undercover provocateurs, complicity with right-wing vigilantes, acts of brutality and murder, trumped-up criminal charges against dissenters—these are some of the ways the law is violated or manipulated by law enforcers in order to repress those who oppose the existing economic system, or sometimes even those who advocate more limited reformist changes within the system.[13]

The lawless use of the law is not the only method of repressing the competing claims of dissenters, workers, and the poor. Police transgressions are but a part of the problem. More encompassing, as already noted, are the *lawful* uses of the law, its special attachment to corporate interests and the way it rigs the rules of class conflict heavily against the propertyless. Both in the way it is written and the way applied, the law favors the wealthy. Nor is this merely the result of the peculiar prejudices of police and magistrates; rather it is of an enduring systemic nature. The law does not exist as an abstraction. It gathers shape and substance from a context of power, within a real-life social structure. Like other institutions, the legal system is class-bound. The question is not whether the law should or should not be neutral, for as a product of its society, it *cannot* be neutral in purpose or effect.

THE BUSINESS OF GOVERNMENT

To say that political officeholders support the interests of industry is merely to repeat what they themselves proclaim. To win the confidence of the business community and help maintain a healthy investment climate and a sound economy are goals that political leaders see as commensurate with the national prosperity and the public interest. As Veblen once expressed it:

> Representative government means, chiefly, representation of business interests. . . . The government has, of course, much else to do besides

administering the general affairs of the business community; but in most of its work, even in what is not ostensibly directed to business ends, it is under the surveillance of the business interests. It seldom happens, if at all, that the government of a civilized nation will persist in a course of action detrimental or not ostensibly subservient to the interests of the more conspicuous body of the community's businessmen.[14]

In this sense one can speak of the business class as the ruling class, that is, as the class whose interests rule society. Not that every businessman makes public policy, nor do corporate elites occupy *all* top government positions, although many, indeed most, important posts are held by persons with direct links to the corporate world. Nor is it that the business class wields power over government with effortless cohesion and unanimity, for there are sometimes sharp differences among business groups—mostly resolved in favor of the larger and wealthier conglomerates. The defining characteristic of the ruling class is to be found not solely in the class composition of its elites, drawn mostly from the top echelons of corporations, government, and other major institutions, but in the class interest that is consistently served. The interests common to the entire business class become the interests of the state, specifically, maintaining high profits, shifting production and taxation costs to the public, making public resources accessible to private exploitation, and limiting and repressing the demands of the working class and the poor, tasks which the state performs whether its policy makers be of wealthy background, like Nelson Rockefeller and Jimmy Carter, or of modest middle-class origins, like Richard Nixon and Spiro Agnew; whether they call themselves Democrats or Republicans, liberals or conservatives.

It is a well-documented fact that government agencies become the captives of the very corporations they are supposed to regulate. Most agencies have been created with the encouragement of the interested industries; they shape their regulations to the needs of these same industries; they engage in what amounts to promotional work to publicize the wants and products of the interested companies; they are lax in enforcing "troublesome" standards and adept at contriving permissive interpretations and applications of existing laws. The men and women who staff the various agencies are frequently drawn from the firms they are to regulate, or end up with lucrative jobs in those firms, or are in any case readily responsive to business needs. The data fed to them come principally from the "regulated" company, and the budgets allocated to them by Congress are determined in part by how faithfully they service the same interests that exert such a telling influence over legislators. The giant firms submit plans that, with minor modifications, become the policies of federal departments. In the name of decentralization and expertise, public regulatory powers are delegated to major business interests, further blurring the line between public authority and private corporate power, to the lasting advantage of business and to the detriment of the less organized, less affluent sectors of the public.[15]

The average business firm is devoted to the production of specific commodities or services for the purpose of profit. Whatever its many operational inefficiencies, it suffers little ambiguity about clients and goals. Its chain of bureaucratic command from top director down to foreman is more or less closed to outside interest groups and the general public. In comparison, public bureaucracies are highly permeable organizations, their authority being greatly diluted by overlapping jurisdictions, statutory restrictions, and most of all by the incursions of powerful private clientele groups. "Bureaucracy has been and is a power instrument of the first order—for the one who controls the bureaucratic apparatus," wrote Max Weber.[16] Like party politicians and legislators, the public bureaucrats serve masters other than the public in whose name they rule. In order to function with any effect, a public agency must maintain support within its political environment, and to do so, it must adapt to that environment. This means staying on good terms with executive superiors, congressional leaders, and the bigger organized interests.[17]

The dramtic growth of the state is not, as some conservatives would have it, solely a result of the aggrandizing propensities of bureaucrats, but is primarily a response to the growing needs of advanced capitalism. As the multinational conglomerates expand, as they face deepening economic crises, so must government expand, now trying to ease the ensuing social unrest with welfare palliatives, now intensifying the use of surveillance, force, and violence against rebellious elements at home and abroad, and all the while carrying at public expense many of the immense costs of private business, including direct grants, subsidies, loans, leases, rebates, research and development, tax shelters, risk guarantees, loss compensations, tariff protections, and safeguards for overseas investments.

These activities do not represent a growth toward socialism but a growth in the socialization of capitalism's costs, with the public paying for much of the original production of goods and services as taxpayers and for the goods and services themselves as consumers. Undertakings that prove unprofitable to private companies but necessary for business are sometimes put under public ownership. Private stocks are then transferred into public bonds, to be held by the same banks, firms, and rich individuals who owned the stocks, the only difference being that now the government directly carries the losses, while profits for bondholders are more secure than they were when the faltering enterprise was in private hands. Such is the case with many municipally owned transit systems that annually pay millions of tax-free dollars to wealthy bondholders while teetering on the edge of bankruptcy. To help meet their growing budgets, federal, state, and municipal governments go deeper into debt to private capital, borrowing at ever higher rates and shorter terms, occupying a position of pecuniary servitude to American banks akin to that suffered by most Third World nations.

The point is often made that government does many things besides defend the interests of the corporate rich, including everything from maintaining public health programs to delivering the mail, functions that benefit the entire populace. To focus only on its relation to the business community, then, is to present a highly one-sided view of the political system.

Several responses can be made to this argument: (1) It is true that even the worst of governments might conduct activities having some kind of diffusely distributed outputs. For instance, the Nazi regime, thinking to win popular support and enhance its image, sponsored occasional charity drives on behalf of the German poor. But even in instances of this kind, the benefits are usually gravely insufficient when measured against public need. (2) The services are funded in regressive ways: thus the Nazi charities were in effect a tax on the working poor to set up soup kitchens for the unemployed poor. Most public services in the United States today are regressively funded.

(3) Benefits are distributed in inequitable ways, as with the many human-services programs that end up being least helpful to those most in need. One might recall that the postal service (to consider a diffuse benefit) was developed at the insistence of the merchant and propertied classes of the late eighteenth century and that today the postal needs of business and advertising firms are heavily subsidized by the

taxpayer. With every public policy that supposedly offers widely distributed benefits, be it nuclear energy, transportation, education, housing, police protection, or whatever, there is an upward class bias in the distribution of costs and benefits.[18]

(4) In addition, policies that ostensibly generate benefits to a wide public usually offer special outputs to a select few. Thus highways serve many motorists but the multibillion dollar highway program is of special benefit to trucking firms, construction contractors, and oil, gasoline, and automotive producers. In any cost-benefit analysis of public policy it should be remembered that the bulk of the *benefits* are likely to be narrowly concentrated and have a *high* visibility for the interest groups actively participating in the legislative and administrative processes. But the *costs* are widely diffused amidst the public and so have a *low* visibility, although the cumulative impact of such costs may become matters of life and death for large numbers of people even if the linkages to the original policies remain obscure.

Few ordinary citizens have any awareness of how they are paying the expenses of private enterprise through the public treasury, being kept in ignorance by the business-owned media and other informational institutions. And few have an understanding of what might be the more removed social and personal costs since it is sometimes difficult to translate the monetary measures of policy into nonmonetary human terms. For instance, the links between the financial policies of banks, urban renewal projects, bad housing, and family pathology are not readily visible and are seldom drawn, being treated by those who claim expertise in these matters as separate problems.

As government becomes more deeply involved in the problems of the economy, various persons have advocated national planning as a solution, including individuals of progressive persuasion who see state planning as a move away from the anarchy of private production and toward socialism. In fact planning, in the present class-power context, is apt to have the opposite effect, reinforcing capitalist operations, legitimating and moving them out of the arena of pressure conflict and into a still less accessible, less visible state apparatus run by and for the corporate class. As S. M. Miller notes:

> Planning should not be regarded as inevitably in the public interest. It is not a neutral device which can be turned easily in one direction or another, nor is it necessarily oriented toward low-income and working-

class populations, as liberals frequently have regarded it. Planning will more likely be in the basic interests of large-scale business in the United States.[9]

Beyond being a technocratic phenomenon, planning is a highly political device, taking place in a context of power and interest. Who plans the planners? Who sets the goals at whose expense and for whose benefit become urgent questions. Within the existing politico-economic system, planning may actually increase inequalities and worsen the conditions of workers and the poor, removing interest conflicts still further from the political arena and into the industrial-governmental boardrooms.

In sum, the nineteenth-century model of government as an entity apart from the private sector, intervening as referee and equalizer, inaccurate even for that time, bears little resemblance to present-day reality. The relationship between private business and public power is not occasional and incidental but ubiquitous, inhering in the nature of capitalist society itself. Rather than being just one among many public-private realtionships, it is the prime one, shaping the public interest itself. Wealth and governmental power coalesce into an encompassing structure that predetermines how other groups might act upon, or even define, their interests.

To say that the public service accorded the large firms results from the fact that government decision makers are dominated by business, and are themselves usually drawn from corporate ranks and are purveyors of business ideology, implies that if it were not so, if officials were less responsive to industry, then policies would no longer favor big business but would serve the needs of the populace. Change would come in capitalist ''democracies'' with changes in personnel, as different policy makers of a different intent would formulate new policies. This position presumes that policy is a product of the will and intent of policy makers rather than the outcome of forces bearing upon them from the wider system. But the giant corporations' power over the key levers of government decision making does not result simply from having compliant representatives in strategic official positions but from having control over the very wealth, resources, labor, and production of society itself, which perforce extracts compliance from officeholders whomever they be.

No government—even one that calls itself ''socialist'' or

"labor," as in Sweden or Great Britain—can ignore or move against the basic needs of the giant corporations without inviting a major crisis that would have intolerable effects on employment, investment, and production. Small businesses can collapse and disappear, but if financial disaster struck General Motors, U. S. Steel, or Citibank, the effects on workers, shareholders, investors, creditors, suppliers, and distributors would shake the entire economy.

> No government could stand idly by. What is more important, no government can ignore the possibility, no matter how remote, that such an incident can occur. Consciously or insensibly, its monetary and fiscal policies must increasingly be arranged with sufficient flexibility that at any time the federal government is in a position promptly to bail out the private managers of large enterprises situated in key positions in the economy.[20]

This also means government must avoid doing things that jeopardize the security of the mammoth firms, taking a lenient position on antitrust prosecutions, on taxes against accumulated profits, on the vigor with which regulatory statutes are applied, doing everything possible in the way of grants, supports, subsidies, and giveaways to keep profits flowing, and passing the costs onto the public in the form of high prices, regressive taxes, and—when budget crises develop—cuts in human services. Whether the government is Democratic or Republican, liberal or conservative, "most doubts will be resolved in favor of the corporations in question."[21]

What then of the democratic principle? Do the broader popular interests have an influence of their own? In the next chapter we will investigate the relationship between the political system and the power of numbers.

NOTES

1. Hans Gerth and C. Wright Mills, *Character and Social Structure* (New York: Harcourt, Brace and World, 1955), p. 220.
2. Robert Dahl, *After the Revolution* (New Haven: Yale University Press, 1970), p. 120.
3. Robert Lekachman, "Humanizing GNP," *Social Policy*, September/October 1971, p. 38.

4. Thorstein Veblen, *The Theory of the Business Enterprise* (New York: New American Library, n.d.), pp. 131–132.

5. Andrew Hacker, *The End of the American Era* (New York: Atheneum, 1970), p. 52.

6. Barry Weisberg, "Raping Alaska," in *Eco-Catastrophe*, edited by the editors of *Ramparts* (San Francisco: Canfield Press, 1970), p. 121.

7. Peter Bachrach, *The Theory of Democratic Elitism* (Boston: Little, Brown, 1967), p. 80.

8. See Andrew McLaughlin, "Freedom Versus Capitalism," in Dorothy Buckton James (ed.), *Outside, Looking In: Critiques of American Policies and Institutions, Left and Right* (New York: Harper & Row, 1972), pp. 120–140; also Alan Wertheimer, "Political Coercion and Political Obligation," in J. Roland Pennock and John W. Chapman (eds.), *Coercion* (Chicago: Aldine-Atherton, 1972), pp. 228–229.

9. David Vogel, "The Corporation as Government: Challenges and Dilemmas," *Polity*, 7 (Fall 1975), 5–37.

10. Jean Jacques Rousseau, "A Discourse on the Origins of Inequality," in *The Social Contract and Discourses* (New York: Dutton, 1950), pp. 234–235.

11. Alvin Gouldner, *The Coming Crisis in Western Sociology* (New York: Basic Books, 1970), p. 307.

12. Ibid.; italics in the original.

13. See the data in Michael Parenti, *Democracy for the Few*, 2nd ed. (New York: St. Martin's, 1977), pp. 127–175; also Theodore Becker and Vernon Murray (eds.), *Government Lawlessness in America* (New York: Oxford University Press, 1971).

14. Veblen, *Theory of the Business Enterprise*, p. 137.

15. Grant McConnell, *Private Power and American Democracy* (New York: Knopf, 1966); Parenti, *Democracy for the Few*; Theodore Lowi, *The End of Liberalism* (New York: Norton, 1969).

16. Hans Gerth and C. Wright Mills (eds.) *From Max Weber* (New York: Oxford University Press, 1958).

17. See Francis E. Rourke (ed.), *Bureaucratic Power in National Politics* (Boston: Little, Brown, 1965), pp. xi, 39 ff. For documentation on the monopolistic collusion between government and business, see Mark J. Green, *The Closed Enterprise System* (New York: Grossman, 1972).

18. Parenti, *Democracy for the Few*, pp. 75–126 and passim.

19. S. M. Miller, "Planning: Can It Make a Difference in Capitalist America?", *Social Policy*, September/October 1975, p. 12.

20. Morton S. Baratz, "Corporate Giants and the Power Structure," *Western Political Quarterly*, 9 (June 1956), 411; see also Bruce Brown's excellent discussion, "Watergate: Business as Usual," *Liberation*, July/August 1974, pp. 16–29.

21. Baratz, "Corporate Giants," p. 412.

13

The Power of Numbers

In an earlier chapter it was suggested that power is not an ingredient flowing from the person of a leader but is, among other things, the result of structured relationships among people. When we say that A has power over B we mean that a relationship exists in which B, for whatever reasons, commits some portion of his or her energy, labor, obedience, or loyalty to A. Great power does not flow from great persons but from great numbers of persons, from the many whose empowering responses are secured through various techniques of socialization, education, propaganda, reward, and coercion. (This is not to deny the importance of great leaders. Political leadership can be a vital resource and leaders may show greatness in their ability to make the kinds of decisions, articulate the sentiments, and manipulate the symbols that help command the responses of others.)

If the source of power is to be found in the empowering responses given to some by others, then groups with the greatest number of adherents, all other things being equal, will have the greatest power or, at least, the greatest potential for power. But, again, all other things are rarely equal, and control over material and symbolic resources enables the elites of public and private institutions to obscure the effect of numbers and direct popular sentiments in ways more in keeping with their own preferences. To ask whether the people have power is like asking whether Saudi Arabia has oil, for the populace are the very stuff of power, yet it is most often the oligarchic few who extract and refine these resources for purposes of their own.

ELECTIONS: THE TAMING OF THE MANY

In the late eighteenth and early nineteenth centuries the propertied elites of the United States and Great Britain looked with trepidation upon the prospect of extending the franchise to the propertyless, their fear being that government would pass into the hands of persons intent upon leveling the stations of the highest to that of the lowest, thereby allowing the improvident multitude to gain for themselves by political means a measure of prosperity that was to be achieved only through thrift and diligent toil. "The tendency of universal suffrage," argued James Kent before the New York Constitutional Convention of 1821, "is to jeopardize the rights of property and principles of liberty." And a year earlier, Joseph Story reminded the Massachusetts Constitutional Convention that a question of highest moment was "how the property-holding part of the community may be sustained against the inroads of poverty and vice."[1] The function of government as these men understood it was, in the words of one, to protect the wealthy from "the plundering enterprises of the majority of the people."

Others among the same class, being less fearful and more farsighted, argued in favor of popular suffrage. Counting themselves as each "the friend to property and the landed interest,"[2] they felt, nevertheless, that no class elite was secure if it failed to make minimal allowance for the expression of public sentiment. They observed that the "tinsel-aristocracy" (Jefferson's phrase) was so fearful of the mob as to cast itself against every known republican principle. But in truth the people were neither brigands nor knaves and if given the chance they would exercise their sovereign power with the same love of property and liberty as moved the very highest. In any case, as Jefferson had taught some years before, great property did of itself command great influence and thus had no need for constitutional subterfuges that denied the common man his birthright.

The arguments of the more liberal-minded groups prevailed in the United States and Great Britain, and popular suffrage was extended in both countries. But the British and American elites were motivated by something other than a gradualist, reformist vision. They had no desire to move toward a new social order but to consolidate the prevailing one under the same political management that had extended suffrage. They initiated changes only in response to serious public turmoil, and these changes—like those before and since—were intended to be not the *first* step in an impending series of reforms but the *last*. The reforms were designed to prevent widespread agitation while securing the rule of a slightly reconstituted oligarchy.[3]

The challenge, as Gladstone observed later in the century, was to "get the working class within the pale of the constitution," that is, move workers toward participation in the forms of political sovereignty without having them transform the existing class structure.[4] Thus the American and British elites expressed confidence in their "ability to manage greatly changed circumstances by old skills, techniques and legitimations."[5] By giving a little, they were able to keep a lot. They anticipated that broad electoral participation would not destroy their class, for they would still play the predominant role, serving as leaders or selecting the appropriate leaders, defining, applying, and interpreting policy and exercising a daily influence over policy makers and over society itself seldom diminished by the periodic clamor of electoral contests.

Furthermore, as just mentioned, the more liberal-minded elites were inclined to think that the poorer classes could be trusted to behave properly. The people would not elect pillagers but would vote for the more "responsible" kinds of persons, since they were more interested in winning modest benefits than in upsetting existing social arrangements. In any case, they would be unable to use the formalized institution of elections to effect radical changes. If properly strained through the ballot box, it was believed, popular sentiments would be a stabilizing rather than destabilizing force.

History was to prove the more liberal elites correct. The suffrage has been an invaluable tool for helping to tame dissident groups. Be they indebted farmers and workers of the early nineteenth century or women of the early twentieth, southern Blacks in the early 1960s or students in the late 1960s, each of these groups, struggling for a wide range of social goals—of which the vote was only one of the lesser—was finally granted the suffrage and told to get the changes they wanted through the ballot. Better that they vote than riot, better that they ring doorbells for candidates than plan insurrection or other disruptive confrontations, so argued those who saw the franchise as a means of transforming the anger felt against the system into an energy working within it and ultimately for it.

With elections, popular turbulence could be directed toward more ordered forms of political participation and into more limited areas of political choice. Protests and ill feelings could be channelized into party contests that absorb the protestors' energies and meager resources, while providing a safety valve—a time to air grievances and search for "solutions." According to the conventional wisdom, elections offer us the opportunity to register our dissatisfaction, stand up and be counted, perform our civic duty, vote for the candidate of our choice, throw the rascals out, lay the groundwork for change, make our system work still better, and participate in self-government.

The vehicle through which the people are mobilized and their voices supposedly heard is the political parties. The primary purpose of the party is to wage campaigns and win elections. For more than a quarter of a century, from Jefferson until Jackson, the parties were ruled by men drawn from the same "aristocracy of wealth and talent" extending from the "best" families of Virginia to the "best" of New England. The Jacksonian period saw a fuller development of popular party organizations and an opening of lower-echelon offices to those of humbler origin. As one historian remarks:

> Political action, which had been the concern of a comparatively few men of wealth acting in concert usually to safeguard their property interests and, thanks to property, having the leisure to do so, now became the province of a large number of (often propertyless) persons who had no other means of livelihood than their occupation with politics.[6]

The emergence of the professional politician at the local level signified not a change in the national leadership but an expansion and delegation of some of its tasks. The mass electorate that emerged during the nineteenth and twentieth centuries with enfranchisement, urbanization, and immigration could not be organized under the casual methods of the Virginia families. The job went to men who enjoyed an ethnic and class familiarity with the common voters and who were enough occupied by the pursuit of office and patronage as to remain untroubled by issues of social justice and political economy.

Supposedly an accommodation to the democratic impulse, electoral politics has remained principally a rich man's game. With the increasing costs of running for office, this is truer today than ever before. The democratic principle rests on a plutocratic condition. In the words of one participant from the McKinley era:

> We care absolutely nothing about statehood bills, pension agitation, waterway appropriations, "pork barrels," state rights, or any other political question, save inasmuch as it threatens or fortifies existing conditions. . . . It matters not one iota what political party is in power, or what President holds the reins of office. We are not politicians or public thinkers; we are the rich; we own America; we got it, God knows how; but we intend to keep it if we can by throwing all the tremendous weight of our support, our influence, our money, our political connection, our purchased senators, our hungry congressmen, our public-speaking demagogues into the scale against any legislation, any political platform, any Presidential campaign, that threatens the integrity of our estate.[7]

Applied to today's scene, that description need not be considered overdrawn. The unorganized voters remain no match for the moneyed influence peddlers with their slush funds, payoffs, expensive gifts, stock awards and lucrative market tips, their corrupt lawyers, judges, bureaucrats, kept editorial writers, and their massive deceits. Party competition for the spoils of office continues to be lively but the focus is on styles, appearances, personalities and a narrow set of policy choices, and seldom on the fundamental questions of the political economy. As Richard Hamilton writes in his extensive study of class and party politics:

> A "competition" and public choice of top officials may occur . . . without any serious attention being paid to the wishes of the general public. The leaders of the contending parties may choose to avoid public demands. One may have a "competition" with no representation, where the parties manipulate public opinion in order to divert attention from basic felt concerns.[8]

The voters give their empowering responses to one or another of two parties whose leaders (1) are financed primarily by large donors, (2) are dependent on business-controlled media for exposure, (3) are themselves drawn from or have close contacts with business elements, (4) work in concert with the industrial sector in defining the agenda of public policies, (5) deflect popular demands in an essentially conservative or innocuous direction, and (6) remain dedicated to the preservation of private enterprise at home and abroad.'

As now constituted, elections serve as a great asset in consolidating the existing social order by propagating the appearances of popular rule. History demonstrates that the people might be moved to overthrow a tyrant who shows himself provocatively indifferent to their woes, but they are far less inclined to make war upon a state, even one dominated by the propertied class, if it preserves what Madison called "the spirit and form of popular government." Elections legitimate the rule of the propertied class by investing it with the moral authority of popular consent. By the magic of the ballot, class dominance becomes "democratic" governance.

According to the classical theory of democracy, the purpose of suffrage is to make the rulers more responsive to the will of the people. But history suggests the contrary: more often the effect and even the intent of suffrage has been to make the enfranchised group more responsive to the rulers, or at least committed to the ongoing system of rule. In the classical theory, the vote is an exercise of sovereign power, a popular command over the rulers, but it might just as easily be thought of as an act of support extended by the electorate to those above them. Hence, an election is more a *surrender* than an *assertion* of popular power, a gathering up of empowering responses by the elites who have the resources for such periodic harvestings, an institutionalized mechanism providing for the regulated flow of power from the many to the few in order to legitimate the rule of the few in the name of the many.

DEMOCRACY AS RITUAL

The preference of many political scientists in the Anglo-American tradition is for a system composed of two competing, centrally organized, and disciplined parties that offer clearly defined stands on issues and give the voters recognizable labels by which they might evaluate performance and hold officeholders accountable. This system also supposedly would leave politicians with sufficient organizational resources to withstand the lures of moneyed interests and would provide cohesive, working majorities within the legislature.[10] In contrast, under a weak undisciplined two-party or multiparty system, it is difficult to get consistent party majorities or hold officeholders accountable to the electorate or mobilize popular sentiment behind progressive legislation.

One might wonder whether the hopes invested in disciplined parties, like an earlier generation's optimism concerning direct senatorial elections, primaries, referenda and recalls, do not place considerations of form and procedure above the realities of power and interest. Advocates of a "responsible two-party system" seem unable to entertain the notion that even the leadership of organized and disciplined parties (as exist in Britain, in some Western European democracies, and in certain American state legislatures), for a host of reasons having to do with the structure of economic power, will persist in being more responsive to corporate wealth than to the ordinary working populace.

Whether they prefer parties that are loosely federated or disciplined, elections that are privately or publicly financed, a presidential or parliamentary system, bicameralism or unicameralism, the different proponents all share a common faith in the democratic myth, the unquestioned faith that elections, party competition, and the existence of a legislature are sure signs of democracy. Democracy continues to be equated with particular political procedures rather than with substantive socio-economic conditions. Hence, countries that have these procedures, along with mass poverty and corporate oligarchic concentrations of wealth (e.g., Venezuela, Colombia, India, certain West Indian republics and, before their fascist coups, Chile, Argentina, and Uruguay), are considered democracies. The existence of these democratic forms—periodic elections (between competing elite-dominated parties) and a free press (owned by business interests)—seem to inspire such an enthusiasm in some people as to leave them unconvinced that things like mass poverty and mass powerlessness are relevant to the question of democracy (except as these conditions might affect the stability of democratic forms). The ritual and procedure, then, are taken as more important than the social outputs they produce.

The competing view, one less familiar to us, argues that democracy cannot exist while the wealthy few control the land, labor, and lives of the many. True democracy comes only when the powers of the state are directed to the interests of the demos, and when the people participate in decisions regarding the production and use of social resources and share more or less equally in the benefits. Party elections and parliamentary skirmishes are the husk and not the heart of democratic life and their presence is neither a sufficient cause nor even a necessary condition of democracy, there being other arrangements such as worker-control committees, community organizations, federated but decentralized production and planning groups, intraparty caucuses within a one-party system, and the like, that might serve as far more popular and more effective representative bodies.

The ostensible purpose of electoral competition among political parties is to hold rulers accountable. According to Western democratic theory, popular elections counteract the oligarchic tendency by institutionalizing the power of numbers. An election, like an opinion poll, is supposedly a measure of mass sentiment, but also a mandatory decision, an exercise of sovereign power by the many. The democratic goal is not only that the many shall have their say but that their say shall have an empowering effect, that it shall be both the public *opinion* and the popular *will*. The right to free speech and dissent, even assuming such a right could be exercised without risk to the dissenter, is not democracy's sum total but merely one of the necessary conditions for holding those in office accountable to their constituency. One can imagine a situation—as exists in our better universities and prisons—in which the constituents might be free to complain of conditions, petition the authorities, read critical newspapers and books, and even write them, while exercising little or no power over decision makers. "Democracy," as it is practiced by institutional oligarchs, consists of allowing others the opportunity to *say* what they want while the oligarchs, commanding all institutional resources, continue to *do* what they want.

While elections and the democratic myth remain a powerful legitimating force for elite rule, there are many citizens, including some who participate regularly and ritualistically as voters, who grow cynical about politicians. Overcome by a sense of powerlessness and a growing skepticism about politics, millions, especially among the more deprived classes, do not bother even to vote. For this they have been admonished for not fulfilling their civic duty and for having no one to blame but themselves when their needs are neglected or violated by the government. It is contended that if the slum dwellers, the underemployed, the elderly, the migrant workers and, indeed, the mass of ordinary wage earners, consumers, and taxpayers have little effect on public policy, it is because they do not bother to organize whatever resources they have within the normal channels of party politics. Supposedly it is not resources they lack, but resourcefulness. If the bulk of the people have nothing else they have their numbers, and if they took time to organize they would enjoy effective political participation.

This argument assumes that nonparticipation is a matter of volition, when in fact the apparent unwillingness to mobilize may be due mostly to an inability to do so. The apathy of the unorganized populace is as much the *result* as the cause of their powerlessness. It is time to consider the possibility that if millions are disillusioned with conventional politics, it is because conventional politics are disillusioning.

Numbers are not power unless mobilized into forms of political action that can deliver some reward or punishment upon decision makers. Otherwise, numbers are nothing more than a potential power requiring for their actualization the use of antecedent resources. Just as one needs capital to make capital, so one needs the power to use power. The ability to convert *potential* resources into *actual* ones is itself a crucial power which presumes the existence of favorable preconditions. This is especially true of the power of numbers, which is "a resource of low liquidity,"[11] necessitating for its effectiveness a substantial command of time, manpower, publicity, organization, legitimacy, knowledgeability, and money. The power of numbers, then, is highly qualified by material and class considerations.

ELITE RESPONSIVENESS AND THE MYTH OF GRADUALISM

Much is made of the allegedly democratic responsiveness of elites in the United States and other Western capitalist societies. In truth, the usual elite response is to resist demands no matter how modest they be. Whether it be a desire to build a "people's park" on unused university land, or getting a traffic light installed in a ghetto neighborhood, or keeping open an old-age home or day-care center or community clinic, or stopping the construction of a highway or nuclear plant or dam, or winning the right to vote or the abolition of discriminatory practices, or improvements in work conditions—none of which is exactly a revolutionary threat to the fundaments of the capitalist system—the usual elite response is delay, obfuscation, denial, mendacity, resistance, and, when necessary, repression. In the struggle with labor, elites have habitually relied upon strikebreakers, goon squads, job suspensions, firings, lockouts, contract violations, court injunctions, media campaigns, restrictive legislation, police, and National Guard—not necessarily in that order—rather than on bargaining in good faith and "reasoning together."

Suffering none of the deprivations of poverty and exploitation, political leaders are able to counsel an admirable forbearance to those who do. They manifest an unyielding dedication to something called "gradualism," which allows them to move at glacial speed toward the gates of reform. Confronted with the demand for change, policy makers find no shortage of compelling reasons for inaction, envisioning imagined horrors and dire developments that might prove damaging to society. And when they cannot imagine where change will lead, so much the worse. Thus, at times even the palest reform and the most peripheral tinkering will be treated with the utmost suspicion

Seeing little necessity for reform, elites are often caught by surprise when the plaints of the powerless explode into riotous confrontation, and they are quick to blame disturbances on a small number of troublemakers and malcontents, the assumption being that people will engage in often dangerously rebellious actions not because they feel so compelled by the conditions of their lives but because some shrewd agitator has been able to lead them along like sheep while making them angry as bulls. If agitators are not only the necessary condition but the sufficient cause of the trouble, then why do they not create mass disturbances at will or at least more frequently, as might be their preference?

Elites can deny that protestors have legitimate grievances but they cannot afford to remain eternally unresponsive to an aroused opinion. The power to do nothing, Richelieu once remarked, is great but it must not be abused. For all that has been said, elites are not omnipotent, nor are they always of one mind. In the face of prolonged and troublesome disturbances, as noted earlier, they will often divide into those who remain adamantly opposed to reform of any kind and those who see a long-term advantage in making minimal concessions, those who believe that giving a little will stem the tide and those who fear that it will open the floodgates. If (1) popular militancy persists and (2) it proves politically difficult to apply mass repression, and (3) there are enough surplus resources to be reallocated without challenging the existing structure of wealth and power, then concessions are apt to be made. At least *some* political leaders are inclined to heed Edmund Burke's admonition that "a state without the means of some change is without the means of its conservation."[12]

This is not to say that concessions are granted in a spirit of moderation and compromise; more often they are wrenched from the clutch of the powerful after bitter struggle, sometimes at a cost in human lives. One of the supposed virtues of the existing system is that change is peaceful and gradual. In fact, it is almost never that. The massive educational and political efforts of abolitionists prior to the Civil War provide a classic example of the difficulties of peaceful change. The abolitionists printed newspapers, gave lectures, held parades and demonstrations, preached on street corners, and eventually crossed the line into civil disobedience by aiding runaway slaves and setting up underground railroads to ferry people out of bondage. They did not resort to violence and were usually against it. Many abolitionists were Quakers or other believers in nonviolence.

Yet violence permeated their struggle. If the abolitionists chose not to be perpetrators of violence this did not prevent them from becoming its victims. They were beaten by proslavery mobs, whipped, tarred and feathered, subjected to the terror of night riders and denied protection by law enforcement agents. Hundreds were lynched. They were jailed on trumped-up charges, dragged before grand juries, and charged with fomenting domestic insurrection. The House of Representatives responded to their demands in 1836 by banning the introduction of all petitions, resolutions, or papers "relating in any way . . . to the subject of slavery, or the abolition of slavery." The House concluded that it was "extremely important and desirable that the agitation on this subject should be finally arrested."

When slavery was abolished it was through a war that the North never wanted, and it came as something of an act of retribution on the rebellious South. Yet it is doubtful that Lincoln would have issued his Proclamation even then had there not been almost a half century of agitation preceding it. The Emancipation itself was only a first small step in the liberation of Black people. In most cases throughout the South, the Blacks' social condition did not change much; their relationship to Whites was still that of nearly total servitude. The point is that change occurred but it was neither peaceful nor from within the system as such. Rather it came only after prolonged agitation, extrasystemic actions, state violence, and loss of life. The most *peaceful* areas of the South were the ones where Blacks remained most closely in de facto slavery long after Emancipation.[13]

Be it the abolition of slavery, the enfranchisement of workers, women, and Blacks, the adoption of reform legislation or the struggles of labor, change came only after prolonged and violent struggles. The history of labor relations, for instance, is enshrouded in the myth of peaceful gradualism, enough so as to convince many that the United States has never suffered the turmoils of class conflict. In reality, pitched battles with workers on one side and police, militia, and army on the other have been common occurences for over a century.[14] It was only in 1935, after the nation had been repeatedly rocked by violent labor agitation, that Congress passed the Wagner Act giving limited collective-bargaining rights to industrial unions. The disruption of industrial production and the threat of revolutionary action convinced enough wise heads that setting up a collective-bargaining procedure (which also placed unions under federal regulation) was, in the words of one writer, "the better part of capitalist valor."[15]

So throughout much of this century, by using direct actions and extralegal methods like strikes, sit-ins, sabotage, boycotts, disruptions, demonstrations, and even armed confrontations, working people have won, along with the right to unionize, such things as minimum-wage laws, the eight-hour day, child-labor laws, unemployment insurance, old age and disability assistance, pure food and drug laws, and occupational safety laws.

But the quality of these victories, as well as the methods needed to achieve them, bears closer examination. Collective bargaining brought a more stabilized, more conservative, and thoroughly nonrevolutionary union leadership to the fore—all at the expense of a few pennies in hourly wage increases. Minimum-wage laws hardly provide a living wage and are set at poverty levels. More than a fourth of the work force has yet to achieve an eight-hour day, having to do forced overtime often without benefit of time-and-a-half wages, or having to hold down a second job. Millions of children still work in service industries and for agribusiness. Over a hundred thousand workers die every year from work-connected illnesses and millions are injured because of inadequately enforced or nonexistent occupational safety standards. Millions of consumers suffer from unsafe foods, cosmetics, and medicines, with the blessing of a Food and Drug Administration that worries more about business profits than public health. Benefits for unemployment, disability, and retirement do not provide adequate support for most of those who must rely on them. Underemployment, job insecurity, and financial need remain chronic problems for millions even in the more stabilized monopoly productive sector.

In short, the progressive social legislation of this century proves to be more impressive in its packaging than in its performance, often failing completely to reach those most in need. Furthermore, elites still control such a superiority of resources as to allow them to extract new advantages from the very concessions they are forced to make, as when the regulatory agencies they initially opposed became factors serviceable to their interest. As noted earlier, the reforms made by the state are not steps toward restructuring the class-institutional relations but measures designed to add to the system's stability by placating troublesome groups, in effect, consolidating the old rule with a slightly changed distribution of desiderata—usually financed by the working class itself.

If political leaders are niggardly with material concessions, they are generous with immaterial ones, spending the better part of their time engineering symbolic responses. Indeed, it is a popular complaint that politicians are little more than specialists in ritualized, verbal responses. If they can do nothing else in the face of disturbances they will at least make a show of concern, alluding to future measures and unspecified solutions, pleading for cooperation and patience, presenting counter-arguments, sometimes calling into question the reliability and patriotism of protestors. They will send their representatives to talk with disaffected elements, call press conferences, and appoint special investigators to hold hearings and issue reports.

The public hearing is usually a haphazard and unsatisfactory device for giving and receiving information. This is one function of such proceedings, but it alone would not account for their continued vitality. A second use is a propaganda channel through which a public may be extended and its segments partially consolidated or reinforced. A third function is to provide a quasi-ritualistic means of adjusting group conflicts and relieving disturbances through a safety valve.[16]

Eventually a report is promulgated, designed to pour oil on troubled waters by giving a narrow definition to the question and suggesting palliatives. Should it actually come up with findings and proposals that run counter to elite interests, officials will ignore these, as did Presidents Johnson and Nixon when commissions they appointed—on everything from urban riots to pornography—repeatedly returned recommendations they disliked.

In addition, leaders will call for further study and discussion of the problem and for sober reflection by all. The protestors will be admonished to work in "the only way that is truly effective"—through the electoral process. As dissenters become increasingly aware of the limitations of debate, petition, and election for purposes of effecting substantive changes, they become less dedicated to election rituals and less attentive to the standard pronouncements emanating from official circles. For the same reason, those who *oppose* change become *more* dedicated to dialogue and symbolic politics, urging protestors to place their faith in reason, in free, open (and endless) discussion, and in the candidate of their choice.

In time, the conviction develops among substantial sectors of the public that political involvement brings few returns, that officialdom pays no heed to the people's needs, and that it matters little who is elected to what office. As stated earlier, what passes for "apathy" is often a muted antipathy, a way of adjusting to one's sense of powerlessness.[17] De Tocqueville's description of the town and regional councils under the old regime of eighteenth-century France is still pertinent. He noted that they increasingly

consisted of members of the [bourgeoisie], representatives of business corporations, and contained very few artisans. Not so easily hoodwinked as many have imagined, the "common people" ceased to take any active part in local government and lost all interest in it. Time and again the authorities tried to reawaken that fine spirit of local patriotism which had worked such wonders in the Middle Ages—but without success. . . . Rulers who destroy men's freedom commonly begin by trying to retain its forms—and so it has been from the reign of Augustus to the present day. They cherish the illusion that they can combine the prerogatives of absolute power with the moral authority that comes from popular assent.[18]

THE COOPTATION OF PROTEST

Edmund Wilson once remarked that Jesus was a radical when he was living, and only since he has been sitting at the right hand of God has he become conservative. If so, it is one of the more impressive cases of cooptation. And it reminds us that God's ways do not go entirely unpracticed on earth, having been successfully applied by, and to, many less illustrious beings.

The ability of any political system to survive depends partly on its capacity to coopt dissident elements and issues. If one approach is to deny, ignore, or suppress popular grievances, another is to embrace them as one's own cause, something political leaders are more willing to do if the embrace helps muffle and blunt the issue. Be it civil rights, poverty, peace in Vietnam, or environmentalism, they will try to adopt stances that can be fitted into the framework of the existing politico-economic structure and ideology.

Along with absorbing and then transforming new ideas and issues, the ruling class sometimes opens its doors, giving official or quasi-official positions to leaders who emerge from the ranks of the dispossessed. Once sitting at the right hand of power, protest spokespersons will find themselves drawn into the labyrinth of government, now effecting minor reforms on behalf of their constituents, now caught in daily operations that absorb the better part of their energies while moving them further from their original goals. At the same time, the promise of advancement within the existing structure may prove to be a compelling reason for their becoming increasingly cooperative with the powers that be, either because they are now possessed by career ambitions or because they hope to exercise a more effective influence on behalf of their followers by occupying a higher position.

Often the latter feeling is a rationalization for the former, although it is difficult to determine at what exact psychological point selfless dedication blurs into self-interest.

Many of those who think they are going to change the system from the inside do not seem to realize that as they work their way within the system, the system works its way within them. Citing only cases personally known to him, Kingsley Widmer wrote:

> A Black militant against ghetto exploitation is now a salaried, and controlled, specialist in putting down riots. A rebel against union autocracy finds himself a favored nominee for a middling position in that bureaucracy. A persistent critic of a university administration's authoritarian behavior now chairs a committee to rebut his own criticisms. An ameliorative dove administers an essentially hawkish foreign program, recently rephrased in the rhetoric of peace. A radical submits to a moderate editor a strong blast against his views; after some rewriting, it becomes the editor's boasted badge of liberality. A revolutionist is politely packaged into an artificial symposium, thus doing honor to the principle of opposition without allowing him to say much. More generally, any sharp criticism which attracts sufficient attention seems to become, after dilution and bottling, some governmental or corporate or media project. Such take-overs denature dissent while providing illusions of change.[19]

From their newly acquired organizational positions, protest leaders develop a keener appreciation of the complexities of the multilayered political system. If they persist in their original mission of trying to implement sweeping changes they will suffer frustration and isolation. Overcome by a sense of futility, they eventually depart from their posts and return to the clamor outside the gates. If they remain within and apply themselves with skillful moderation, they may be able to get certain programs adopted and certain marginal changes implemented, sometimes without complete sacrifice to their independence and ideas. But they have to learn which proposals are "practical" and acceptable within the existing power system and tailor their aspirations accordingly. As they develop a taste for position and power, however tightly circumscribed it be, and as they apply minor ameliorations to major problems and thus gather a feeling of their own efficacy, their previous sense of urgency gives way to an undefined optimism. To recall Sorel's classic comment:

The optimist in politics is an inconstant and even dangerous man. . . .
[His] projects seem to him to possess a force of their own, which tends to
bring about their realization all the more easily as they are, in his opinion, destined to produce the happiest results. He frequently thinks that
small reforms in the political constitution, and, above all, in the personnel of the government, will be sufficient to direct social development in
such a way as to mitigate those evils of the contemporary world which
seem so harsh to the sensitive mind. As soon as his friends come into
power, he declares that it is necessary to let things alone for a little, not
to hurry too much, and to learn how to be content with whatever their
own benevolent intentions prompt them to do.[20]

Sometimes the mere experience of repeated personal contact with
representatives of the ruling class leaves a protests leader open to their
perspective. Enjoying, and even feeling flattered by, the serious attentions they accord him and by their appeals to his reasonableness and
good sense, the leader feels somewhat bound to live up to that image,
trimming his demands, and in other ways trying to demonstrate his
goodwill and sense of responsibility. (Some trade-union leaders provide classic examples of this.) In order to be effective and not alienate
those in power whom he believes he is reaching, he urges his followers
not to attempt any precipitous action and to cease their remonstrances
lest they cause the potentially sympathetic elites to balk. The elites
themselves make clear that his credibility with them, and their willingness to treat with him, depend on his ability to control his people.
Thus he takes it upon himself to try to contain his followers, not
realizing that this is also the first and last goal of the ruling group. At
no time is it made clear why an authority that has been moved only by
the pressure of mass agitation is to be believed when it claims it will initiate reforms only when such pressure is removed. The important accomplishment from the elite viewpoint is to break the momentum of
the protest, for it is seldom automatically or easily regained.

The call for patience by a rebel leader, whose protest originally
was premised on a burning sense of impatience with the status quo,
can be an early symptom of cooptation. Not that the leader is consciously betraying his people, although he may be capable of that;
rather he has contracted the elite's sense of endurance about the problems suffered by others and he begins to wonder if the impatience of
his followers is not due to their imperfect appreciation of the facts of
life as he now understands them. Without quite realizing it (and it is

the nature of cooptation that those being coopted do not believe the process is happening to *them*), he comes to share some of the feelings of the established parties while discarding much of the original impulse that brought him to leadership within the aggrieved group. His followers will be more perceptive than he of the transformation he has undergone and will accuse him of having "sold out," a charge he interprets as an unfair personal attack on his integrity rather than as a correct assessment of the objective role he is now playing.

To conclude: those interested in fundamental changes in the existing society should not underestimate the coercive, repressive, and preemptive capacities of the ruling class. Crucial among these are the powers of the state. From election laws to property laws, from city hall to the federal bureaucracy, from taxation to spending, government helps those who can best help themselves and this means not those wanting and needing sweeping transformations in the class structure and in the ways wealth is produced, distributed, and used. To deal with disaffected elements, the elites have a variety of symbolic outputs as close at hand as the next election or next press conference. Along with this they have the ability to discredit, obfuscate, delay, and "study," what Neustadt calls the "almost unlimited resources of the enormous power of standing still."[21] In addition, they have an array of minor concessions, readjustments, blandishments, and cosmetic reforms that are more effective in tuning up than in transforming the machinery of the capitalist state. And should all else fail, elites have at their command the most decisive of political resources— the one that pluralists never talk about—the forces of violent legal repression: the clubbing, gassing, beating, shooting, arresting, rampaging agents of law and order.

NOTES

1. The remarks by Kent and Story along with various other selections from the Massachusetts, New York, and Virginia State constitutional conventions of 1820–1830 can be found in Thomas Mason (ed.), *Free Government in the Making*, 3d ed. (New York: Oxford University Press, 1965), pp. 408–440.

2. See the comments of P. R. Livingston at the New York constitutional convention, reprinted in Mason, *Free Government in the Making*, pp. 419–420.

3. Allan Silver, "Social and Ideological Bases of British Elite Reactions to Domestic Crises in 1829–1832," *Politics and Society*, 1 (February 1971), 189. Silver is con-

cerned with the British oligarchs of the early nineteenth century who sought to undercut the Radical Political Unions but much of his analysis can be applied to the American elites of the same period. The concerns of these elites might be compared to those of the framers of the U.S. Constitution. See the discussion in Michael Parenti, *Democracy for the Few*, 2nd ed. (New York: St. Martin's, 1977), pp. 54–60.

4. Gladstone, quoted in Herbert Aptheker, *The Nature of Democracy, Freedom and Revolution* (New York: International Publishers, 1967), p. 14.

5. Silver, "Social and Ideological Bases," p. 197.

6. Matthew Josephson, *The Politicos, 1865-1896* (New York: Harcourt, Brace and World, 1938), p. 70.

7. Quoted in Matthew Josephson, *The Robber Barons* (New York: Harcourt, Brace and World, 1934), p. 352.

8. Richard F. Hamilton, *Class and Politics in the United States* (New York: Wiley, 1972), p. 4. A more detailed development of the points made above can be found in Parenti, *Democracy for the Few*.

9. See the data compiled and discussed in Hamilton, *Class and Politics in the United States*, and Parenti, *Democracy for the Few*.

10. The classic statement of this view is by the American Political Science Association in *Toward a More Responsible Two-Party System*, a special supplement to the *American Political Science Review*, September 1950 issue.

11. William Gamson, *Power and Discontent* (Homewood, Ill.: Dorsey, 1968), p. 95.

12. Edmund Burke, *Reflections on the Revolution in France* (Chicago: Regnery, 1955), p. 37.

13. On this point, see Charles H. Nichols, *Many Thousand Gone: The Ex-Slaves' Account of Their Bondage and Freedom* (Bloomington: Indiana University Press, 1963). This book provides one of the best treatments of life under slavery, superior to more recent and better publicized works.

14. See the accounts in Jeremy Brecher, *Strike!* (Greenwich, Conn.: Fawcett, 1974).

15. James Coleman, "Elections Under Capitalism, Part 2," *Workers' Power*, September 1-14, 1972, p. 10.

16. David Truman, *The Governmental Process* (New York: Knopf, 1951), p. 372. Truman knew of what he spoke. Faced with a serious student uprising in 1968 while vice-president of Columbia University, he called for a public hearing and investigation—at which students read the above quotation back to him.

17. See Gordon Fellman and Barbara Brandt, *The Deceived Majority: Politics and Protest in Middle America* (New Brunswick, N.J.: Transaction Books, 1973). For some earlier statements, see Morris Rosenberg, "Some Determinants of Political Apathy," *Public Opinion Quarterly*, 18 (1954), 349–366; and J. E. Horton and W. Thompson, "Powerlessness and Political Negativism," *American Journal of Sociology*, 68 (1962), 485–493.

18. Alexis de Tocqueville, *The Old Regime and the French Revolution* (Garden City, N.Y.: Doubleday, 1955), p. 45.

19. Kingsley Widmer, "Why Dissent Turns Violent," *The Nation*, April 7, 1969, p. 426.

20. Georges Sorel, *Reflections on Violence* (Chicago: Free Press, 1950), p. 9.

21. Richard Neustadt, *Presidential Power* (New York: Wiley, 1960), p. 42.

14

Change and Continuity

It has been argued in these pages that a capitalist economic system creates a capitalist-dominated society and that ruling-class interests, by virtue of their control of wealth and production, insinuate themselves into almost all areas of ideology and institution, exercising not just economic power, but social, cultural, and political power. This fact is the overriding condition of the existing social structure.

The resistance one encounters to this idea is itself symptomatic of the way business ideology permeates political consciousness—including the consciousness of many of its critics. The Ralph Nader-type of muckraking, for instance, seldom indicts capitalism *as a system* but faults particular corporate malefactors for their "excesses," thus reducing systemic forces to problems of individual turpitude. The deleterious social effects of capitalism are treated as "abuses," irrational outputs of a basically rational system rather than the converse, rational (i.e., expected, inevitable) outputs of a basically irrational system. Corporate firms are faulted for some of their worst monopolistic and profiteering sins, but *capitalism* as such is accepted as the best of all possible systems, needing—if critics like Nader are to be believed—a return to its earlier, purer, more competitive forms. But the competitive forms have proven impossible to sustain because of monopolistic forces within capitalism itself. The would-be reformers call for a return to an economic system that flourished under social conditions no longer existing. Elites have a large tolerance for these kinds of criticisms and "solutions."

IS IT ALL ECONOMICS?

In arguing that a capitalist economic system creates a capitalist-dominated society, it is not my intention to discount cultural, psychological, and other such factors. There is no neat compartmentalization of the "economic" as something apart from the "noneconomic." Rather than dismissing noneconomic factors, I have tried to show how they are closely linked to the class-dominated social structure and, as such, *play a vital part in reproducing the conditions necessary for the continuation of the existing system.*

Far from arguing that "it's all economics"—and I know of no intelligent socialist who does—I have repeatedly stressed that ruling elements maintain themselves not only by raw economic power but, more significantly, by achieving "cultural hegemony," to use one of Gramsci's favorite concepts, by winning the empowering responses of the many through a variety of socializing and legitmating ways, many of which have become so deeply imbedded in our practices and institutions as to appear quite removed from economics as such. Over time, these cultural-psychological forces can act with a momentum of their own, with no guarantee that they will *always* move in elite-dominated directions (about which more will be said presently), although they do so often enough because of the limitations set by the social structure.

What is often missing from orthodox treatments of culture and society, and what has been introduced into this discussion, are the concepts of power and interest. This analysis has tried to move away from the idea of culture as merely an accidental accretion of time and habit, and toward thinking of it both as a *product* and *instrument* of class interest. Anyone who would object to this idea might be reminded that the ruling elites of capitalist society themselves treat culture as a vital instrument of class power. Whether they ever put it in those words or not, they consciously try to keep a tight control over the command positions of social institutions and over the flow of symbols, values, information, rules, and choices which are the stuff of culture. A good portion of this book has dealt with this elite effort. Regardless of what their apologists in the social sciences might say, elites have never thought of leaving cultural beliefs and practices to chance or to unrestricted popular development.

To be sure, many of the behavior patterns of powerless groups represent their own adjustments to social conditions, for example, "the culture of poverty," and are not directly imposed by the ruling class. If anything, elites might even disapprove of such behavior on class-based aesthetic and moral grounds. Yet even the adaptations made by nonelites are to life conditions not entirely of their own creation, to say the least, but represent adjustments to the oppressive realities of the social system and can be seen as being, to a large degree, by-products of that system.

CHANGE WITHOUT CHANGE

If the ruling class so successfully perpetuates the conditions of its own domination, how then does change occur? And of what kind is it? There exist two seemingly contradictory opinions regarding social change: "We live in a fast-changing world. Traditional ways are forever yielding to new practices and norms. Indeed, change itself is the norm." And the contrary view: "Change is a most difficult thing to effect in human society. Most institutions, including government, are resistant to it. Most changes are merely new coatings on old substances." Both impressions are correct, for they refer to different phenomena. The first is speaking of the dramatic transformations in technology, production, and consumption within the framework of a developing capitalist society, the kind of change treated positively by elites and equated with "progress." The second refers to the redistribution of social desiderata, the struggle for social justice, and the ability to transform patterns of control and authority through collective action, a kind of change looked upon with fear and loathing by the rulers of society. The first is largely a creation of capitalism, the second a threat to it.

Yet changes of the first kind involve transformations in production, markets, life-styles, and popular demands and expectations that become a force (or sometimes a hindrance) for those seeking changes of a socio-political and class nature. The task of a ruling class is not to prevent change—which is impossible—but to minimize and control its effects, the ultimate goal being not progress or social justice but class survival. The more "socially conscious" corporate leaders are keenly attuned to this fact. While making every pretense at being dedicated to change and social betterment, their overriding concern may be summarized as follows: "If there be change, let it be of a kind we can control." As David Rockefeller told his business colleagues:

> Any adaptation of our system to the changing environment is far more likely to be workable if those who understand the system's problems [i.e., corporate management] share in designing the solutions. So it is up to businessmen to make common cause with other reformers . . . to prevent the unwise adoption of extreme and emotional remedies, but on the contrary to initiate necessary reforms that will make it possible for business to continue to function in a new climate. . . . [N]ow with the social contract again up for revision, new social and environmental problems are generating increasing pressure for further modification and regulation of business. By acting promptly, business can assure itself a voice in deciding the form and content of the new social contract.[1]

Change is tolerated, and even given the imposing designation of a "new social contract," with the anticipation that it will not be "extreme and emotional" and can be kept compatible with the basic interests of the business system. Any other kind of change is unacceptable even to "socially conscious" magnates like Rockefeller.

As noted in the previous chapter, the concessions won by non-elites, while of a progressive nature, have been contained within the existing class structure. With time, most of these reforms have been accepted by the ruling elites, being regarded not as departures from the system but as part of it. The same is not true of present-day demands for fundamental change. Yesterday's revolution was a necessary component of our fine tradition, celebrated by conservatives in bicentennial cermonies. Tomorrow's revolution is dreaded like the plague, the work of diabolic persons who should be dealt with harshly.

For many corporate leaders reform of any sort is seen as a threat.

The existing society is treated in the more conservative mind as the best of all possible worlds, a fortunate product of history that should not be tampered with. Edward Banfield offers us this remarkable passage:

> A political system is an accident. It is an accumulation of habits, customs, prejudices and principles that have survived a long process of trial and error and of *ceaseless response to changing circumstances*. If the system works well on the whole, it is a lucky accident—the luckiest, indeed that can befall a society. . . . To meddle with the structure and operation of a successful political system is therefore the greatest foolishness that men are capable of. Because the system is intricate beyond comprehension, the chance of improving it in the ways intended is slight, whereas the danger of disturbing its workings and setting off a succession of unwarranted effects that will extend throughout the whole society is great.[2]

Statements of this sort were uttered in 1787, in 1860, and in 1929. Presumably Banfield would have disagreed with them at those times for he gives no evidence of opposing the reforms of earlier generations, such as the extension of the franchise, the direct election of the Senate, the abolition of slavery, the development of social welfare legislation, and the emergence of trade unions. But what is acceptable about these past reforms is that they are of the past. The ability to change, celebrated to exaggeration as the peculiar genius of the system, is treated as a "meddling" of potentially disastrous dimensions when applied to today's polity. Past changes are to be embalmed in an unchanging present. The "ceaseless response to changing circumstances" must itself cease. By refusing to make changes, conservatives like Banfield mistakenly hope to stop the process of change itself.

In their distrust of political change, elites have the support or acquiescence of other sectors of the public including some nonelites. As noted earlier, there is a tendency for individuals to see the *established order* as synonymous with order itself; hence, the overthrow of this order is feared as the end of all order. So people tolerate official violence perpetrated in the name of the existing system but are terrified at the first signs of active resistance against the social order. In more specific terms, they fear a worsening of their own conditions, a loss of whatever little comforts, possessions, and security they have. But the question is whether these propensities are innate to the human psyche or a product of particular conditions. It has been argued here that the elite-dominated social system works with cyclical effect upon individuals, creating conditions that produce mentalities functional for the system's own perpetuation. Thus material exploitation and powerlessness produce damaged persons possessed of a low self-esteem and intense scarcity psychology who, in turn, are less able to act in resistant and self-realizing ways. And if elite social controls are successful in reproducing the conditions of obedience and defeat in the working class and other groups, then the reluctance to move in self-affirmative ways is a "realistic" or certainly understandable response to real conditions.

There is ample evidence, much of it discussed in this book, that individuals have been socialized into an essentially conservative perspective and that many of them perceive the business community as fulfilling a beneficial and providential role. Therefore, it might be argued, the performance of the political system on behalf of the interests of corporate wealth, and the favoritism shown to business in almost every area of public policy, are not at odds with popular attitudes on this subject. If the people support the system then the system is democratically representative, being what the people want. But it is one thing to argue that citizens accept the existing institutions and economic structure as a fact of life and another to argue that this structure and its institutions are products of their will. For, it is worth repeating, while the populace may accept the capitalist system—to the extent they understand what it is and have been introduced to no other system—this does not mean the inequities and deprivations they suffer are of their own choosing and liking. Far from being democratically created, the social consensus is a product of undemocratic conditions. Nonelites accept the status quo out of fear of something worse and the apparent lack of any opportunity to move without risk toward something better, while elites accept the status quo because of a heartfelt self-interest and desire for things as they are. Furthermore, a closer investigation of the history of the "muted levels" of society shows that along with the compliance and even devotion to the existing order, nonelites have been repeatedly moved to protests and insurgencies.

ARE ELITES OMNIPOTENT?

Is not this portrait of the ruling interests overdrawn? Do elites always know what they are doing? Do they never make mistakes? Are they never governed by irrational impulses? Do they always act in their own class interests? One might answer these questions as follows: maybe elites do not *always* act in their own interests but they do so often enough. Certainly there are few examples of them deliberately acting *against* their interests. Nor does it mean that they always act successfully in their own interests even if they always try to. No one *always* knows what he or she is doing; everyone can make mistakes and suffer confusions. Indeed, many conflicts arising *among* elites are differences over what might be the best tactics for maintaining their common class interests.

If corporate-political elites cannot always determine with unerring certitude the best course for themselves, they nonetheless have a far greater ability than other groups to define their interests, set up viable strategies, allow room for mistakes, control the agenda, and press for gains. Elites are neither omnipotent nor omniscient but they have material, institutional, and ideological resources that provide them with options inaccessible to nonelites, allowing them to occupy the high ground in almost any struggle and enabling them to turn immediate concessions into long-range legitimations.

Many things that move beyond their control and are not of their own creation are nevertheless used to good advantage by them. The pattern is consistent enough to indicate that not simply luck is at work; rather it is the organization of power which creates the conditions of good fortune and moves things in a direction that serves elite interests. Thus the capitalist class may not have deliberately created racism or sexism, both of which existed long before capitalism, but racism and sexism are greatly fortified by the hierarchical authority, individualized competition, economic deprivation, and scarcity psychology of capitalist society and have the kind of divisive and distracting effects that serve capitalist class interests.

One need not make the claim that the interests of corporate wealth prevail in *every* way on *every* issue. But it is one thing to observe that the ruling class is not all-powerful in all things (for no social interest in any society can claim omnipotence), and another to conclude that power in the United States is inclusively distributed, usually countervailing, democratically accountable, and free of gross exploitations and nequities.

Are elites conspiratorial or do they operate through democratic means like other groups? Some social critics have been faulted for seeing ruling class conspiracies where there supposedly are none. The contention in this book is that elite power is principally systemic and legitimating rather than conspiratorial and secretive. No ruling class could last very long if it depended primarily on conspiratorial maneuvers. At the same time, no privileged ruling class could survive if it did not sometimes conspire, if it did not consciously and secretly plan, coordinate, and control many matters. Elites themselves make repeated claims to confidentiality, nonaccountability, and secrecy on the grounds that the existing order would be jeopardized ("national security") were they obliged to operate in the open. If conspiracy is not a sufficient cause for capitalist rule, it seems to be a necessary condition.

In recent years, the American public has been treated to a series of revelations regarding elite conspiracies dramatic enough to catch even the biased myopic eye of the news media: the Pentagon Papers, dairy-lobby payoffs, wheat deal and oil price conspiracies, widespread bribery of Congressmen, illegal corporate campaign funds, a secret air war in Cambodia, covert and violent interventions in Chile and other countries, Watergate break-ins, and illegal domestic operations of the CIA and FBI. For those of us who have moved beyond the schoolbook version of American democracy these revelations were neither shocking nor surprising. Why have others thought it so improbable that ruling-class elements would use covert, conspiratorial means to advance their interests? Would it not be more unlikely to assume that they leave things to chance, that they seldom conspire to secure their powers and profits in the face of competing demands, and that they operate only through the overt, troublesome, and often ineffectual channels of formal democracy?

The legitimation of class rule is an extraordinary accomplishment but never a finished one. Elites must constantly strive to reproduce the conditions of their hegemony, and in that task they face real difficulties—some of which may be treated briefly here:

(1) Class rule is not only willful but also systemic, that is, it must operate within the dynamics of a capitalist system that, over and above the desires of any individual elite, imposes its own necessities, and these must be responded to if the system is to be maintained. Among the problems of rule, then, are those that inhere in the capitalist economy itself, manifested in such things as the declining rate of profit and the shrinkage and even disappearance of long-term investment markets, along with a deepening fiscal crisis, a rise in the cost of exports, an increase in foreign competition, recession, inflation, the maldistribution of goods and services, private glut and public insolvency, a growing tax burden, and urban and environmental devastation. As the noted economist John Gurley concludes:

> By 1975 the U.S. capitalist class had experienced a decade or more of deterioration in its ability to draw surplus value out of the free enterprise system. Deflationary policies, expansionary programs, growth measures within a set of direct controls, large-scale unemployment, dollar devaluation—none of these had thus far turned the clock back to the 1950s. The causes of the decline in capital's fortunes appear to be so deep-seated that they will not easily be swept away.[3]

This is not the place to attempt a detailed investigation of the problems of advanced capitalism.[4] Of interest to us is the way the crisis affects people whose loyalty rests in no small measure on the presumption that "the system is working" and that it "delivers the goods." The capitalist system contains within it failures and injustices that cannot always be hidden or ascribed to innocent causes or blamed on its victims. Although the schools, the business-controlled media, and institutional representatives may impose their distractions and deceptions on the public, certain conditions of reality intrude directly upon people's experiences so as occasionally to give them some independent means of critical discernment. Thus the "fuel shortage" of the winter of 1974–1975, which suddenly developed into a full-blown "energy crisis," only then mysteriously to disappear as soon as gasoline and fuel prices doubled, was taken by the public for what it was—a price-rigging hoax perpetrated by the oil companies for the purpose of increasing profits. As the disparity between the claims and performance of capitalism becomes increasingly evident, the population becomes more critical of big business and its associated military and governmental institutions.[5] In some industrial nations, substantial portions of the working class and intelligentsia have rejected capitalism and given support to Socialist and Communist parties.

The unsettling coupling of high popular expectations and poor economic performance causes politico-economic leaders to call for a lowering of expectations. Being unable to do anything about the economic system, they admonish the people to tighten their belts, to prepare for austerity, and stop demanding so much. The vision of the ever-better life, so much a part of the American myth, is now questioned by the very elites who once offered it as proof of the moral and material superiority of the private-enterprise system.

(2) Elites face the problem of having their deceptions not work as well as they need to. It is often said that conflicts arise because of a failure of communication, but many struggles begin not because communication has *failed* but because it has succeeded, not because of a lack of understanding but because people come to understand what is happening all too well. An impoverished peasantry, rising in rebellion against a wealthy, repressive oligarchy, is not suffering from a lack of understanding of how ruling interests are maintained and how its own interests are violated, but has a keen appreciation of class realities. The student rebels of the late 1960s, accused of not understanding how the university worked, responded that, quite the contrary, for the first time they *were* understanding how the university was run, by whom, and for what interests and such understanding was the very cause of their unhappiness. What university officials were confronted with was not a breakdown in communication but a breakdown in deception.

As the official image of established social institutions, or of the society itself, is exposed for what it is—an official lie—disaffection and cynicism increase. If the disaffection becomes mobilized into protest and resistance, then repressive measures become more necessary and more explicit. As repression increases, the undemocratic and oligarchic realities of social institutions become still more evident. Communication keeps improving all the time and this is what worries the ruling elites. Failures in *mis*communication go hand in hand with increases in conflict. There is nothing inherently pacifying about communication. It works to end conflict only if miscommunication is the main source of conflict and only if other more substantive interests are reconcilable. A "better understanding" may mean the end of a false consensus and the surfacing of fundamental differences that challenge the elite-dominated peace.

As difficulties of control increase, elites must rely more on lies, subterfuges, illegal actions, and official violence, revelations of which lead to a further weakening of elite legitimacy. The reliance on coercion is less a manifestation of power than a symptom of ruling-class weakness, of its failure to win the empowering responses of the many and its need to extract a begrudging compliance. To quote Charles Merriam:

> Power is not strongest when it uses violence, but weakest. It is strongest when it employs the instruments of substitution and counter attraction, of allurement, of participation rather than of exclusion, of education rather than of annihilation. Rape is not an evidence of irresistible power in politics or in sex.
>
> We cannot exile and imprison and execute many, after all; so why not draw them in rather than cast them out of the community in which there may be offered substantial advantages and emotional satisfactions? So reason the more prudent rulers.[6]

(3) Yet the problem may not be that rulers are unwilling to "draw them in," that is, include the masses in the good things, but that they are unable to do so. The question is not only to what extent are ruling elites willing to change their ways, but to what extent are they *able* to change and yet maintain their dominance and preserve their capitalist system? By its very nature, cooptation works only on a limited, selective basis, and cannot be counted on when the society is facing crises of major proportions.

If the elites were able to accomodate the needs of the many and still retain their own privileges and powers, there is no reason to think they might not do so. Certainly it would lead to a more stable and complacent populace, one that would not make troublesome demands on ruling class prerogatives. But the system does not have those kinds of slack resources to be distributed, and the structural imperatives of capitalism are such that the social needs of the many could only be met if there are major transformations in the ways wealth and labor are used—which would bring us to something other than capitalism.

Many demands for reform (viz., stop urban decay, eliminate poverty, end unemployment, tax the rich not the poor, drastically cut the military budget, stop United States interventionism in other countries, etc.), while giving every appearance of being nonrevolutionary changes within the system, actually strike at essential arrangements in the class-power-ideological structure. To respond to these "reforms" would necessitate such a fundamental change in the ownership, and use of domestic and international wealth as to undercut the ruling class's position in American society and in the world, a development of revolutionary rather than reformist dimensions. In short, there is a limit to what the haves can allow the have-nots, and the reason elites often turn to repression rather than reform is because reform is not a realistic choice within the existing system.

The unwillingness of elites to make the kinds of alluring, inclusive reforms that Merriam refers to, then, does not result simply from opacity, rigidity, and selfishness—although elites manifest enough of those qualities—but from an inability continually to avoid or reconcile the contradictions between the interests of the few and the interests of the many. It is not that rulers are wanting in prudence, but wanting in options.

(4) The successes enjoyed by competing social systems in other nations lend the legitimacy of substance and practice to revolutionary ideas that were once treated as chimerical and utopian. In addition, the need to contain the spread of these ideas in other parts of the world demands imperialistic ventures that prove costly in lives, money, and morale, leading to further domestic protest and disaffection. As with earlier empires, today's ruling class finds itself sometimes having to bleed its base in order to protect its periphery, Vietnam being only the most dramatic and costly instance of this to date.

(5) As the disparity between what is preached and what is practiced, both at home and abroad, becomes more evident and elite controls over the material and symbolic environment become less certain, competing notions emerge and the search for alternative practices is taken up in earnest by disenchanted groups. Questions about the fundaments of the system, heretofore the esoteric fare of a few radical intellectuals, begin to circulate among larger numbers of people.

In times of crisis and ferment one can speak with good cause of "the contagion of ideas." The very myths and ideologies that served elite interests so well now produce unexpected spin-offs, as when the precepts of the democratic creed are given a literal interpretation by disadvantaged groups. The litany of equality, liberty, and prosperity, designed to legitimate elite rule, can be a double-edged weapon, introducing powerful symbols that stir nonelites in self-assertive directions. While the ruling class finds it advantageous to have people believe that they are free and self-governing, it runs the risk of injecting ideas into the political culture which prove troublesome when taken seriously. Those who are taught they are free and equal might see they are not, but having been so taught, they are still possessed with the expectation that they *should* be free. And if this expectation advances, and they begin to believe they *could* improve their condition, they are likely to mobilize themselves against the established rder in some way.

(6) In addition, each new generation in some way seeks to make a statement of its own experiences and is both unwilling and unable to see the world through the eyes of the generation before. All infants born into a society are its potential enemies in that they have no commitment to its particular illusions, fashions, beliefs, and practices. Elites do not enjoy an automatic continuity of obedience. The young must be instilled with the right attitudes. But the socialization process operates imperfectly; hence the notorious unreliability and unpredictability of society's youth.

Events overtake us. The system is riddled with contradictions that intrude upon orthodoxy. The snugness of the established order is experienced as a suffocation by many. And despite widespread indoctrination and supervision there emerge pockets of heterodoxy, inventive applications and alternative forms of social existence that threaten to infect ever larger numbers of people.'

Elite control over the socialization process, while thorough and deep, is not absolute. The experiences and consciousness of a whole society, and of a whole world, are always more diverse than those which the ruling class can regulate and contain. Hence, although orthodoxy is widely propagated, adherence to official viewpoints is far less firm than rulers would desire.

As the crisis of capitalism deepens, the political struggle may take one of several directions. (1) A large movement toward the left may emerge, consisting of increasingly hard pressed sectors of labor, the poor, racial minorities, youth, intellectuals, and some of the more literate and progressive elements of the middle class, developing into an eventual confrontation or series of confrontations of revolutionary dimensions, gathering additional impetus from victorious revolutionary forces throughout the Third World and perhaps even in Europe.

(2) Mass discontent may be mobilized but in a rightward direction, one that accepts the corporate system and the hierarchical society and concentrates on nonclass issues, built upon the fears and anxieties provoked by military defeats abroad, economic recession at home, and the weakening of authority and decline of traditional cultural and ideological institutions. Today one can see early signs of such a rightist protest, focusing on issues like the abolition of legal abortion, school busing, opposition to equal-rights laws for women, gays, and minorities, restoration of the death penalty, and antiunion "right-to-work" laws. Rightists from the John Birch Society and other such groups have won leadership positions in these movements and have begun to link these immediate issues to their own virulent anticommunism, racism, and militarism. Support is drawn mostly from the newly rich, small business people, and lower-middle-class elements, with growing incursions being made among the working class.

(3) Most likely in the years immediately ahead, despite some polarization to the left and right, the existing system will continue as it has—with a growing dependency on government planning and spending to bolster the capitalist economy and a strong reliance on selective repression to keep dissent from mobilizing in a leftward direction. This will be coupled with an increasing deterioration in the quality of the consumer economy, in public services, and in the natural and social environment.

The function of a revolutionary left is not only to hasten the demise of the existing system but to make sure that if and when the time of great upheavals comes, when the conditions of habitual obedience and acquiescence are thrown off and the people begin to move, a political consciousness will have been developed that ensures their moving in a progressive revolutionary direction rather than a fascist counterrevolutionary one.

One thing is certain: the conservative continuities of authority and institution that seem so immutable, so commanding, and so ubiquitous will themselves be subjected to the forces of change. The human spirit, whether in its noble or aberrant forms, cannot be contained eternally in one particular set of social arrangements. No social system lasts forever, although most have thought it their destiny to do so. Changes in ecological balances, material resources, methods of production, technologies and population, the incursions of competing systems, the demands of competing classes, the inability of rulers to find new solutions that allow them to maintain old interests, the advance of popular ideologies, new expectations, new human identities and collective strivings—in the face of these kinds of dynamics, societies over the centuries either are transformed drastically or decline and fall under their own weight; either they metamorphose like certain insects or collapse like dinosaurs. But even dinosaurs live a long time. And in this book I have tried to explain why.

NOTES

1. *Wall Street Journal*, December 21, 1971, quoted in James O'Connor, *The Fiscal Crisis of the State* (New York: St. Martin's, 1973), p. 227.

2. Edward Banfield quoted in Bradbury Seasholes, *Voting, Interest Groups and Parties* (Glenview, Ill.: Scott, Foresman, 1967), p. 130. Italics added.

3. John G. Gurley, *Challengers to Capitalism* (San Francisco: San Francisco Book Company, 1976), p. 157.

4. See O'Connor, *The Fiscal Crisis of the State*; Gurley, *Challengers to Capitalism*, pp. 31-61, 151-163; and Paul A. Baran, *The Political Economy of Growth* (New York: Monthly Reviews Press, 1957); Michael H. Best and William E. Connolly, *The Politicized Economy* (Lexington, Mass.: Heath, 1976).

5. See the opinion polls cited in Michael Parenti, *Democracy for the Few*, 2nd ed. (New York: St. Martin's, 1977), pp. 42-45, and the discussion therein.

6. Charles Merriam, *Political Power* (New York: Collier Books, 1964; originally published in 1934), p. 179.

7. A study of the causes, methods, and possibilities of popular rebellion cannot be undertaken here but will be the subject of a later work by me.

Index